Questions Kids Ask about Sex

Honest Answers for Every Age

The Medical Institute
for Sexual Health

Edited by J. Thomas Fitch, M.D.

with Melissa R. Cox

Revell

Grand Rapids, Michigan

© 2005 by The Medical Institute for Sexual Health

Published by Fleming H. Revell
a division of Baker Publishing Group
P.O. Box 6287, Grand Rapids, MI 49516-6287
www.revellbooks.com

Paperback edition published 2007
ISBN 10: 0-8007-3217-0
ISBN 978-0-8007-3217-2

Second printing, July 2007

Printed in the United States of America

The Library of Congress has cataloged the hardcover edition as follows:
Questions kids ask about sex : honest answers for every age / Melissa R. Cox, editor.
     p.   cm.
   Includes bibliographical references and index.
   ISBN 10: 0-8007-1878-X (cloth)
   ISBN 978-0-8007-1878-7 (cloth)
   1. Sex instruction for children. 2. Sex instruction for youth. 3. Sex instruction.
 I. Cox, Melissa R.
 HQ57.Q47 2005
 649'.65—dc22   2005013670

Published in association with the literary agency of Alive Communications, Inc., 7680 Goddard Street, Suite 200, Colorado Springs, CO 80920.

J. T.

Thank you for dreaming that this book could become a reality. Your patience, persistence, and sheer determination have been the source of strength for all of us.

The Medical Institute

Alan

Thanks for dreaming with us so many years ago about this project: without your insight we would not have made it here.

Melissa Cox and J. Thomas Fitch

Logan and Keegan

This project was a passion prior to your births. Your curiosity was the basis for many questions, and your innocence motivated us all. Here's to your future! Thanks for being our creative inspiration.

Melissa Cox

Contents

Part 3 The State of Sex Today

Acknowledgments

This book would not have been possible without the tireless efforts of all the individuals involved. The Medical Institute for Sexual Health would like to thank each and every one of them for their contribution and passion to help motivate parents to talk with their children about sex.

Writing Team

Melissa R. Cox, Highlands Ranch, Colorado
J. Thomas Fitch, M.D., Pediatrics, San Antonio, Texas
Patricia Francis, M.D., Pediatrics, Moraga, California
Wilson Wayne Grant, M.D., Pediatrics, San Antonio, Texas
Marilyn A. Maxwell, M.D., Internal Medicine/Pediatrics, St. Louis, Missouri
Joe S. McIlhaney Jr., M.D., Obstetrics/Gynecology, Austin, Texas
Margaret J. Meeker, M.D., Pediatrics, Traverse City, Michigan
Paul A. Warren, M.D., Behavioral Pediatrics, Plano, Texas

Contributors

W. David Hager, M.D., Obstetrics/Gynecology, Lexington, Kentucky

Joneen Krauth Mackenzie, RN, BSN, WAIT Training, Denver, Colorado

Lynn Lutz, Ph.D., Dallas, Texas

Mary Anne Nelson, M.D., Cedar Rapids, Iowa

Curtis C. Stine, M.D., Tallahassee, Florida

Research Editor

Anjum Khurshid, MBBS, MPAFF, MA, The Medical Institute, Austin, Texas

Reviewers

Lisa Beck, Colorado Springs, Colorado

Reed Bell, M.D., Pensacola, Florida

Kate Hendricks, M.D., M.P.H., Austin, Texas

Gaylen M. Kelton, M.D., Indianapolis, Indiana

David Roper, San Antonio, Texas

Brooke Spencer, San Antonio, Texas

Lynne Tingle, Ph.D., Charlotte, North Carolina

The Medical Institute
for Sexual Health

The Medical Institute for Sexual Health is a nonprofit organization committed to the health, hope, and happiness of all people. We have discovered that one of the greatest risks to an individual experiencing these things is being involved in sexual activity outside of marriage. Science clearly shows that unmarried youth who become sexually involved are at great risk of long-term consequences including nonmarital pregnancy and sexually transmitted infections.

Considered a leader in communicating about youth risk-behavior issues, The Medical Institute provides individuals and community organizations with resources for purchase that help initiate conversation with young people and parents. Currently The Medical Institute distributes almost one hundred thousand pieces of material each year to individuals and organizations across the United States and throughout the world.

Leaders at the Centers for Disease Control, the U.S. Health and Human Services Department, the White House, and state-level government offices, as well as educators and parents across the nation, seek out advice from The Medical Institute about sexual issues affecting our nation's teens.

With a national advisory board of medical doctors, counselors and psychologists, educators (including abstinence leaders), and parents, The Medical Institute for Sexual Health is based at P.O. Box 162306, Austin, TX 78716-2306. To order resources, call 512-328-6268 weekdays, 8 a.m. to 5 p.m. (Central Standard Time).

You can also reach The Medical Institute by email at medinstitute@ medinstitute.org or on the Web at www.medinstitute.org/contact/contact. htm. The Washington DC office is at 3250 Prospect St. N.W., Washington, DC 20007; the phone number is 202-342-7444.

Editor

Melissa Cox is vice president of Cox Creative, Inc., a full-service marketing and advertising firm in Denver. Previously she served The Medical Institute for Sexual Health as director of marketing and public relations, developing and producing acclaimed resources such as the cutting-edge videos *Sex Is Not a Game* and *Just Thought You Oughta Know*, which won a Telly Award for "finest work in film and video on cable television."

She was editor of Focus on the Family's *Physician* magazine and managing editor of the best-selling *Complete Book of Baby & Child Care*.

Contributors

J. Thomas Fitch, M.D., is a pediatrician in San Antonio, Texas. He's especially interested in helping the parents of his adolescent patients understand how they can help their children avoid involvement in risk-taking activities like alcohol and drug use, as well as nonmarital sexual activity. He's become a national expert on condom effectiveness and was one of the expert panel members for the National Institutes of Health Condom Effectiveness Panel. As past president of the Texas Pediatric Society, he's given numerous professional presentations to colleagues and has been published in a variety of periodicals. He is a clinical professor in the department of pediatrics at the University of Texas Health Sciences Center in San Antonio, Texas. He was a content editor for Focus on the Family's *Complete Book of Baby & Child Care* and is a member of Focus on the Family's Physician Resource Council, as well as the chairman of the Medical Institute's board of directors.

Patricia Francis, M.D., a pediatrician in Lafayette, California, has been in private practice since 1985. As the mother of two daughters, she's focused on issues impacting young women, including eating disorders and sexually transmitted diseases. Dr. Francis volunteers for a number of organizations in the Bay Area. She's a member of a variety of professional medical organizations and was a content editor for Focus on the Family's *Complete Book of Baby & Child Care*. She is also a member of The Medical Institute's national advisory board.

Wilson Wayne Grant, M.D., a pediatrician with one of the busiest private practices in San Antonio, Texas, works with children from at-risk populations. He's a child development specialist with more than thirty years of experience and a unique ability to communicate with his patients at their level—plus a special interest in helping teens make wise choices. He's written many books, including *From Parent to Child about Sex*, *Growing Parents Growing Children*, *The Caring Father and Strategies for Success*, and *How to Help Your Child with Attention Deficit Disorder*. He's a member of a variety of professional medical organizations, has served as the medical director of the South Texas Children's Habilitation Center, and is on the clinical faculty of the University of Texas at San Antonio Medical School. He is also a member of The Medical Institute's national advisory board.

Marilyn A. Maxwell, M.D., is a professor of internal medicine and pediatrics and the associate director of the combined Internal Medical and Pediatrics Residency Program at St. Louis University. Previously, she was medical director of People's Health Centers, Inc., a large, federally funded, community health center where she established an adolescent clinic that specifically addressed teen health issues. Many of her patients were unwed mothers and adolescents with sexually transmitted infections. She's a member of numerous professional organizations and was a content editor for Focus on the Family's *Complete Book of Baby & Child Care*. Currently she serves on the executive committee of the bioethics section of the American Academy of Pediatrics. She also serves on Focus on the Family's Physician Resource Council and The Medical Institute's National Advisory Board.

Joe S. McIlhaney Jr., M.D., an obstetrician gynecologist in Austin, Texas, established The Medical Institute for Sexual Health in 1992. He left his private practice of twenty-eight years in 1995 to join The Medical Institute full-time. During his tenure as an ob-gyn, he was active on the medical staff of St. David's Community Hospital and focused on reproductive technologies, contraceptive techniques, sexuality education, sexually transmitted diseases, and social behavior education. Along with three other physicians, Dr. McIlhaney was instrumental in bringing in vitro fertilization and embryo transfer to Austin. During his time in practice, he wrote five books with an emphasis on the problem of STDs. Currently he speaks and writes about the twin epidemics of sexually transmitted diseases and nonmarital pregnancy. He's the author of six books, including *1,001 Health-Care Questions Women Ask* and *Sex: What You Don't Know Can Kill You*. He has been an advisor to President George W. Bush on issues related to STDs and nonmarital pregnancy. He currently serves on the Presidential Council on HIV/ AIDS, the advisory committee to the director of the Centers for Disease Control, and the research task force at the National Campaign to Prevent Teen Pregnancy.

Margaret J. Meeker, M.D., is a specialist in child and adolescent medicine working in Traverse City, Michigan. A national speaker on teen health issues, she's passionate about helping young female adolescents. She's the author of *Epidemic* and *Restoring the Teenage Soul*. She is a frequent contributor to a number of parenting publications. She's a member of The Medical Institute's national advisory board.

Paul A. Warren, M.D., is a behavioral pediatrician in private practice in Dallas. He specializes in working with children with developmental and behavioral problems and serves as a consultant for special-education services to multiple school districts. He's written three books and co-authored nine, with an emphasis on the emotional issues that prevent children from thriving. He's served as a guest lecturer for many organizations and has been featured on numerous national radio programs. He's a member of Focus on the Family's Physician Resource Council. He's a member of the Medical Institute's national advisory board.

Introduction

The Medical Institute for Sexual Health developed *Questions Kids Ask about Sex* to help parents like you navigate this often-difficult subject of talking to their children about sex. You probably picked up this book because you know you need to start the conversation, but you're just not sure how to go about it. You're not alone, and this book was designed exactly with you in mind.

The medical doctors, educators, and fellow parents with the Institute compiled more than four hundred questions from educators, physicians, and parents across the country. We also combed through teen chat rooms and educational websites to find out what kids are eager to know. The questions and answers presented in this book aren't intended to be the be-all and end-all, but rather a helpful starting place for your journey of helping your kids achieve a future full of health, hope, and happiness.

For some of you, talking with your kids about sex is very embarrassing. For others, it's not as big of a deal. Our hope is that the answers offered here will enhance the experience for all of you by providing practical and accurate tools that can foster deeper discussions (and more meaningful relationships) with your kids.

The first part of this book (chapters 1–6) was developed to provide you, the parent, with a basic philosophical context in which to frame your discussions with your children.

The second part—bulk—of the book (chapters 7–13) is divided into age-oriented sections, with answers to questions parents ask listed first, followed by answers to questions kids ask. The answers for younger kids are written so that you can use them line-for-line or rephrase them in your own words. For adolescents, questions were written in such a way that you can simply hand the book over to your adolescent, go over the response together, or create your own response based on the information provided.

We wanted *Questions Kids Ask about Sex* to be something you can pick up repeatedly over the years as your children mature. Throughout this book, therefore, you'll find sidebars with practical help on key issues of character building and fostering friendships. These are topics that are applicable to every phase of life and certainly affect one's understanding of sexuality.

A final, short section, part 3 (chapters 14–15), introduces you to the discussion of sexually transmitted infections and contraceptive options. This provides you and your child with a complete understanding of the risks associated with nonmarital sexual activity.

In all, our goal is to empower you to talk about sex more freely, confidently, and effectively. In exchange for your investment, we believe you can help your children experience an incredibly satisfying sex life within the context of marriage—a sex life that's free of guilt, pain, and disease.

Remember, sex is not a four-letter word. And research shows your kids want to hear about this issue from you.

Part 1

Framing Your Discussions

Where's the Party?

The World Is Waiting for Your Child; Are You?

Have you ever considered the influence pop culture has on your child? Sex sells, and believe it or not, your child is the target audience. Beer commercials shock viewers with beautiful bodies, bountiful breasts, and seductive music. MTV allures viewers with hours of spring-break reporting showing girls and guys dressed in nothing but whipped cream. A myriad of "reality dating shows" encourage young people to abandon all reservations—even threesomes are encouraged. "Artists" bring us such popular tracks as "It's Gettin' Hot in Here" and others that work hard to break down any inhibitions that might still be lingering.

Is it any wonder children (and even many adults) are confused about sexuality? Misinformation permeates the airwaves, and sexual innuendo creates unrealistic fantasies about what sex "should" be. Adolescents look forward to the party advertising has created—truly believing it will fill their longing for personal happiness—but are disillusioned when the reality leaves them empty and cold.

The question at hand: can young people avoid this trap of dissatisfaction?

Impossible Standards

Advertisers promote pleasure, including sexual pleasure, as the pinnacle of life. Whether the product is an exotic cruise or frozen food, beautiful people are portrayed as happy people. Happy people are individuals who drink and smoke. And happy people are also sexual people. Music videos clearly paint this picture. Is it any wonder young people are so consumed with sex?

So is it the media's fault that kids are having oral sex in seventh grade and babies in ninth grade? Is the media responsible for young adolescents reenacting porn flicks at home alone in the afternoon? Could they also be responsible for the trend of same-sex experimentation among young teens?

Or is Hollywood just an innocent bystander trying to entertain an increasingly cynical population?

Some experts believe that the media merely represents the world around us. Others feel that the media profoundly influences and directs our culture and has contributed significantly to the increased interest in sexual pleasure and sensuality.

Realistically, both viewpoints are true: the media does indeed reflect our culture when it comes to sexuality and our fascination with pleasure, and it also drives and directs and profoundly influences our culture at the same time.

Nowhere is this more evident than in the culture of our young people. Think about it. Adolescents are numb to the sexual references and behavior they see and hear on a daily basis. While rates of sexual activity among teens seem to be decreasing, sexually transmitted infection rates are skyrocketing. Of the almost 19 million new sexually transmitted infections (STIs) each year, over 50 percent occur in people under the age of twenty-five.[1]

If you're a parent of a young child, this may seem insane. If you have a child in high school, you may be cynical and have a sense of despair when it comes to helping your child embrace healthy sexuality.

It's time to open your eyes and not lose hope! Your child doesn't have to be the victim of cultural influences. You are the most powerful influence in your child's life (even though he may not seem to listen). The media may create smoke and mirrors, but your child knows you're the real thing! Your child wants you to talk with him frankly, honestly, and often about how sex fits in the context of life.

Avoiding Mixed Messages

Buried within the fabric of our culture are several distinctly different messages about sex and sexuality. The first is that sex is the most important thing in life—how one looks and dresses and one's sexual feelings are simply a measure of our existence. If sex is just a part of our physical and emotional makeup, then seeking to satisfy one's sexual desires through purely physical relationships would be justified. The problem with this viewpoint is that it's all about personal pleasure—not about personal relationships—which always leads to using other people. The result of this "user-friendly" message in our society has been an alarming rise in teenage pregnancy, sexual addiction, sexual identity difficulties, and sexually transmitted infections. But of even greater concern is an increase in the loneliness, hurt, heartache, and depression that accompanies sex apart from a deeply satisfying, intimate relationship.

Another, equally destructive message suggests that sex is a secret (different from private and intimate) part of life that should never be discussed. This mind-set indicates that sex and sexuality aren't parts of the gift of life. The message goes something like this: "A good person doesn't experience sexual temptations, sexual thoughts, or sexual feelings." Obviously, this is a lie. Sex is an integral part of life, and sexual feelings are unavoidable on the journey of life. This negative view of sex has resulted in increasing ignorance, shame, and secretiveness about sex and sexuality. That translates into an increase in teenage pregnancy, sexually transmitted infections, sexual addiction (such as pornography), and sexual identity difficulties, but most of all loneliness, heartache, shame, and guilt.

Both of these lies leave teens in an impossible bind—sexuality and sex is simply a biological and emotional drive one has the right to gratify in any way one sees fit, or sex is a filthy, dirty, and shameful thing to be avoided at all costs.

Consider a more balanced approach to sexuality. This approach suggests that if sex is integrated into life in a healthy, productive way, it will enhance life and help a person experience fulfillment. Because of this, sex doesn't become compulsive or damaging; rather, it's experienced as the gift it was made for—to enhance the intimate bond between a husband and a wife. This approach also provides for discussion complete with accurate, age-appropriate medical information accompanied by psychological, spiritual, and ethical values essential to healthy human sexual expression.

Not Just Another Sex Manual

This book is written from a unique perspective. The authors believe that sex is a beautiful gift. This gift is not a physical feeling or activity, nor a biological drive. Sex and sexuality are deeply relational, emotional, and spiritual (as well as physical) issues. Knowing this can help young people embrace their sexuality with power and knowledge.

We'll discuss a number of issues throughout the book. These underlie our passion and excitement for writing about sex and sexuality:

- Healthy sexuality requires that every person respect other people. True pleasure comes from recognizing the worth of others and the value of relationships.
- Sexual health comes from a positive self-image based on strong character traits such as self-control, personal responsibility, honesty, and kindness.

Parent Power

Four Ways to Stay Connected with Your Child

1. **Learn together.** What is he learning in school that you can learn about too? Read the books he loves, watch movies you can both enjoy, and intentionally look for things you can do together like travels or hikes and walks.
2. **Listen, listen, listen.** Before you tell your child what to do or get angry with him, ask him to help you understand what makes him behave a certain way.
3. **Live out your values.** Modeling is the best teacher of all. Your opinions on how he views his body and sexuality matter.
4. **Love unconditionally** and tell your child so, even if you don't like how he's acting or the choices he's making. Make your home—and you—a safe place.

- Sex within the right kind of relationship—a monogamous marital relationship—is healthy and good.
- Sexual desires are normal and healthy; a decision to act on these sexual desires is controllable behavior.
- Self-control is healthy and necessary for achieving satisfaction. People who operate only on their physical and emotional feelings find little joy and happiness in life.
- Avoiding early and promiscuous sexual activity is an emotionally and physically healthy choice.
- Parents are the most powerful influence in a child's life. Parents have the ultimate responsibility for teaching character to their children, and they have the primary right and responsibility to be involved in their children's education—especially about value-laden topics such as character and sexuality.

Perhaps you're overwhelmed with the status of our culture—the mixed messages of the media, the negative messages about sexuality, and the overwhelming nature of the responsibility of teaching your children about character and healthy sexuality. Don't be discouraged. Talking with your kids about sex and sexuality is just another adventure on your parenting journey. It can be fun! And the benefits will last a lifetime.

The Big Deal Is You!

You Do Make a Difference

You are the most influential factor in your child's life. When teens are asked, "Who holds the most influence in your life?", surprisingly, rock stars and athletes don't top the list. An overwhelming majority of teens answer, "My parents."

Children are created to be relational beings. The first relationships they develop are usually with their parents. Young people desire intimacy and the opportunity to communicate about the most important things in life—including sex. Unfortunately, many parents feel unprepared to discuss sex with their kids. Think about it: when (if) your parents talked to you about "the birds and the bees," was it painful, perhaps even terribly embarrassing?

Times have changed. Our sexually saturated society doesn't allow you the option of not talking about sex and sexuality with your child, because so much information, or should we say misinformation, permeates the culture around us. Today the options are clear. You can either choose to initiate and direct the conversation, or you can let culture's preconceived ideas dictate your child's beliefs about sexuality. Believe it or not, ignoring the issue often brings about a disastrous outcome of ignorance and perhaps a great deal of pain and loneliness for your child in the future.

As a parent, your greatest challenge and opportunity should be to provide information about sexuality to your child. It's important to remember that you can make a difference. Your child is looking for you to shape her life, not just physically and emotionally, but also in the areas of character and sexuality. You must also remember, however, that you are not responsible for the outcome. Each of us is born as a free agent with the right to make choices. Nevertheless, the fact remains that you are responsible, through what you say and do, to prepare your child for a life of healthy sexuality.

Building a healthy relationship with your child is the most influential thing you can do to help her develop strong character and healthy sexuality.

Know Yourself

Who are you? Before you can know your child, you have to know yourself. No parent is perfect. No parent has every issue figured out. Baggage from the past is standard fare for most parents. The truth is that life is hard, and it's the rare person who has completed the journey without any scars. Parenting is not a call to be perfect—just to be real. You don't have to ignore your pain; just commit to not letting your hang-ups taint your child's future.

If you're married, keeping your marriage strong and the lines of communication open with your spouse is crucial. It's healthy for a child to observe that mom and dad don't always agree, but they can talk about the issues of life, relationships, character, and sexuality.

Even if you're no longer married (or were never married), the best thing you can do is keep talking to your former spouse or another trusted adult about your child's growth, character development, and sexuality.

Know Your Child

To effectively teach your child about healthy sexuality and character, you need to know your child. You need to understand his individual temperament and respect him as an individual. Unfortunately, few parents really know their own kids—who they are inside and out.

So, how do you get to know your child? Spend time with him throughout every stage of his development. Spending time means entering into his world—knowing his strengths, weaknesses, joys, passions, and fears—and not just trying to give him a view of your world. It's literally the art of giving one's self by saying, "I care enough about you that I want to come into your world." Chapter 6 will provide some ways of doing this. Knowing your child is an important part of understanding the power of your relationship in developing healthy character and sexuality in your child.

Let Your Kids Know You

Letting your kids know you doesn't mean sharing all of your mistakes and weaknesses. Rather, you should share how your own experiences have impacted your journey. Allow your child to know that you have felt the same emotions she is experiencing. Help her see that you have walked in her shoes. When you allow your child to know that you experienced some of the same struggles growing up and had many of the same questions, she's less likely to feel alone in her quest for maturity.

The Power of Parents

One final aspect of developing a healthy relationship with your child is learning how to serve her relational needs. All children need relationships in order to fill up the areas of character and self-identity inside them. This doesn't mean spoiling your child by giving in to her every whim—indeed, quite the opposite. The challenge for you is to provide your child with time, attention, affection, affirmation, and comfort while at the same time giving appropriate structure, limits, and guidance. All of these things will contribute to a healthy sense of identity, so your child can develop her own self-esteem and self-confidence.

Parents are powerful. You are more influential than you might have imagined! If you're thinking, *I've tried everything, and my child is still a disaster*, don't be discouraged. You aren't responsible for the choices your child makes. You are only responsible for teaching and modeling a healthy life and developing, to the best of your ability, a healthy relationship with your child.

How's Your Sex Life?

Would you describe it as great? Before you can talk to your child about sex, it's important to figure out how you feel about the matter firsthand. Magazines provide plenty of advice on how to "spice up" your boring bedroom or how to drive him crazy with a flip of a switch, but do all of these tips truly equate to great sex? Research indicates that the people who have the best and most frequent sex are people who are married, monogamous, and religious—quite the opposite of any Hollywood stereotype.[1]

The real question of this book is, do you want your kids to have an incredible sex life? Hopefully your answer is a resounding YES! If you're like most parents, you want your kids to have a better life than you experienced: personally, professionally, and even physically. Maybe you've never thought about sex in terms of how it relates to your child's personal growth. Now would be a great opportunity to start thinking about how you can help your child achieve a phenomenal sex life in the future.

Great Sex Starts with You

You already know: you are the most influential person in your child's life when it comes to sexual issues.[2] Your behaviors and attitudes about sex (spoken and unspoken) will forever be imprinted into his life. Some parents are scared to talk to their kids about such a personal issue. Others are flat-out unprepared (academically and/or emotionally).

Since you are probably not a physician and don't hold degrees in anatomy or physiology, take heart. You're not alone. One of the benefits of being a parent in today's sexually saturated society is that there are plenty of resources and places to go for advice on this topic—but make sure the advice supports your worldview.

Perhaps embarrassment is preventing you from delving into sexual issues with your child. Consider this: MTV isn't embarrassed to talk candidly with him about sex. Why should you be embarrassed to talk with him about such an amazing subject?

If fear is holding you back from exploring this important topic, it's time to examine the root cause of such fear. Are you ashamed to talk with your kids because you had many partners early on and are embarrassed about the mistakes you've made? Maybe you've never experienced sex in the context of a committed, healthy (emotionally, physically, and spiritually) relationship, or perhaps you were abused as a child.

Or maybe you're just not emotionally ready to talk with your child about sex because you were raped, or he was conceived while you were under the influence of alcohol or drugs, or you weren't married when you got pregnant. Perhaps your sexual addictions or an affair have cost you your marriage and family, and you're not ready to be vulnerable with your child about the pain of your past.

Remember that your life experiences can be used as either building blocks or stumbling blocks in your child's life. Why not use your experiences from the past as tools to grow from?

All of these issues are understandable, but they aren't strong enough to allow you to stay silent. You need to deal with your issues so you can protect your children from the pain you've experienced in the sexual realm of your life.

Where Does Healing Begin?

Experiencing healing opens the door for you to positively influence your child's life. There are several steps you can take to begin the healing process:

Listening to Your Child

The Key to the Heart

1. **Stop what you're doing.** (She knows if you're trying to do something else at the same time.)
2. **Look her in the eyes** when she's talking—give focused attention.
3. **Don't interrupt or finish her sentences**—let her speak her thoughts.
4. **Reflect back** what you heard her say.
5. **Ask her questions to clarify or help** her find the solution herself if she's asking for advice.
6. **Only offer your thoughts if asked** or if you want her to think about your point of view.
7. **Thank her for sharing** with you and tell her how much you enjoyed it.

1. Take an honest look at your life. Healing will come after a genuine review of your life experiences and mistakes. This includes looking at how others have let you down and how poor choices you made have impacted your life.
2. Share with a trusted friend or a professional counselor. Find a reliable person with whom you can share not only the experiences described above but also the feelings that came from your experiences. Healing is unlikely outside of relationships, and talking with a trustworthy friend or counselor can provide a tremendous sense of relief from the pain and sadness of your past.
3. Forgive. This is perhaps the most difficult part of the process. Forgiveness of those who have wronged you, and forgiveness of yourself for making mistakes in the past, are essential to free you to help your children develop a healthy sense of self-worth and sexuality. Forgiveness isn't the same as forgetting—and it doesn't matter if the person has asked for or earned forgiveness. It's truly

a process of letting go and moving forward. Forgiveness is a gift you give yourself!

4. Learn more. It's never too late to become a student again. In the process of talking with your kids about sex and their sexuality, take the opportunity to glean new information from trustworthy sources so you can positively shape your children's future relationships.

It's Never Too Late to Start

Embracing a positive outlook on sex and sexuality will help you communicate more effectively with your child about this incredible subject. Releasing your pain will empower her with skills to enhance her sex life in the future. If your child is in high school and you're just starting this process, ask her for forgiveness and try to repair any misinformation you might have (or have not) communicated in the past due to your lack of insight and knowledge.

There's never been a more exciting time to be able to give your child the gift of a positive and strong message about her growing sexuality. Remember, your child will learn about sex from someone. The question is—will it be from you?

What a Girl Wants

Attention, Affection, and Affirmation

If you've been to the movies lately, you know what a girl wants: power, prestige, beauty, wealth, and a strong man to take care of her at the end of the day. Box-office hits show young women doing anything and everything men can do, but with a sensual style that can knock others off their feet. For young women to be successful, Hollywood suggests they must be smart, beautiful, athletic, adventuresome, powerful, and, of course, sensual and seductive.

Unfortunately, Hollywood's extreme view of size-two women does incredible damage to vulnerable young women in search of their identity. Many young girls starve themselves for attention from young men. You don't have to be a rocket scientist to know that the primary need of young women is to be nurtured. Girls want to be successful, smart, and sexy, but most of all they want to be loved, valued, and cherished.

Girls' Greatest Traits

As girls grow up, two features stand out. First of all, girls are highly verbal. They love to talk about anything and everything, including their feelings and experiences. Second, they love to be nurtured and to nurture others. An important part of being nurtured is being affirmed and valued for who they are—whether or not they're short, tall, smart, thin, athletic, or dainty. Being nurtured also includes the need to be cared for and protected.

Playtime for a young girl usually represents the relational pieces of life. Many girls love to play with dolls, dress up their Barbies, cook in the kitchen, and have tea parties. (All of these activities are done with friends, real or imaginary.) If the word *stereotype* is screaming through your head at this point—hang in there. The reality is that whether a girl plays with a ball or a Barbie, her natural tendency—when compared to boys—is to focus on the relational aspect of the game rather than the physical.

Material Girl

Product developers and advertising experts spend millions monopolizing on young women's desire to be nurtured. Products focus on glamour, fashion, and how to catch the right man. In commercials (and music videos), women more often talk with their hips than their lips. Unfortunately, the messages young women receive about their role in society focus primarily on the physical and leave relational issues to chance—or worse yet, suggest that if you have the physical package, you'll be satisfied relationally and emotionally. Plastic surgeons profit from women's desperation to look more attractive. (Have you been Botoxed lately?) These cultural influences reinforce the false idea that young ladies can get their needs met by looking and acting seductive.

Avoiding the Trap

If you truly want your daughter to have a fabulous sex life when she's married, it's important to help her understand that sensuality and sexuality

Magical Moments of Childhood

Dream with Your Daughter

It's important to celebrate your daughter throughout her life. Some things you might do to make her feel special and to open up situations when you might dream together about her future include:

- **Giving her a dozen roses** (or her favorite flower) when she makes good grades
- **Helping her decorate** her room (maybe fifty times!)
- **Pulling together a special outfit** for her to remember an important event
- **Writing her love letters** and providing her with a special box to put them in
- **Taking her to dinner or making her a special meal** where you'll treat her like a princess (this is especially good for dads to do so she'll have high expectations for the men in her life)

aren't the same thing. Teach her how to accomplish her goals without using sex as a weapon.

To help you achieve this task, let's look at the role of mothers and fathers. A mother's love is primarily one of nurturing and caring for her young daughter. If a mother truly invests in nurturing her daughter as she grows, she will realize that she's valued and worth being cared for, regardless of her outward appearance. Remember, you are inundated with messages about your own appearance and may subconsciously respond by commenting on your daughter's weight. Don't fall into this trap—or you'll be just as guilty as those you're protecting her from. This will lead your daughter to believe that it's her physical appearance that makes her valuable. Instead, compliment her on character qualities such as courage, sensitivity, and integrity.

At the same time, a father's love is primarily one of protectiveness. It's mostly experienced as affirmation and protection as a young woman grows up. The more time a father gives to his daughter, the more he teaches her that she's valuable and that she can have her needs met because there's a man willing to offer his love and affection to her. It's not hard to understand that when a father's love is missing, a young woman will look to other men to meet her relational needs. In doing so, she may become seductive, flirty, or even sexually active at an early age because she desires and needs the protective, affirming love a father gives.

The greatest gift a father can give his daughter is attention, affection, and affirmation.

If you're a single mother (and your daughter's father isn't involved in her life), it's imperative that you seek out a positive male role model to influence your daughter. You might seek out one of your immediate family members, a teacher or coach, or a leader in your church. This man may help make up for the loss of a father.

Another critical component to preparing your daughter for a life of great sex is to be sure she witnesses healthy marital relationships—relationships where a husband and wife show respect for each other. If you're not married, it's important to identify and expose your daughter to healthy marriages so she understands the benefits. These relationships will help your daughter recognize how a woman should be treated, and they'll help her set realistic expectations for her future marital relationship.

Love of Self

As a young woman sees positive relationships modeled through her parents and other important mentors, it's also important that she learn to value herself. She needs to know she's valuable as a person, regardless of her specific talents or beauty.

As your daughter matures, teach her how to protect herself from inappropriate relationships and dangerous situations that may rob her of her self-confidence. Remind her that she doesn't need to be seductive and aggressive in seeking male affection to have value. This will be a challenge, especially in light of the cultural and peer pressures she'll face in a sexually saturated society.

Remind your daughter: sex is sexist. If a girl becomes sexually active outside of marriage and has multiple partners, she's the one who will be hurt (both physically and emotionally). The reality of most sexually transmitted infections is that the women experience the pain and problems related to the infections.

As a parent, you're needed by your daughter more than you will ever know. Remind her of her value daily, because if you don't, someone else will—and the results may rob her of the personal and sexual satisfaction she desires in the future.

Let the Adventure Begin

The Makings of a Man

Sticks, stones, guns, swords, bats, and balls—these are the tools in a boy's toy box. From these tools, one can assess that boys of all ages desire adventure, conquest, and competition. The process of parenting young boys and helping them mature into young men is one of delicate balance. Relationally, young boys may not require the intensity of hours that young girls do, but boys desperately need guidance from their parents as to what journeys to take and what battles to fight.

How many times have you heard "Boys will be boys" to explain the behavior of boys and young men? Boys are expected to be aggressive risk-takers and seek to break any limits that might be applied to them. As a parent of a son, you have the incredible opportunity to allow your son to explore, but also the responsibility to remind him that his actions have consequences.

Pushing the Limits

Boys tend to seek adventure as they try to find out where they fit into this world. Boys are less likely to engage in relational play focused on nurturing and caring for people and are much more focused on venturing out, conquering, and exploring their world. As a boy grows and matures, his physical, emotional, and even sexual drives will be more intense than those of girls. Additionally, some boys tend to have more trouble dealing with anger, verbalizing their feelings, and acting on their emotions and sexuality than girls do. Because of this, it's imperative for your son to learn how to effectively communicate his needs.

Counter Culture

Most advertisements geared toward men focus on adventure and sexual fantasy, regardless of whether the product is the trendiest beer or the latest stuffed-crust pizza. Since young men are bombarded day and night with sexual messages from the mass media, you must be vigilant in helping your son realize that sex should not be just about conquest or a physical encounter. This is why the family structure surrounding young men is so important.

Family Matters

If you want your son to have great sex—in a loving and lasting relationship—it's going to take more than words. Young men need to see healthy relationships. The concept of learning by example is key here.

A mother's role in her son's life is imperative. Her ability to nurture him and to meet his physical and emotional needs early on is unlike any other. Often, nurturing love is what strengthens and encourages a boy to grow and become strong physically, emotionally, and eventually sexually.

A father's love, however, is equally important. As with young girls, a father's relationship and kind of love is primarily affirming and protective to a young boy. Dads are uniquely qualified to help their boys understand the world around them. This love is inescapably essential to the emotional and sexual health of a young boy. When a father makes the effort to spend time and play with his son and protect him from the dangers of the outside world, it contributes significantly to the young man's growing sense of self-worth. Additionally, fatherly love will help a young boy grow and mature with the ability to be comfortable in his own skin. If fatherly love is missing, it should come as no surprise that a young man will probably spend the rest of his life looking for that affirmation and protection from others.

What Makes a Man?

As your son matures, there are a couple of concepts you need to instill in him.

Self-Control

Since boys experience their world by exploration and also experience their physical, emotional, and even sexual drives to a stronger degree than women, learning self-control is imperative to the development of your son's self-esteem, confidence, identity, and ultimate success. Self-control needs to be taught, enforced, and modeled by strong parental relationships and hopefully modeled by a strong marriage.

Respect

Another important lesson for boys to learn is respect for others, especially women. Life offers plenty of opportunities to teach young men about the importance of respecting and caring for other people. Playing sports, building tree houses, and even rough play are opportunities to learn about self-control, rules, and respect for others.

Respect for others' feelings is an imperative trait for a young man to possess—especially if he desires to someday be a husband and father. Boys need to learn how to control their feelings and emotions without being disrespectful and violating the boundaries of their parents. As a young man matures and is more involved with his peers, his boundaries will be challenged and his self-control mocked.

In the process of learning about respect and self-control, a boy should also learn how to receive physical affection and give it to other people. (This is often very hard for many boys—and fathers for that matter.)

You need to understand, educate about, affirm, and celebrate all of the emotional and physical changes that happen in your son as he matures. Far too often, boys experience the process of puberty, sexual feelings, wet dreams, and erections without any support, education, or advice from their parents (especially their fathers). Your son needs to be informed about the physical changes occurring in his body so that he understands they're a positive transition into manhood rather than a reason for fear, shame, and embarrassment. Helping your son embrace his masculinity will provide him with the opportunity to avoid learning about his newfound sexuality from his friends—often excellent sources of misinformation or valueless notions.

Real Men

One of the most difficult lessons you'll encounter along the road to your son's sexual development will be helping him distinguish "talk" from "truth." We all know that locker rooms are full of boys bragging about their accomplishments—whether they be on or off the playing field. You need to help your son understand (if he doesn't already) that boys exaggerate, especially in the realm of sexual activity. Remind him that not everybody is having sex and that his friends may be talking trash to build their own self-esteem.

In addition, you need to help your son realize that real men demonstrate self-control in order to accomplish long-term goals. For boys, sexual satisfaction is a short-term goal. And often they don't think about the potential long-term problems that might result from having nonmarital sex just one time with one girl.

Make Life an Adventure with Your Son

When connecting with your son, look at things that he really enjoys:

- Develop a hobby together, like taking guitar lessons at the same time
- Volunteer to serve others together
- Take him fishing, hiking, skiing (some "boys only" venture!)
- Teach him how to make his favorite meal
- Read books with him

Another issue to prepare your son for is pornography. Unfortunately, porn starts to enter young boys' worlds earlier than you might anticipate. Many experts believe that most young men have been exposed to their first pornographic images by the time they're eight years old, whether it be through the Web, movies, or magazines. As a parent, you must talk with your son about the power of pornography and how it can inhibit him from experiencing a fantastic sex life.

Finally, you need to prepare your son to withstand peer pressure from his female friends. In today's culture, it isn't uncommon to hear about girls being sexually aggressive toward boys. Young men need to be prepared to say no to physical advances, and they also need to be taught how to avoid falling into the traps of aggressive women.

Too often adolescents (especially boys) are left to discover their sexuality with Hollywood—and their peers—as their only teachers. In order to empower the next generation of young people with the tools to develop an incredible sex life, we must provide them with models of healthy relationships, realistic expectations, and the knowledge that the greatest sex awaits them if they can first master the art of developing healthy emotional relationships without falling into the trap of settling for meaningless physical ones on the journey to adulthood.

Rules of Engagement

Ways to Listen So They Will Talk

Some say talk is cheap, but not talking to your child about sex will be costly. Before you dive into this important topic, remember that sex is a deeply personal and relational topic. Talking about sex can't be a onetime event. Let your child know that you want to be his guide on this very important and exciting journey as he learns about his sexuality. It may take him some time to warm up to the idea if he's older—but before you're offended by his responses to your efforts, remember that your relationship with him will determine how much he wants to know from you. Keep in mind that this journey is a process of engagement, teaching about the very essence of life, relationships, and sexuality.

The art of talking about sexuality will evolve as your child grows. Initially, the answers you provide may be very matter-of-fact, but as he matures, you'll want to wrap your answers in the context of relationships and couple answers with the character traits, morals, and religious values you're trying to teach. An important part of this journey of talking about sex and sexuality is to provide affirmation and permission to ask more questions in the future. You might say something like, "I'm glad you asked that. I know that's a difficult question to understand."

Relationships Matter

All relationships, especially parent-child relationships, should be grounded in a healthy respect for one another. In other words, as a parent, your primary concern needs to be what's in the best interest of your child.

There is no other way to develop a healthy relationship with your child than to enter into her world. As we mentioned earlier, this means understanding what her current needs, interests, and passions are. You can't delve into the life of your child except by playing with her and understanding and listening to what she thinks, feels, and enjoys.

As your child matures, she'll undoubtedly have more and more questions about sex and sexuality. In fact, she'll not only have more questions but more experiences. These questions might arise from scenes in a movie, or exposure to pornography and the stimulation that comes from that, or experiences such as masturbation or hearing about sexual abuse that happens in the community. Each of these will allow you opportunities to boldly answer questions and affirm the thoughts, ideas, and growing identity of your child.

Tips for Success

Most parents wonder how they can become more effective at influencing their child's thoughts on sexuality. Here are a few tips that might help you on this important excursion:

- Start early. Work your way up to talking about sex. Enhance your one-on-one skills with your child by discussing appropriate personal health and safety issues as he grows. It will be easier for both you and your child to talk about sex if you've already developed a rapport and pattern for discussing sensitive subjects. These might include personal hygiene, dealing with strangers, resisting peer pressure, avoiding substance use, and anticipating puberty changes.

- Believe in your child and build his confidence (and self-control). Both children and adults tend to overestimate the number of teens who are sexually active. Never assume your child is incapable of resisting temptation. Instead, equip him with knowledge, confidence, and unconditional love and support. Help him establish high goals and expectations for himself, and regularly praise him for his success.

- Look for teaching opportunities and use them. Many parents admit they have a hard time finding a good starting place for a discussion about sex, but if you're observant, you'll find natural "launching pads" for discussion all around. It might be a provocative commercial on TV, a popular singer's attention-getting wardrobe, or a graphic sex scene in a movie.

- Relax and create an open environment for talking (and listening). Your child can tell when you're uptight. In order to foster an environment that's conducive to meaningful discussion, you need to be calm and confident. Encourage your child to ask anything he wants (and thank him when he does). If you don't, he'll probably seek an answer somewhere else. Don't overreact to something he says, even if it's not what you expected to hear. The goal is to make your home the preferred place for discussions. Don't just talk. Ask questions. Listen to his responses.

- Give accurate, age-appropriate information. Listen closely to the questions you're being asked. Don't get lost in details if your child asks a very general question. Consider his age and what's appropriate for him to know, but also remember that kids today experience puberty earlier than ever. Kids are also exposed to sexual imagery and vocabulary more freely and at a much younger age.

- Don't be afraid to say, "I don't know." Admitting to your child that you don't know the answer to his question could be the one thing that helps your relationship thrive. He needs to know you have limitations. Rather than letting this slow you down, use your lack of knowledge as an opportunity to research the issue in more depth together.

- Anticipate the next stage before it happens. It's always better to be proactive than reactive. You can be an even stronger advocate for your child by preparing him for what's ahead. Being proactive gives you the opportunity to discuss with your child appropriate responses to a variety of situations that might arise.

- Be aware of your actions. As you become comfortable talking with your child about sexual issues, be careful about bringing up discussions during what might be an embarrassing time for him (such as when friends are around).

- Teach your child how to develop healthy relationships. As you talk to him about the importance of saving sex for marriage, it's important that you provide him with alternatives on what to do with his emotions and physical desires. Learning how to develop strong friendships is a skill every child needs. Many young people grow up without learning about healthy friendships, so it's no surprise that when they begin to seek a relationship with the opposite sex, they skip the friendship phase. Teach your child what healthy friendships look like. Also, encourage him to develop healthy relationships with adults other than yourself. These individuals can serve as great role models, resources for questions, and support for your child's psychological and emotional growth.

- Integrate your family's faith and values into the discussion. Never underestimate the power of faith when it comes to your child making a decision about becoming sexually active. According to the National Longitudinal Study of Adolescent Health (the largest study of adolescent behavior ever), students who reported having taken a pledge to remain a virgin were significantly more likely to delay their sexual debut.[1] In another poll, teens cited religion as the second-strongest influence in their lives, just behind their parents.[2]

- Love your child unconditionally. Remind him how much you love him—for who he is, not what he does. And if he blows it, don't take his mistakes personally. Step up to the plate and help him through the crisis.

As you digest this information and delve into the second section of this book, remember that the answers provided are merely a foundation to get the conversation started. Be creative and open to exploring conversations you never dreamed of having with your child. *Your kids are listening. Will you be the one talking?*

Questions, Anyone?

What Parents Need to Know

You probably heard "There's no such thing as a stupid question" over and over again while you were in school. Nothing could be truer when dealing with sex and sexuality. If you haven't figured it out by now, parenting is a journey in humility that may include telling your child that you don't know the answers to her questions, but you're willing to help her find out.

If you're like most people, the conversation with your parents about sex stopped just short of getting interesting. Perhaps you found the answers to your sexual questions on the playground or in the bedroom with your first love. Or maybe you made some great decisions while you were a teen and waited to experience sexual intercourse as it was meant to be, on your honeymoon. The bottom line is that you probably know the fundamentals about sex and even have an idea about how to address some of the deeper issues, but you may not have the exact words to answer the questions your kids are sure to ask. This book is meant to be a springboard for the questions you will undoubtedly encounter as your child grows. It also might answer some of the questions you may have lingering in the back of your mind—but were afraid to ask.

Think of this—talking to your kids about sex may turn out to be some of your fondest memories as you reflect on your parenting journey in the future. You may not know how to start the conversation, so take your time—the right opportunity will present itself. Lighten up and let the adventure begin!

Why is it important for my child to learn about sex from me?

Your child is going to learn about sex from someone. You know him better than anyone else, and you know how much information is too much too soon. This knowledge makes you the best teacher for the subject. Sexuality is one area of life where the correct information, delivered in the correct context with the correct emotional atmosphere year after year, is crucial to healthy growth. Ignorance about the true meaning and purpose of sex is indeed dangerous.

Discussing sex and sexuality shouldn't be a onetime conversation. The conversation should continue throughout your child's life. The benefit of talking with him about sex is that you can respond to the environment around him. If he's been exposed to overtly sexual messages during a movie, you can respond immediately, before he's affected by the experience.

Also, sex is best taught in the context of your family morals and religious values. For the health of your child, it's essential that the emotional and moral tone of his sex education be compatible with that of your family. (Research strongly indicates that the young people who make the worst decisions are those who have no foundation from which to develop their own decisions and moral structure later in life.[1]) Facts are important for the conversation, but they're not nearly as important as the tone used to deliver the message.

When should I start teaching my child about sex?

Now. Talking about sex and sexuality is something that begins in early infancy as you start to respond to your child as she becomes curious about her body. Your daughter may seek information about what it means to be a girl. She may be curious about her body parts, and one thing is certain: her curiosity will continue to grow as she does. If you start talking early about these issues, the conversation will never seem awkward or inappropriate. After all, your goal as a parent is to teach your child about the world—sexuality is just one of many important topics to address.

Can I tell my child too much too soon?

In our culture, images and talk about sex are everywhere. Sexual awareness is tossed on your child much sooner than you would wish. In this atmosphere, you'll face the challenge of preparing him to understand sexual issues without burdening him with facts and feelings he can't emotionally handle. Any discussion about the details associated with sexuality should be developmentally appropriate for your child's level of understanding. If for some reason you do present information that's over his head, he will likely brush it off and not be bothered. Remember, the spontaneous questions he asks will provide you with the best idea of where he is and what he wants to know.

What are the dangers of teaching too little too late?

If you aren't timely in sharing the facts of sexuality with your child, her first impression about sex could come from an uninformed peer, a preying older child, or a sex-education program that may not reflect your family's values. In the absence of information from you, your child will likely be confronted with sexual situations she is not intellectually or emotionally prepared to handle.

What can I do to feel more confident in talking to my child about sex?

Just do it! The more you talk, the better you'll feel. Yes, talking to your kids about sex can be embarrassing, but it can also be fun. Don't act like you have all the answers. If you make the process an educational journey, both you and your child will benefit greatly. Don't be afraid to say, "I don't know." Don't be afraid to admit your failures.

Once you start talking, you'll be surprised at how easy it is to discuss the issue of sex. Remember, you don't have to describe every detail during your first conversation. Start early, talk often, and be open. Your confidence will develop gradually.

If you're still dealing with your own hang-ups about sex, it's time to work through the issues. There's no time like the present to become comfortable with your own sexuality. Yes, you may have been sexually abused or wounded in other ways, but now is the time for a fresh start. Your child deserves the best, and he deserves to hear about sex and sexuality from you.

How important is a child's family life to developing a healthy attitude about sexuality?

The quality of a child's family relationships plays a vital role in her developing sense of her own sexuality. In fact, the overall atmosphere of the home is more important than her parents' ability to present the facts perfectly. A home where a child feels accepted and where family members are comfortable with their sexuality sets the stage for healthy sexual attitudes in the future.

On the other hand, if the atmosphere in the home is cold, inconsistent, or lacking in role modeling or unconditional love, a child will have difficulty developing healthy sexual attitudes even when she's presented with the very best factual education regarding sex. A healthy, loving home is the first step to a healthy understanding of sex.

How can I help my child have a wholesome attitude about his body?

A quick tip—attitudes are largely caught rather than taught. Your child will generally mirror your attitudes when it comes to his body and sex. If you have a sense of shame about your body and sexuality, he may adopt the same attitude. If you're comfortable about your body and sexuality, he will be as well. You can reinforce healthy attitudes by talking matter-of-factly to him about the beauty of the human body.

I'm a single parent; does that affect how I talk to my children about sex?

Many parents are rearing children without the help of another parent. Being a single parent makes many aspects of parenting harder, but not impossible. As a single parent, like any other parent, you'll need to prepare yourself with the facts in order to answer your children's questions effectively. There may be times when you have to say, "I haven't had that experience, but here's what I think." Also, think about enlisting the help of a trusted relative or other adult to fill in with information on specific issues when a parent of the opposite sex isn't available. Most important, your being single doesn't mean you shouldn't talk about sexual issues; your children want to hear from you—your opinions and experiences are valuable.

I didn't start talking to my child at an early age; is there any way I can catch up?

It's helpful to start talking about sexuality early with your child. But if you missed out on the early stages of sex education, you can start where you are and make the best of it. It's better to start now than to not talk at all. With a teenager, you can start the conversation by apologizing for dropping the ball. Then ask him if he has any questions, and start with a clean slate. If you're honest about your failures, you'll find that your kids are more forgiving and flexible than you thought possible.

Which age is most important when it comes to teaching about sex?

This question is difficult to answer because each stage of development is so important and unique. The preschool years are critical in establishing comfort in talking about the body and sexual issues. Subconscious attitudes and feelings are rooted here. The school-age years are important for teaching information about the body, reinforcing your child's attitude toward herself, and establishing boundaries in relationships with both sexes. The preteen and teen years are crucial—from both an educational and a behavioral standpoint. During these stages of development, the physical facts of anatomy and bodily function will be detailed for the rapidly growing adolescent. This is a time of emotional upheaval when sexual curiosity and desire are driving forces. Given the surging hormones and accompanying temptations in our society, this is also a time when parents must be vigilant in providing a great deal of information and support.

What is a healthy attitude toward sex, anyway?

Basically, it's an attitude that understands sex is more than the picture painted by popular culture. A healthy attitude says sex is more than:

- Intercourse
- Animal attraction
- A process of gratifying needs or longings
- Stimulation of the senses
- Recreation or a way to have fun
- A means of manipulation

Sex is a wonderful, precious gift. One's sexuality, fully understood and mastered, stimulates growth and opens the door to the full meaning of relationships. Healthy sexuality frees us to be whole persons rather than imprisoning us and limiting our options. Healthy sexuality is intimately intertwined with love. While sexual urges ebb and flow, they reach healthy completion only in a loving, committed, and permanent relationship—marriage. Anything less shortchanges the people involved.

How can I best protect my child from sexual abuse?

Not only do we hear about sexual abuse more freely today, but evidence points to a true increase in abuse. The sexual overstimulation of our society accompanied by a breakdown of behavioral boundaries contributes to the epidemic of child sexual abuse. In addition, children today are in contact with so many more people outside the home than ever before.

The following protective steps are based on recommendations from the American Academy of Pediatrics:

- Talk to your child about sexual abuse. At every age, teach him boundaries for intimate contact and talk. At his level of understanding, help him to know that some behaviors by adults or older children aren't appropriate.

- From an early age, teach your child which body parts are private and to be touched and talked about only in the home. If anyone tries to violate this privacy, urge him to let you know.

- Listen when your child tries to tell you something. Often children won't come out and describe directly the actions of a person who has violated their privacy. But they often hint at their concerns. Be sensitive and listen carefully when you sense that your child is trying to tell you something but is having difficulty putting it into words.

- Let your child know that you won't be angry with him when he tells you something that someone else did. Let him know by your words and facial expressions that you won't blame him.

- Never let your child go home or go to a game with someone you don't know. Close supervision is a must. Get to know the parents of your children's friends. Get to know the sitters and child-care providers you use.

- Most important, let your child, whatever his age, know that you will always listen to his concerns. Frequently spend unstructured time with him so that you'll have the opportunity to pick up on cues indicating any concerns on his part.[2]

Is it necessary to use special materials such as books, magazines, charts, or videos when teaching my child about sex?

At times, teaching tools of various sorts may be helpful in teaching the facts of sexuality. A picture book that you can read to your preschooler may be helpful in opening the door to discussions about body parts or the birth process. A color atlas of the body will clarify the presentation of information about puberty to the preteen. A video- or audiotape series that parents and teens watch or listen to together may be a catalyst stimulating talk with teenagers. It's important to realize, however, that such items are only tools, not the main course of study. The most important tool, by far, in teaching children about sex is open dialogue between parent and child—of any age.

How can I best transmit my values about sex to my child?

You have great power in molding your child's feelings, attitudes, and behaviors. You can do several things to maximize this potential. First, talk to her about sex. The more accessible you are to her, the more likely she will be to look to you for answers to her most pressing questions, including those involving values. Second, openly share your values. Let her know what you think and why. Third, engage your kids, particularly teens, in conversation about your family's values. Use teachable moments to talk about the pros and cons of different sexual practices that are all too familiar to your teens, since they see such behavior in public, on TV, or in the movies. Most important, live a life worth modeling. Values are caught—not taught.

What is the school's role in teaching my child about sex?

Parents are ideally the best teachers for their children when it comes to sexual issues. However, in the last thirty years, schools have assumed a more prominent role in talking with kids about sex and other risk behaviors. Many believe that schools started discussing these vital issues because many parents weren't educating their children. Some people counter that schools are now aggressively assuming more of a parenting role in order to bring conformity to society. In more recent times, schools have been pushed to be more proactive in teaching about sex as the world has been confronted with the epidemic of AIDS and other sexually transmitted infections. Whatever the reasons, there's no doubt that schools in every area of the country and for every age are actively teaching more and more about sex.

There are two areas where you have the right, as well as the responsibility, to observe closely what schools are doing in the area of sex education. First, it's important in our overly sexualized society that schools don't present too much sexual material too early, before the children are ready to deal with it. The second area of concern is the presentation of information about sexual behavior in such a way as to imply that values don't matter and that sex in all of its forms is okay as long as it is "safe sex" or "safer sex" (which generally means promoting the use of condoms). As a parent, the most important thing you can do is stay involved in your child's education—don't check out. Your involvement will go a long way toward making sure he receives the best education in all subject areas.

Are there any health implications associated with homosexuality?

Yes. Science clearly suggests that individuals who participate in gay, lesbian, or bisexual behaviors are at greater risk than heterosexuals for experiencing certain problems. Research shows the following:

- Men who have sex with men are at greater risk for contracting many dangerous or even life-threatening sexually transmitted infections, including HIV, hepatitis B, and anal cancer, compared to heterosexual men. Other STIs of concern among men who have sex with men include anal syphilis, urethritis, and a range of oral and gastrointestinal infections.[3]

- Men who have sex with men account for over half of all AIDS cases in North America.[4]

- Hepatitis A is more prevalent among men who have sex with men than among heterosexuals.[5]

- According to the National Health and Nutrition Examination survey, the prevalence rate of hepatitis B is about five times higher among men who have sex with men than among those who are exclusively heterosexual.[6]

- Herpes is one of the most common anal and rectal infections among homosexually active men. The existence of open sores from genital herpes infection enormously increases the risk of acquiring HIV.[7]

- Homosexual youths are two to three times more likely to attempt suicide than are their heterosexual peers, and 30 percent of all youth suicides are committed by homosexuals.[8]

Regardless of a teen's sexual identification, she should be strongly encouraged to practice abstinence until she's married to prevent the long-term health implications associated with unhealthy sexual activity.

What's my role in helping my child develop healthy friendships, and how do those relationships help him avoid future high-risk behaviors?

Friendships are key to your child's emotional and sexual development—they are the glue of life. Helping him develop strong and positive friendships will go a long way toward building his self-esteem and preparing him for his future.

As he grows and matures, so will his ability to develop friendships. Your own friendships with colleagues, your spouse, and your kids will help prepare the foundation for your child's future relationships, including his marriage. Many parents falsely believe that they don't have the power to influence their child's friendships. You do! If you're involved in his life, you will influence not only him but his friends as well. (See the "Fostering Friendship" sidebars.)

What's the problem with buying my child whatever she wants? How does this relate to her future decisions regarding sexual activity?

By providing your child with all she wants when she wants it, you're setting her up for future failure. Delayed gratification is a concept that you need to teach her from an early age. If you give her everything she wants, then she'll expect that to be the norm as she grows. If you teach her to wait for the things she wants, you're providing her with the skills to wait for what she wants even when her hormones are raging.

How important is it that I teach my child about character traits?

Very. A book on healthy sexuality would be incomplete without a discussion on character development, for the two are intricately intertwined. (That's why you'll see "Character Builders" throughout this book.) Think about it:

- How do you choose to wait until marriage to have sex if you have no self-discipline to put off instant gratification?
- If honesty isn't part of your character development, then you'll lie to convince a sexual partner that you've never had a sexually transmitted infection.
- If loyalty to a relationship isn't present, then its stability is challenged.
- If respect is absent, then sex becomes a commodity.
- If love and unselfishness are missing in a relationship, then sex for one's own pleasure becomes the focus.

Character development must start early and should never end. You, the parent, are the best teacher, and the best curriculum is how you live your life on a daily basis. Using character words in daily conversations with your children will help them understand what being a person of character is all about. Many elementary schools have recognized how important character training is to produce responsible students, but it's really our job as parents to instill these traits in our kids.

What can you do?

- Be intentional about modeling character traits.
- Show humility by admitting when you blew it and should have acted differently.
- Applaud your child when he demonstrates one of these traits by his words or actions.
- Use your child's failure to be a person of character as a teachable moment, and give him another try, rather than punishing him.
- Constantly look for examples in the newspaper, TV and videos, books, and articles that show positive character traits for your children.

The following list of character traits will be highlighted in the various age groups. However, they all apply to every age group. This list isn't complete, so add your own traits as they seem relevant. A good resource for learning more about character traits is *Teaching Your Children Values* by Linda and Richard Eyre.[9]

- **Honesty:** being truthful and trustworthy; not lying, cheating, stealing. It's the inner strength and confidence that is bred by exacting truthfulness, trustworthiness, and integrity.
- **Kindness:** being friendly, generous, thoughtful of others; also showing compassion.
- **Respect:** treating others and things as if they had value and honor. This includes manners and courtesy. We should have respect for differences, life, elders and parents, property, nature, and the beliefs and rights of others.
- **Determination:** setting your mind to accomplish something; to decide and resolve to go a certain path.
- **Orderliness/cleanliness:** picking up after yourself and keeping things organized; taking care of your body in hygiene and grooming.

- **Responsibility:** taking on an obligation and carrying it out. It's being reliable and accountable for your commitments and being dependable.
- **Loyalty:** showing commitment to your family, friends, school, employment, faith, and country.
- **Courage:** the attitude of facing and dealing with anything recognized as dangerous, difficult, or painful, instead of withdrawing from it. Courage is doing something that's hard, like not following the crowd but acting on one's convictions, even if it's unpopular.
- **Self-discipline:** being able to motivate and manage yourself and your time, your appetites, your anger, and your health.
- **Sexual purity:** having as a goal that a sexual relationship belongs in marriage and restraining yourself until that commitment is made public in the marriage ceremony. Purity includes understanding why this is the best choice for emotional, physical, and spiritual reasons.
- **Unselfishness/love:** individual and personal caring that goes beyond yourself. It's thinking of the other over your own needs and sacrificing for the caring or needs of another.

Every day, as parents, we are challenged to educate and equip our children in ways we never were. Remember, as you talk with your child about these important issues, you are equipping him with the tools for a successful future—one without regret. Press on!

Part 2

The Answers You Need & They Want

7

Baby Steps

Infants to Four-Year-Olds

"Mommy, I have a penis!" Did you laugh in amazement the first time your son made that statement? Or did you shriek in horror as you realized where his statement might lead you—or where he might repeat his new knowledge? Whether you're ready or not, talking with your kids about the issues of sex and sexuality actually begins before they can even speak. As we mentioned earlier, your attitudes, actions, and words will profoundly affect your child's view of these issues.

There's no doubt about it, young children enjoy rubbing and touching their genitals, whether they are twelve months old or four years old. It's your job, however, to help your child understand that even though she may enjoy the touch, there's a proper place and time for this activity. As a parent, you have an incredible opportunity to help your young child embrace the beauty of sexuality while at the same time teaching her

Character Builders

Kindness will be key to healthy sexual understanding, and it's never too early to start teaching your child to care about others.

- **Model kindness** by sharing with your young child when you both can help someone in need—such as bringing dinner to a new mom or helping watch a friend's child in an emergency.
- **Find ways your preschooler can show kindness** to a family member by playing the "Kindness Game." (This is a game in which each child is rewarded and praised for each kind act done for another family member or individual outside the family.) Make a sticker chart for rewarding each success.
- **Comment on any book**, video, or TV show where someone acts kindly toward another.

the proper context and relationships for sex. As she explores her world and brings up questions about sexuality, challenge yourself to answer her questions with confidence and creativity. The investment you make now in shaping her actions and attitudes will reap amazing dividends for her in the future.

Parents' Questions

■■ **When does sexuality develop?**

Giving and receiving love, which is intimately related to one's sexuality, has its roots in the earliest days of life. Everyone's primary need to experience love and trust is met through stable caretakers who hold, cuddle, feed, and talk to the baby. Physical touch, eye contact, and soothing words give your baby a sense of warmth and security. The act of feeding, whether breast- or bottle-feeding, provides not only nutrition but physical closeness and feelings of pleasure, trust, and security. Exposure to this love and affirmation early in life leads to deep, loving relationships later.

When should sex education begin?

At birth! Affirming your newborn infant as an individual through cuddling, touching, and a soothing voice communicates a sense of personhood and reinforces his developing identity. The messages your infant absorbs moment by moment early in life set the stage for a healthy self-identity throughout his life span.

Later, a more deliberate means of sex education builds on this early, nonverbal modeling as your child becomes more verbal and aware. Then you'll be able to teach proper words for body parts as well as model healthy attitudes about the body and sexuality.

How do I teach my young child about the body and its proper functions?

In both sexes, the reproductive organs are completely formed at birth. The external genitalia of both boys and girls, however, increase little in size during the first ten years or so of life. Then at puberty, the genitalia of both sexes explode in rapid growth. Your job will be much easier if you teach your child the proper names for the genitalia and body functions at an early age. Use proper anatomical terms rather than slang words. Boys have a penis, not a "ding dong." Girls have a vagina, not a "hole." Teach your child the proper uses of words like *urinate* and *bowel movement*. Using precise names of body parts now will facilitate communication when children are older.

My four-year-old has taken to touching her genitals frequently at home and sometimes in public. How should I respond?

Preschoolers' curiosity naturally extends to the body and how it works. They ask questions about it. ("What is my belly button for?" "Why am I different from Julie?") With their questions and actions, they're discovering how their body looks, feels, and functions. Some degree of touching the genitals at this age is quite common and natural. You shouldn't be frightened or concerned if your toddler or preschool boy or girl touches or plays with the genitalia while taking a bath or getting ready for bed.

Such situations present you with great teachable moments. For example, you may say, "Yes, this is your penis." Pointing to the navel, you may ask, "What is this?" Later, pointing to the scrotum, you can ask, "What is this?"

On the other hand, the child who is rubbing or pulling at her genitalia in public should be corrected gently but not scolded. You might say, "It's not appropriate for you to touch your vagina (or penis) in public. That part of your body is very private. Remember, we don't touch our private parts in public." With this approach, you're giving your child guidelines for behavior but not making her feel guilty.

How do I teach my child the proper names for body parts and body functions?

Among the very first words your son or daughter learns are names of family members and personal pronouns such as *he* and *she*. Names of body parts come quickly at the same time. Attitudes previously taught through looks, gestures, and tone of voice are reinforced by words.

Bath time presents a great opportunity to teach about the body. As more water splashes on the floor than on the skin, questions and answers fly back and forth between you and your child. Nose, ears, and toes are identified. When your son touches his penis and asks, "What's this?",

Character Builders

Developing Honesty Starts Early

Figuring out how to deceive and get away with it—especially when it comes to sexual health—can poison one's future for a lifetime. You should always be thinking about teaching honesty at home.

- **Preschoolers learn the power of words.** They observe the lack of consequences when lying to their parents gets them off the hook even though the child knows he's guilty. ("Johnny spilled the milk, not me!")
- **Model honesty in all you say and do**, such as not lying on the phone when a solicitor calls.
- **When it's obvious your child has told a lie, point out the facts** that support that. Now is the time for him to learn what truth and lies really mean.
- **Role play to teach**—play a game where you tell him either a truth or a lie and have him guess which it is.
- **Read children's books** with examples of truthfulness.

simply respond, "Your penis. You know all boys have a penis and girls don't. They have a vagina."

How do I encourage my preschooler to develop a healthy identity as a boy or a girl?

A baby is never just a baby—from the very moment of birth, we think of the baby as "he" or "she," never "it." The most obvious difference between the sexes at any age is the uniqueness of the male and female genitalia. As children mature, secondary sex characteristics, such as the appearance of breasts, hair distribution, body shape, and pitch of voice, also help identify one sex from the other.

Gender identity is defined as all those things that a person says or does to define himself or herself as being either a man or a woman.

As their language develops, children see others as either "he" or "she" and see themselves as uniquely a "he" or a "she." Healthy personal development requires a child to be comfortable with her gender. This healthy sexual identity is affirmed not only by identifying with adults and peers of the same sex, but also by comparing oneself with the opposite sex.

In our society, sex-specific behaviors overlap a great deal. There's no broad line dividing gender roles. You shouldn't feel that you must impose strict sex stereotypes on your children. Instead, it's helpful for you to reinforce a healthy gender identity by expressing through verbal and nonverbal means your pleasure in your child as a person.

▮▮ Who is most important to the infant, the father or the mother?

Both parents play crucial and unique roles in the life of infants and preschoolers. The breast-feeding mother has an essential task in the physical nurturing of her infant. In the act of nursing, she also provides a sense of warmth and security through the cuddling and touch that is a part of feeding. The father's contribution in bottle-feeding the baby as well as holding and loving him is also vital.

Beyond these different tasks, fathers and mothers interact with infants in significantly different ways. While mothers tend to be comforting and cuddling, fathers tend to be active in their involvement—stimulating the infant to more motor and cognitive activity. Fathers represent the outside world, introducing the infant to life beyond mom's arms. Both roles are crucially important to the healthy development of the infant's identity.

A young child benefits when both parents are involved in teaching about sex. Since the healthiest sex education occurs spontaneously, both parents should be prepared to answer their child's questions as they arise. Children of both sexes will see their sexuality in a more natural light when both parents have served as role models and have been actively involved in conveying facts and attitudes.

Fostering Friendships

Friendship in the earliest stages of development is primarily with the parents and family. As your child gets closer to her fourth birthday, playmates have an integral role in learning early friendship skills. Keep the following things in mind as a parent of a child this age:

- **Cultivate friendships for yourself.** Your own level of friendship is a great model to your very young child as to the importance of friends.
- **If you're married, focus on keeping your marriage strong.** Remember, the best marriages happen between two people who not only love each other but are each other's best friends.
- **See yourself as your child's friend as well as parent.** Through play, conversations, and shared family experiences, the earliest roots of friendship are learned.
- **Expose your child to structured, supervised time with peers.** Many children this age don't develop close friendships, but certainly three- and four-year-olds are capable of doing so and will enjoy being around other children with the comfort and safety of supervising adults.

Early exposure to parental friendship and peer playmates helps reinforce to your child that relationships—not materialism or other substitutes—are the stuff with which hearts and souls are filled to fulfillment. These early relationships will teach your child about compassion and respect for others.

■ Is it normal for my son to dress up as a girl?

It's normal, and even expected, that some boys of this age will enjoy the excitement of "dress up." While boys often dress up in men's clothes or action-hero costumes, some will experiment with dressing up in girls' clothing. This isn't necessarily a problem, and you should allow some latitude. At the same time, directing your son toward more appropriate dress-up play would be encouraged.

If your son wants to exclusively dress as a girl and begins to do this even in secret while frequently saying he'd prefer to be a girl, you should be concerned and seek professional help.

Why does my son prefer to role-play as a girl when he plays with his friends?

Many boys will experiment with the roles of both boys and girls during this age. When a boy consistently prefers to play as a girl, there's greater reason for concern. This may be because of the lack of a male role model, an overenmeshed relationship with his mother, or struggles with gender identity. While it's important for all young boys to have a strong male role model in their life, if your son is struggling with his gender identity, it's even more important. Encourage your son to play with boys his same age, and make sure his playgroup is one where he feels safe and included.

Is having my child sleep in my bed a problem for his psychological development?

Opinions vary about children sleeping in bed with their parents. Certainly an occasional night in bed with you is not something to be concerned about. Usually your bed represents a place of safety and security, and sleeping there is considered a treat by most kids. Generally issues raised about this practice aren't sexual in nature. Certainly a child being in bed with the parents can have some sexual implications for the parents.

A larger issue for the child who shares a bed with his parents is the necessary milestone of learning how to soothe himself and get to sleep on his own at bedtime. Learning to fall asleep and stay in one's own bed during the night is part of a healthy growing-up experience. As your child reaches school age or even earlier, this becomes a major issue and a developmental milestone.

My preschooler is always asking questions. Often these questions are about sexual issues. How should I respond?

Most likely you're overwhelmingly aware of your child's incessant questions. Every sentence begins with why, how, or what. Sooner or later, this curiosity touches on concerns about her origins and methods of arrival.

The usual question at age four is, "Where did I come from?" With this question, your child could be asking any number of things. You can assess what she really wants to know by asking, "What do you mean?" Her response to this question will let you know if she's inquiring about birth or whether she's asking a theological question ("Who made me?") or a geographic question ("Did I come from Alabama like Johnny?").

In fact, the response "What do you mean?" is one of the best tools you have to teach your child of any age about sex. In asking "What do you mean?", you learn several things at once: you can find out what generated the question in the first place. "Johnny told me he grew in his mommy's tummy. Did I?" You learn what your child already knows about the subject, which in turn helps you know where to start with your answer. Once you know these facts, you can build on what she reveals to answer her question most appropriately.

How do I explain "making love" to my preschooler?

Your preschooler isn't likely to ask about this term directly unless he's heard it used by an older person or heard it on TV.

Again, the most helpful thing to do is ask questions: "What do you think 'making love' means? What have you heard about it?" Your child's response will clue you in to what he has heard and help you determine how you should respond.

If he seems to have a vague or general curiosity about the meaning of the term, you might reply something like this: "'Making love' is the way your daddy and I show that we love each other. We hug each other very tight and lay close to each other."

If you get the impression that your young child has some hint of the nature of intercourse, then it's important to give an accurate but simple account. You might reply, "When a mommy and daddy 'make love,' they get very close to each other, and the daddy puts his penis inside the mommy's vagina." Or, "When mommies and daddies make love, the daddy plants his sperm inside the mommy. This is the way babies are made."

▮▮ How can I best protect my child from sexual abuse?

See page 59.

▮▮ What is the relationship of toilet training to sexuality?

Learning to control bladder and bowel function is a normal, necessary part of healthy child development. This control is separate and distinct from sexual function, but it's a symbolic transition, as it's the first time children are given the chance to control their bodies. A tenuous relationship does exist, since both functions (toileting and sexuality) are associated with the same part of the body and thus use some of the same language. Immature minds (of all ages) tend to link bowel, bladder, and sexual functions together in some cynical way. This is why you hear so many jokes about genitalia, elimination, and sexual activity.

In a related way, toilet training may affect how a child feels about her sexuality. If shame and coerciveness are associated with toilet training, she may relate these negative feelings to her understanding of sexuality because of the anatomical closeness of the toileting and sexual functions. If she's made to feel guilty about toileting, she may transfer this sense of guilt and shame to attitudes about sexuality.

▮▮ Is it okay for my preschoolers to bathe together? Until what age?

Preschool siblings of opposite sexes often bathe together. This has no negative consequences. In the context of healthy family relationships, this experience can provide those teachable moments when the differences between male and female bodies can be discussed.

Your children should stop bathing together when one or both of the children are uncomfortable with it. This may occur as early as age four—it is more likely by the age of five or six. You should be sensitive to the indication from any of the children that he desires more privacy and honor that desire.

When should I stop washing my child's pubic area during bath time?

With younger children, it's appropriate for you to fully or partially bathe your child. In fact, the young child almost always needs help. Even with the older child, such as the early school age, occasional help in cleansing the genitalia may be needed. If your child indicates a wish for privacy in bathing, you should honor her request except for those times when help or inspection is needed.

In general, the goal is to have her assume responsibility for self-help activities such as bathing as early as possible. In fact, most children three and older should be able to wash their whole body with minimal help, except in special circumstances.

When does it become inappropriate for my child to see me naked?

Young children are often present with parents of either sex as they dress. This is natural. As your child gets older and more verbal, he may ask questions about the shape and look of your body—this curiosity extends to parents of the same sex as well as of the opposite sex. Again, such questions are normal and healthy. This provides another teachable moment for the discussion of anatomy.

Privacy should become more the rule when the parent or child is uncomfortable with the exposure. In general, by the time your child is four or five, you shouldn't be naked intentionally around him. Accidental exposure now and then isn't a problem during the preschool and early school-age years.

When is it no longer appropriate for my child to run around the house naked?

Typical toddlers and younger preschoolers have no sense of embarrassment about their bodies and love to run around the house naked. This is a natural desire and doesn't mean your child will vacation at nudist camps in the future. Between the ages of four and six, most kids develop a sense of privacy and limit the amount of time they spend naked.

There are certain situations, however, such as when guests who might be stimulated or bothered by the nakedness are in your home, when your child shouldn't run around naked. Simply explain to her that being naked in public or when guests are in the house isn't good manners. Unless you're uncomfortable with your child's nudity, allow her to outgrow this phase on her own.

Is my young child affected by seeing sexually explicit material?

Children, regardless of their age, are impressionable and curious. Although you may think kids don't understand what they're seeing—rest assured they do. Without the facts from you, your child will interpret any sexually explicit material in a distorted way. Your goal should be to talk to him first about relationships, sexual intercourse, and respect for others' bodies—rather than allow a movie with inappropriate content to do the teaching.

It's important for you to train him to recognize inappropriate material and if he's been exposed to it, to tell you about it. Keep asking him if he has any questions about something he's been exposed to, so that he knows you're concerned.

The Answers You Need & They Want

What should I say when my son utters, "Mom, I want to marry you"?

Your child is becoming aware of two things: his maleness and that his future will hold a deeper relationship called marriage. Tell your son, "I'm already taken by your father, but someday when you're older, I hope you find a wonderful girl to marry and are as happy as your dad and me. When that happens, I will always be your mom and a good friend."

Should I allow children of the opposite sex to spend the night with my child?

Decide this on a case-by-case basis. If a child of the opposite sex is a good friend and his parents are out of town, it's not a big deal. If your child is asking for a friend who's two to three years older than her to spend the night, that's not appropriate. Remember, it's important to start discussing appropriate relationship boundaries with your children at this age. A good response to this question would be, "The only boy we want to have spend the night in our home is your future husband." Tell your daughter that her friend can come over and have dinner and then go home at bedtime.

When is it inappropriate to change my child's clothes in public?

About the time your child turns three, he'll no longer want you to change his clothes in public. You need to listen to his cues, as well as take into consideration the people around you. If you're out in public or at a mall, look for a bathroom or dressing room to change your children in. If you change your infant in public, be discreet. (It's also polite to ask the people around you if they mind.)

Should my toddler see me showing affection to my spouse?

Yes! Your toddler should see you showing affection to your spouse on a daily basis. Watching you show consistent affection to your spouse (e.g., kissing, hugging, hand holding, verbal praise) will go a long way in helping your child feel secure and will help model a positive marital relationship for her future.

What sort of affection for my spouse is inappropriate for my toddler to see?

Inappropriate affection to display in front of your child would include deep kissing, aggressive touching, fondling of the genitals, and other sexual behavior that should be conducted privately.

I'm a busy parent; how important is it for me to spend one-on-one time playing with my child?

Playing with your child is one of the most important investments you can make. Spending time engaging in a playful manner will not only relieve your stress, but will go a long way toward instilling confidence in your child. He needs to engage with you at his level; it doesn't matter whether you chase him around the house, throw a ball, or play video games. The time you invest playing with him today will ultimately protect him from engaging in high-risk behaviors in the future.

I'm a single father; how important is a female role model to my child?

Regardless of your marital status, if you're rearing your children without a positive female role model, the consequences can be damaging. The old adage "You can't be all things to all people" is especially true for your children. A positive female role model can provide your daughter with a person to help her understand what it means to be a woman and also answer questions that might be embarrassing for her to ask her dad.

A positive female role model's presence in your son's life can help him understand how men and women function differently and help him appreciate the differences between the sexes. A female role model in your son's life will also offer him the opportunity to "practice" respect for women. Boys very much want to learn how to get along with the opposite sex, but they need a female role model to actually practice how to do this. While avoiding stereotypes, a female role model in a boy's life can help him learn about gentleness and tenderness as well as provide the opportunity to ask her about the many "mysteries" of girls. Having both a male and a female role model in your child's life, boy or girl, demonstrates the complex beauty of how men and women complement one another.

I'm a single mother; how important is a male role model to my child?

A positive male role model is important to both boys and girls. A man has the ability to give your daughter attention to help her understand that she doesn't need attention from other boys to feel valued. A male role model can help your son develop his masculinity. Often single mothers shelter their sons from rough play, and this decision can impact healthy male development. Additionally, a positive male role model can help your daughter understand how young boys are turned on by certain dress or action and can help your son understand how to control his impulses and respect women.

Questions Children Ask

Where did I come from?

With this question, your child may be asking any of a number of things. Occasionally he may be asking a geographic question, really wanting to know what city or town he came from. Often he's seeking assurance that

Character Builders

Introducing Respect to Your Child

Respect for others should be an ongoing discussion throughout a child's life. Disrespect leads to selfishness, meanness, and bullying toward others.

- **Model respect** in how you treat other family members with your words and tone of voice.
- **Discuss how you respect your body** by taking good care of it—eating well, getting exercise, keeping yourself clean, and getting enough sleep.
- **Talk about how people around you are different.** When your preschooler makes a hurtful and disrespectful comment, role-play a similar scenario of a rude comment toward her and ask how she felt about that. Give her some new words that would say something nice about that person instead.

he belongs to the family by asking, "Who do I belong to?" He may be asking a spiritual or philosophical question; he may have heard that God made people, and he's trying to find out if God actually made him.

Certainly many preschoolers who ask "Where did I come from?" are wondering how they were made—and have a vague idea of the truth. So before plunging into a long explanation of pregnancy and childbirth, it's best to ask your child, "What do you mean?"

If it's apparent he's curious about the birth process, you can answer this way: "You grew in your mother's body. All mothers have a special place where babies grow. It's called the womb or the uterus. When you were ready, you came out of your mom's body."

How do babies get out?

Mommies have a special opening between their legs called the vagina that allows a baby to come out when the time is right.

When a baby comes out, how can you tell if it's a boy or a girl?

Boys and girls have different bodies. When a baby is born, parents can tell by looking at the penis or the vagina if the baby is a boy or a girl.

How does the baby get inside the mommy's body?

Mommies make tiny eggs in their bodies. The eggs are released, and when the egg meets up with the sperm from the daddy, the egg begins to grow into a baby. It takes both a mommy and a daddy to make a baby.

How does the daddy's sperm get inside the mommy's body?

When mommies and daddies make love, the daddy puts his penis inside the mommy's vagina and passes sperm from his penis. When one sperm joins with one egg, a new life is formed.

Will I have a baby too?

If a girl asks this question, you can answer, "Yes, when you grow up and get married, you'll probably have a baby." If a boy asks this question, you can answer, "No, boys don't have a special place for babies to grow like girls do."

Why do mommies have breasts?

Women have breasts so that they can feed newborn babies. Breast milk is the perfect food for babies.

What is a penis?

The penis is the fingerlike part of the body that hangs down between the legs of boys and men. It is how boys pee. When a boy grows up, his penis gets larger.

Will my penis fall off?

No, your penis will always be a part of you. It's like your nose or your ears; it will grow bigger but never fall off.

Can my friend touch my penis?

No. Your penis is a part of your body and belongs only to you. It's private. No one should touch your penis unless something is wrong with it and it needs to be checked by your doctor or your parents. You shouldn't touch another boy's penis either. And you shouldn't touch a girl's vagina.

Why do I have a belly button?

A belly button is where your umbilical cord was attached when you were inside Mommy. It's how you ate and drank while you were in Mommy's belly.

Does it hurt to have a baby grow inside the mommy?

Not usually. Sometimes mommies feel the baby kick, but it's not painful. Often mommies will feel pressure as the baby gets big and they get tired a lot.

Why do mommies go to the hospital to get the baby?

Mommies don't get the baby at the hospital. The baby grows inside the mommy. She goes to the hospital so that the doctor can help the baby come out.

Luke and I (a boy) are going to get married when we grow up.

While you and Luke may be best buddies now, boys don't marry boys, and girls don't marry girls. I'm glad Luke is your buddy, and I hope you're friends for a long time, but you want to marry a girl so that you can have children like your daddy and I had you.

Mom, I'm (a girl) going to marry Billy when I grow up.

It's great that you already know you want to marry Billy when you grow up. Finding someone you love and want to be with will be an important decision you have to make in life. Many girls don't have the benefit of having great friends like Billy.

Why do girls sit down to go to the bathroom?

Girls go to the bathroom sitting down because their genitals are inside their bodies and their urethra (the tube that moves the urine) is between their legs.

Why do boys stand up to go to the bathroom?

Boys can go to the bathroom standing up because their urethra (the tube that's attached to the bladder and moves the urine) is in the penis. Since the penis is on the outside of the body, a boy can pee while standing up. Boys do sit down to poop.

First Comes Love

Early Elementary: Five- to Seven-Year-Olds

"Logan and Lauren sitting in a tree K-I-S-S-I-N-G. First comes love, then comes marriage, then comes baby in the baby carriage." You may remember this childhood taunt from your days on the playground. Aren't you amazed by how fast your child has grown up? Sometimes it's hard to believe she's already in school. You might have noticed that little boys and girls aren't as innocent as they were when you were in first grade. Times have changed, and unfortunately, kissing games have made their way to kindergarten.

As a parent, this is a wonderful age to find out how your child sees the world around her. Take the time to ask questions about her friends, and dig a little deeper into the games she's playing. While children at this age aren't exploring very many questions about "sex," they often use their imagination and playtime exploring and creating the perfect relationships between boys and girls.

This is also the age of bold exploration and excitement about their bodies and what their bodies can do. Modesty and privacy may become an issue. Don't be offended if your child doesn't want you to join her in the bathroom anymore. Keep your eyes and ears open, and be ready to be inspired by her confidence and newfound independence.

Parents' Questions

▮▮ What effect do outside influences have on my school-age child when it comes to sex?

Outside influences will definitely impact your child's view of sex. It's up to you, however, to determine whether those influences will be positive or negative. If you're working to prepare him for the world he'll live in, these outside influences can be great teaching tools. If you're trying to protect him from the harm of the world, however, his world may be rocked.

As he enters school, it's a good idea to get to know his teachers and his friends' parents. Also, if you know he's been exposed to a movie you don't approve of or to foul language, take the opportunity to explain why what he's been exposed to doesn't reflect your family values. Communicating openly with your child during this stage of life is very important. Your being involved in his activities and getting to know the people around him will not only protect your child but also prepare him for the world.

▮▮ How can I guard my child from the unhealthy influences in the world?

Your goal should be to prepare (as well as protect) your child for the world she'll encounter. You need to talk about the unhealthy influences she might experience and role-play responses that will help her react appropriately to situations she'll encounter.

Additionally, this isn't the time for you to exit your child's life. She needs you more than ever to stay involved. Make an effort to volunteer in her classroom. Invite her friends over and get to know their parents

Character Builders

School-age children are smarter than preschoolers about telling lies or half-truths, but they usually will still be caught in their discrepancies.

- **Keep** your own words and actions honest.
- **Discuss** how consequences will be worse if your child lies about a wrongdoing instead of admitting he was guilty from the start. Be clear what each consequence will entail; then stick to it.
- **Affirm** your child any time he chooses to tell the truth when he could have gotten away with a lie. Thank him for his honesty.
- **Ask** your child how he felt when a friend lied to him. Discuss how honesty and trust go hand in hand.
- **Show** him instances in the media where people were caught lying and the consequences that ensued.

as well. When she spends time with other families, talk to the parents about your standards for movies, TV, and computer games—this will help them avoid exposing her unnecessarily to negative influences.

Finally, listen to her to gain insight into how she sees the world. Ask questions about what she thinks about various things, and you'll learn a lot. The bottom line is to be involved in your child's life and let her know you're available and want to be with her.

How can I build up my child's self-confidence and help him to think for himself?

Self-confidence is an essential skill that every child needs in order to navigate the difficulties associated with peer pressure. Investing in your child's confidence now will protect his sexuality in the future. Kids who have a "can-do" attitude are usually able to withstand peer pressure and make good choices for their future.

Modeling self-confidence is the best thing you, as a parent, can do for your child. After all, actions speak louder than words. Additionally, make an effort to affirm your child. Tell him you love him for who he is, and show him affection with hugs and kisses. In addition, celebrate his achievements. Focusing more on the process and character building than on the actual end result tells him he is capable and worthy.

What should I do if I don't know the answer to my child's questions?

Say "I don't know." Then use the experience as a teaching opportunity. If your child has the attention span to do so, invite her to research the answer with you. If not, let her know that you'll start looking for the answer and get back to her as soon as you know it. Make sure to set a time to talk about the issue again. Your failure to follow through could eliminate any future conversations on the issue.

When should I start talking to my child about sexual intercourse?

A few children at this age might come right out and ask the big question about sex or how a baby gets made. It's important to understand what your child is looking for by asking additional questions. He might be looking for something very simple and not "What is sexual intercourse?" If he clearly wants the straight facts, a simple answer is in order. In addition to discussing body parts, it's very important to discuss context (that is, "when you are a grown-up and married") and that sex is something very special between two people who love each other and are married. Whatever you communicate to your child you should ask him to repeat back to you, since kids at this age often have vivid imaginations.

How do I explain the process of making love to my child if she should ask?

At this age, most children don't want a long, drawn-out, moment-by-moment explanation of sexual intercourse. Usually they just want to know how babies are made and what making love (or any other term they're questioning) actually means. This is a great opportunity to tell your child how special love can be between a husband and a wife. The fact is that you love each other so much that you want to hug and kiss and be as close as possible. When you are alone together, you like to be naked when you hug, and there are special feelings that happen when dad's penis fits right inside mom's vagina. It feels good all over. It's a great way for a husband and a wife to say, "I love you." Remind your child that sex is intimate and special and is meant for marriage. She might give you a range of reactions, from "gross" to just plain "okay" and then run off to play. When discussing sexual issues, stress to your child that she shouldn't talk about these things with her friends or siblings. Again, ask her what she heard to make sure she didn't think you said something different than you did.

What if my child isn't asking any questions about sexual matters?

He's normal! Most children this age don't ask questions about sex. If your child asks questions, answer them with simple and short answers; then ask if he understood what you said. Most kids aren't looking for long dialogues but just want to get something confusing sorted out. If you want to bring up a sexual issue and your child isn't asking, initiate a conversation based on something you both have heard or seen recently. Life offers plenty of opportunities to talk about the matters of love, respect, and sex—just look around your neighborhood or on the TV.

▐▆ What should I do if my child walks in while I'm naked?

This depends on how you feel about your child seeing you naked. If your child saw you naked while she was younger, this incident won't be a big deal. However, if she suddenly seems to be embarrassed by seeing you naked, reach for a towel or something to cover up, and then talk with her about knocking before entering your room. This can be a great opportunity to talk about closed doors and privacy.

▐▆ What should I do if our child walks in while we're having sex?

If your door isn't locked and your child is suddenly in your room during sex, be firm, but ask him to leave because you want some special time alone together. If he's in shock from what he's seen, tell him that this is the way parents show affection for one another. Don't overreact! It will make an uncomfortable situation worse. Often his response to the situation will mimic yours. As traumatic as this experience is for you, it probably will be more confusing for your child. You can discuss what he did or didn't see once your clothes are back on.

Prevention is the best approach to this embarrassing situation. Install a lock on your door, and tell your child that if your door is closed, he should knock and be given permission before entering.

▐▆ When should I introduce the subject of AIDS to my school-age child?

HIV and AIDS are very complex subjects that an elementary-age child might not run into or ask about. You don't need to bring up the topic at this age unless your child's school addresses it in the classroom. If there are any children in the school with HIV, then it should be brought up to all classes so that misinformation isn't spread around the playground. (See pages 110 and 117.)

What should I do if my child has been sexually abused?

See page 59.

How do I warn my child about sexual predators without scaring her?

As parents, we must teach our children that some adults aren't trustworthy. This is a concept that they've seen over and over in movies and cartoons. Basically, tell your child not to interact with strangers. You also need to tell her that if a stranger approaches her in a threatening way, she should run and yell that this person is not her parent. It's imperative as your child grows to remind her that no one should touch her private parts (except for a medical professional). If someone touches or views her genitals by force or coercion, she needs to tell you immediately—even if the person specifically said not to tell her parents. This way, she has your permission to come to you.

Additionally, get to know the parents of the friends your child spends time with. It's hard to believe, but most predators are family friends or acquaintances known to the family. Finally, never leave your child with someone you don't know or haven't run a background check on.

How do I reinforce a sense of privacy at this age?

Often children at this age become embarrassed about nudity—yours and theirs. In order to show respect for your child's privacy, you shouldn't interact with him when he isn't clothed. If he wants to take a bath or shower without you in the bathroom, then let him. If he no longer wants you to stand in the public restroom stall with him, hold the door shut on the outside. Respect his need for boundaries. Privacy is something that comes naturally to most children. If your child isn't showing a need for privacy, modeling can help him get there.

Character Builders

Every adult has certain responsibilities at home, at work, and in the community that negatively affect others if they're neglected. The sooner our children learn that they have important responsibilities, the better able they will be to exercise it. Here's how:

- **Show your kids by your actions** that you carry out the responsibilities you've committed to—going to work on time, shopping for groceries, making meals, doing the laundry—the list is unending! (And you could use their help.)
- For impact, **ignore a responsibility** (not a crucial one, but one that impacts all—such as the laundry), and see how people in the family are affected.
- **Make a list** with your child of what responsibilities he can take on as a family member, such as setting the table, keeping his room picked up, and emptying the trash. It's better not to pay your child for these tasks, because everyone needs to contribute to the household.
- **Discuss** how when one promises something (like taking out the trash), it takes being responsible to get it done.
- **Show the connection** between being responsible and earning more freedom.

Is it normal for my child to want to touch her genitalia at this age?

Kids love to touch their genitals. It's quite normal for children to explore their anatomy and learn the correct names for the different parts. This becomes a problem when your child wants to touch herself often and in public. You need to explain that this is not a behavior people do in public. You shouldn't punish your child, but you should explain that other people feel uncomfortable watching her rub her genitals. If the behavior continues, ask your child to leave the room and find a private place until she's finished.

What should I do if I find my child playing with a friend, and they're both naked?

If you discover your child and a friend playing "doctor," it's important to ask them what they were doing and why. Make sure that one of them wasn't forcing the other to do something uncomfortable and that they weren't simulating intercourse. Many children this age have seen enough on TV and in the movies to get the motions down.

If they were simulating sex, you need to have a discussion about privacy and respect for each other's bodies. Remind your child that it's okay to be naked with his parents, his younger or same-sex siblings, and his doctor, but it's not okay to be naked with anyone else. Ask him to repeat what you said so it's clearly understood.

Curiosity shouldn't be punished. If the behaviors continue, it's appropriate to have some consequences laid out (friend can't come over, play date is over, and so on). By all means, tell the parent of the other child so that you both can approach the problem as a team. This isn't an issue you should get angry about or shame your child over. The key is to let him know that there are boundaries to all of our behaviors.

My little girl was pinched in her privates by a friend. What should I do?

Aggressive play at this age isn't uncommon, and when this play is unsupervised, sexually aggressive incidents may occur. You should take steps to address the inappropriateness of this behavior as well as affirm your daughter for sharing this behavior with you. If you're cool, calm, and collected, you can give good information about avoiding aggressive behaviors and people, including peers, who violate personal boundaries (such as touching, tugging, pulling, or punching one's genitals or touching one's body without permission). If you feel the behavior is persistent and aggressive, talk to the parents of the child and even the child himself. If the activity persists, you may have to take action to separate your child from this "friend."

Should my son and daughter have separate rooms?

If space in your home permits, this is a great time to allow your children to have separate rooms. If your children must share a room, however, it's a good idea to hang a curtain or some other barrier that will allow them to have "their own space." This is the time in life when your children's sense of privacy is developing, and helping them have a "space" to themselves will provide them an opportunity to develop their own sense of identity.

What types of TV shows are appropriate for my child to watch?

A rule of thumb for TV viewing during this stage of development should be: your child shouldn't watch any show that you haven't previously seen. It's very tempting to just let your kids sit in front of the TV while you get dinner made and do chores. The problem is that even cartoon networks and "kid-specific" channels have programming that's inappropriate for the early-elementary audience. Children this age should watch programs that contain only positive content. Children do process sex, foul language, and violence, but not in a mature way. Images will be distorted in ways you don't have control over.

It's best to watch programs with your child so you can comment on the programming. This will have a great impact on how he'll interpret what he sees. Make watching TV an active event by asking questions during viewing to find out how your child is processing what's been shown on the screen.

Should I allow my child to go to PG-13 or R-rated movies?

No. The entertainment industry has set a rating standard in regard to movies. PG-13 and R-rated movies contain material that will be too

Character Builders

Now is the time when you can expect your child to take on the responsibility of getting dressed, taking a bath, brushing her teeth, and picking up around the room. Here are some helpful ways:

- **Make your expectations clear** by charts of what is part of the daily routine. If your child can't do a task on her own, then do it together until mastery is accomplished.
- If messes are made, **help your child take responsibility** for the cleanup, even though it may be easier for you to just do it.
- In rooms, **make use of bins and boxes** with lids and labels to help your child organize all her stuff. Insist on picking up and putting away before another activity is started. Routinely give or throw away things that are broken or not used anymore to avoid clutter.

graphic for your child to understand, whether it's due to foul language or explicit sexual scenes. Unfortunately, many children's movies have PG ratings and aren't appropriate for young kids—just because it's animated doesn't mean your child should see it. Again, exposing her to explicit images, sarcasm, violence, and foul language will only lead to behavioral problems in the future. Remember, you're the parent. Don't just tell your child no; provide alternative activities and explanations that support why you don't want her to see a particular movie.

Is it appropriate to permit my child to go around the house naked?

Some families are very comfortable with nudity, and if it's not embarrassing to anyone, then there's not a problem with it. But starting around age five, most children begin developing a sense of privacy and become uncomfortable when they or others are nude. This is a great time to talk about respecting others' privacy and modeling modesty.

Should I allow my children to take baths together?

This issue really depends on the comfort level of your child. He'll let you know when it's time to kick his siblings out of the tub. Young children think taking baths together is a lot of fun. As your child becomes school-age, he might express an interest in having some privacy during bath time. The key is to listen and respect his desires.

Should I allow my child to take a bath with a friend?

If the children are of the same sex and are comfortable with each other, there's no problem with bathing together at this age. However, you should ask your guest's parents whether or not they care if the children take a bath together. Children of the opposite sex who aren't family members shouldn't take baths together.

What should I do if I hear my child using foul language?

Many children like to impress their friends and siblings with swear words. When kids are young, most likely they don't have a clue what the words mean. Before you get angry, the first thing you should do is ask your child what the word means. If she doesn't know, explain to her that there are certain words your family doesn't use. If your child knows what she's saying, establish an appropriate consequence for the behavior and also explain the word's meaning. It's important to find out where she's hearing the words and make sure she isn't hearing them from you or your spouse. Since modeling is the best teacher, it's hard to scold your child if she's repeating words learned from your mouth.

The Answers You Need & They Want

How important is school when it comes to shaping my child's attitudes about sex?

Your home should be the primary source of your child's information about sex. The school should only support what you're doing at home. Unfortunately, many schools have taken over the job of sex education because too few parents are doing the job. Many schools have a sex-education curriculum for kindergarten through twelfth grade. As a parent, you need to find out just what your child's school teaches. You have a right to review all of your school's materials, including the sex-education material. Take advantage of your right and ask to review it.

The influence the curriculum will have on your child depends on what stand it takes on the different topics of sex education. If the material supports what you're saying at home, that's great. But if it doesn't, you'll need to either pull your child from the class or be prepared to talk with him about how your family values differ from what was taught in school.

The best approach, and the one that will minimize the school's influence, is to talk about sexual issues before they're brought up at school. Then your child will see you as the expert, rather than his teacher.

How do I find out what the elementary school is teaching about sex?

Ask. As a parent, you have the right to review all of your child's curriculum. You don't want to come across to her teacher as a difficult and demanding parent, but on the other hand, it's important to know what she'll be taught in this area. You can ask the teacher if you can review the curriculum so you can know how to best support it at home with discussions with your child. Or you can volunteer to work in the classroom on those days, or ask to review books on different topics that the teacher might use. By talking and working with your child's teacher in other areas, you won't seem confrontational. If you're concerned with some of the topics and discussion points in the curriculum, ask the teacher why these materials were chosen.

Should I allow my child to spend the night with a group of kids at a sleepover?

Sleepovers have become very popular through the school years, especially for birthday parties and special occasions. In the early-elementary years, children really need a good night's sleep and don't have the desire to stay up late watching movies and gossiping about the opposite sex, so it isn't necessary to start group sleepovers at this age. There's always a concern that your child will be exposed to TV and movies that you might not approve of, so if he does spend the night, make sure you know what will be going on.

Organized overnights with Scouts, or other groups where there's a large ratio of adult-to-child supervision, are great opportunities for children to learn to be away from home for a night or two. Since some children are fearful of leaving home, this might be a good way to introduce a little independence. Spending the night at a friend's house, where you know the family and their standards, is also a fun way to practice being away from home. Certainly, if your child doesn't want to sleep away at this age, don't encourage it. (Also, be prepared to trek out during the night to pick him up—this moment could be priceless in reminding you that your child isn't as mature as you might think.)

Should I be concerned if my child tells me about her friend who has a boyfriend or girlfriend?

Kids today are exposed to so much talk about "boyfriends" and "girlfriends." Before you freak out, ask her what she means by her friend having a boyfriend or girlfriend. Most of the time at this age, it just means something simple, like her friend thinks her "boyfriend" has a nice smile or he's cute. Usually, there's no real relationship beyond being friends. Most of the time, they don't even speak to each other! Occasionally kids might brag about having "kissed" each other on the lips, but it's more of an accomplishment than a true reflection of any feelings.

Take this opportunity to discuss relationships in general with your child. What does it mean to be a boyfriend or girlfriend or a friend in general? What is the difference? Stress that looks aren't what makes a good friend. Keep your ears open for future conversations on this topic, because it will come up often over the years as your child redefines these terms.

What should I tell my child about his father's new girlfriend living with him?

This is a difficult concept for kids to grasp after a divorce. In addition to trying to have a "normal" relationship with each parent, kids secretly desire that their parents will reunite. As parents start to rebuild their lives, the process often will include a new relationship. Cohabitation is an easy way to avoid commitment but makes it awkward when it's time for your child to visit. If you disagree with your former spouse's values, have a discussion with your child (with respect for the other parent) and say that you wish it were different.

It's very important that you not influence your child's opinion of his dad (or mom), but your input will help him process the differences at his father's house. Be sure to listen to his feelings before and after the visit. Encourage him to share his feelings with his father as well, if appropriate. Additionally, if your child is uncomfortable, you might talk with your ex about how to remedy the situation.

Is it normal for my son to play exclusively with girls?

No. At this age, it's the rare boy who prefers to play with girls only. Starting around age six, boys will give up the companionship of opposite-sex friends and move into an "I hate girls" mind-set. This is the time when boys want to build clubhouses and don't want girls around. This isn't sexism; in fact, it's part of healthy and normal gender identification.

If your son desires to play only with girls, it would be wise to seek input about his behavior from a professional who shares your values. Many parents may be uncomfortable with their son's behavior but choose to ignore it because others will insist it's not a problem. This preference could be a sign that your son needs more one-on-one time with his

Fostering Friendships

Friendships for the five- to seven-year-old begin to change in nature from playmates to the first experiences of true friendship. These friendships become deeper and more self-directed because of the earlier lessons about compassion and respect for others. Keep the following things in mind as you teach your child friendship skills:

- **Be your child's friend!** Share life events, conversation, and play together.
- **Help your child identify peers with common interests.** Invite friends over and watch the kids interact; then help your child determine which children are easier to get along with. Encourage your child to branch out and meet children she normally isn't drawn to.
- **Cultivate a relationship with the parents** of your child's friends.
- **Talk with your child about the basics of friendship:** (1) good friends care for and respect each other, not ridicule or tease each other; (2) good friends are supportive of rules and family standards. Laying this foundation now prepares your child for the future, when she's older and peer pressure becomes very real.
- **Encourage your child's unique gifts and abilities**, noting how these things can be used to develop friendships.
- **Emphasize character traits of kindness and sharing** in friendship relationships.
- **Organize play dates** and structured group activities with a small group of other children.
- **Remember that your child will still prefer same-sex friendships.** Strong relationships with same-sex friends lay the foundation for healthier opposite-sex friendships later.

father. Also, this would be a good time to help your son be around boys with similar interests. If you have the time and resources, you may also want to identify an individual sport, such as bowling, biking, tennis, or swimming, that your son can excel in to boost his confidence.

Is it too early for my child to show signs of gender confusion?

No. Gender confusion can certainly manifest itself between the ages of five and seven. It isn't common for a boy this age to consistently prefer to play only with girls, be overly attached to his mother, dress up like a girl, or even consider himself a girl, and you should seek professional help. A girl who likes to play athletic and aggressive games while avoiding more "girl-like" behaviors and games isn't of great concern unless she's convinced she is actually a boy.

Children this age need strong, supportive relationships with parents and adults of both sexes. They also need clear direction and boundaries for behavior and activities. These adults need to be committed to affirming the children for the gifts and temperament that have been given them.

How can I prevent gender confusion in my child?

Questions about one's gender may be unavoidable in a child, boy or girl, who isn't stereotypically "all boy" or "all girl." Some identity issues arise from feelings and confusion within the child. These questions should be addressed by parents who are affirming and loving to their child, helping that child to understand his or her maleness or femaleness while avoiding behaviors that reinforce the image of gender confusion (such as encouraging your son to play with baby dolls or allowing your daughter to only dress in boys' clothing). Other children may experience gender confusion simply because of questioning or ridicule by peers, adults, or even parents. Children in this situation need affirmation, strong role models, and possibly professional help.

How do I prevent my son from experiencing gender confusion while at the same time helping him appreciate his gifts?

The first things you can do if you see your son acting differently than other boys are to appreciate his special gifts and stay involved. If your son is sensitive, kind, social, artistic, and gentle, this doesn't mean he won't grow up to be a strong man. The primary factor that affects a young boy's identity is how his father responds to his personality. If his father doesn't appreciate his gifts, a boy may identify with his mother, and then he'll likely experience some gender confusion.

Mothers need to allow their sensitive boys to be boys. If your son is being teased or pushed around, don't rush in to save him; without being overprotective, let him learn how to express himself. Fathers, don't ridicule your son because he's artistic; rather, spend time exploring the hobbies he enjoys. Embrace his personality and help him experience your world with his giftedness in mind.

At this age, your son is very aware of his differences, and counseling may be necessary to help him understand his strengths.

What should I (a mother) do if my son doesn't like (or rejects) his father?

Sometimes young boys don't identify with their fathers because dads are away from home most of the time or ignore their sons when they are home. Before you react harshly or encourage your son's dislike for his father, dig deeper into the reason behind his statement. Often young men choose to shun their fathers because they have felt rejection from them.

Boys desperately need three things from their fathers in order to bond with them: affection, attention, and approval. If your son isn't getting his needs met, he may interpret his father's behavior as personal disinterest in and rejection of him. If he's feeling rejected, the natural thing to do is to reject his father. By all means, don't encourage his behavior. Remind your son that his father loves him and thinks he's amazing.

Then talk with your husband (or son's father) about your son's actions, and encourage him to invest more time with his son and to look for opportunities to bond. Encourage your son to not reject his father, but rather to give his dad the opportunity to be involved in his life.

◼ How can I (a father) develop a strong relationship with my son?

Cultivating a strong relationship with your son will take a lot of commitment and involvement on your part. This starts when he's young and continues through his adolescence. Start early by engaging your son in roughhouse play. Let your son tackle you and believe that he's taken you down. Also, let your son shower with you. If you start this at an early age with your son and his brothers, it ultimately fosters a common, relaxed, anatomically based identity and breaks downs the mystery around the male body.

Additionally, take your son with you on errands out of the house. Let him help you fill the car with gas. Take him to the hardware store or out to buy flowers for Mom. This will communicate to your son that he's special.

Finally, be the last person to tell your son goodnight. Read him a story and say a quick bedtime prayer. Your being the last person in his room will provide him comfort and emotional assurance that he'll be safe through the night.

Questions Children Ask

◼ Where do babies come from?

One way a husband and wife show how much they love each other is by hugging each other very close. To be as close as they can be, they hug without any clothes on, and a tiny cell, called a sperm, comes from the husband's penis and swims up into his wife's uterus and comes together with one of her eggs. Together these two cells start a baby!

The baby grows inside the mom's uterus until it's ready to come out through the mom's vagina. The uterus gets bigger as the baby grows, just like blowing up a balloon. Once the baby is born, the uterus gets small again. All of this takes nine months to happen, and it's quite an amazing process!

Why do boys have a penis?

The penis helps a boy go to the bathroom and later in life helps make babies. Just behind the penis is a sack of skin (the scrotum), and inside it are two small, round balls called testicles. It's always important to show respect for all parts of our bodies and not talk about them in public.

What is sexual intercourse?

Sexual intercourse is one way that a husband and wife show each other how much they love each other. You might see a married couple kissing, holding hands, and giving hugs. But sex is getting even closer together than that. In fact, a husband and wife usually lie together naked in bed (it seems to be most comfortable and private there) and get so close that the man puts his penis into his wife's vagina. (For more information, see page 131.)

How does a baby get inside a mom's tummy?

A baby's life starts when a dad's sperm and a mom's egg join together. This happens when the mom and dad hug close together so that the sperm from his penis goes into her vagina to find her eggs. This tiny beginning of a baby moves into the mom's uterus (a place inside a mom especially made to grow babies). The baby will spend about nine months growing in the uterus before it's ready to be born.

The Answers You Need & They Want

Character Builders

■ How do babies get out of the mom?

After spending nine months growing inside the mom's uterus, the baby is ready to be born. The uterus opens up into the vagina, and the vagina is the passageway that the baby comes out of. It's between the mom's legs, close to where she goes to the bathroom. When the baby is ready to be born, the mom will go into labor for a number of hours. During labor, the mom pushes her baby through the passageway so her baby can come into the world.

■ What is a vagina?

All girls have three openings in their private areas. The first is near the front and allows urine to come out. It's called the urethra, and the opening is very small. The second one, in the middle, is larger and is called

Character Builders

As your child enters school, he'll desire independence to do things himself—get dressed, tie his shoes, and ride a bike. Determination is a trait that can help him gain independence. Learning determination now can protect your child in the future when he has to make decisions about being sexually active or pursuing his future.

- **Set small goals** for yourself and then talk about how you can accomplish them. Some examples might be exercising three times a week, skipping seconds at dinner, or finishing a project at home.
- **Give your child some small things to accomplish.** This reinforces accomplishment of goals. Let him participate in ones he feels he can do. Help him plan how to do them. These could include a craft, finishing a chore, or saving for a special item.
- **Take any opportunity you see** in stories, news articles, or friends' experiences **to talk about how determination helped someone** accomplish a goal.

the vagina. The vagina allows babies to be born when a woman is older. The third opening or hole in the back (called the anus) is medium size and is where poop comes out.

What is AIDS?

AIDS is a disease caused by a dangerous virus that makes the body so weak that it can't fight off other germs. It's very hard to catch the AIDS virus, and children don't do any of the things that would cause them to get AIDS.

What is a period?

A period is the flow of blood that a woman has about once a month that comes from her uterus and through her vagina. A period shows that a

Character Builders

At this age, kids start to really notice what others have that they don't—especially toys and videos. To curb bad habits, it might be wise to do the following:

- **When your child wants something you don't want to buy, discuss your reasons and then move on.** If you keep getting badgered, a warning that you'll take away something already in her possession can put a stop to the whining.
- **Teach the meaning of value.** If she wants something special, it's not too early for her to do extra chores to earn part of the cost. Most times she'll lose interest and won't really want it after all.
- **Teach the difference between "need" and "want."** List together the things she really needs to have (even that's debatable) and her wants or extras.

woman's body is able to take care of a baby inside her uterus if a man's sperm comes together with one of her eggs.

Why don't boys have breasts?

Boys do have breasts, but they don't grow like a woman's breasts. The main purpose of a woman's breasts is to make food for newborn babies. Since boys don't have babies, they don't need to make breast milk. That's why boys have breasts that don't grow.

What is sex?

Sex can mean a few different things. There are two sexes—male and female. Sex can also mean sexual intercourse, making love, or several other slang words that you might hear. Sexual intercourse is an activity that should be enjoyed by a man and woman who are married. One of the reasons a man and woman have sex is to make a baby and start a family. This works the best in marriage. Many people who aren't married have sex, but they often experience a lot of problems because of their choices.

Breaking Free

Late Elementary: Eight- to Ten-Year-Olds

Soccer games. Boy Scouts. Karate. Homework. Xbox. Sleepovers. Do you remember a simpler time? A time when your Saturdays were spent watching cartoons and making breakfast for your kids? Those days have been replaced with games, practices, multiplication tables, and more and more activities.

Whether you like it or not, your baby isn't one anymore. He's become a confident student, athlete, and talented young man. (At least he thinks so.) Now is the time to start talking about his future, if you haven't already done so. As your child longs for independence, it's your job to teach him the responsibility that goes hand in hand with independence.

This is also a time when you can build his confidence by showing interest in what he likes to do, rather than forcing him to be involved in your interests. Many kids this age are dying for their parents to show an interest in their dreams and desires. Even though your child longs to be grown-up, he secretly wants you to quit work early and come home to play catch with him.

Your mission during this stage of your child's life, if you choose to accept it, is to start letting go, while at the same time providing him with the skills to make good decisions. The fatal mistake many parents make at this juncture in their child's development is to gradually drop out all together. Your child needs you to affirm him and help him make sense of the world he encounters. As he begins to change physically and emotionally, he needs you to be there to encourage and support him. This is indeed a pivotal time in his development.

Parents' Questions

▮▮ When does puberty begin for boys and girls? Is it the same for both?

Puberty is defined as the time of life in which boys and girls physically begin to change and develop into men and women and become able to have children. Puberty begins, on average, between ages nine and eleven for girls and ten and thirteen for boys. Some start developing even later than that, and a very few begin earlier (which could be a sign of a hormonal problem).

▮▮ When should I start talking to my child about puberty?

You certainly want to talk to your child before she starts puberty. And since you don't know when she'll start, this conversation should happen earlier rather than later. If you have a daughter, you should start talking about puberty between ages eight and nine. If you have a son, start talking between ages ten and eleven. However, if you have a family history of early development, you might want to consider even a year earlier.

Your child may resist a conversation about puberty, but your attitude can play a role in her comfort level. Be positive and let your child know

The Answers You Need & They Want

Character Builders

If your child is still caught lying at this age, you must make the consequences more serious. Otherwise lies will persist into the preteen years, and you'll find other serious issues arising, such as drugs, sex, and alcohol.

- **Be an honest person.** Your child may call you on even half-truths she hears you stating. Don't make excuses; just admit you're wrong.
- **Remind her how much worse the consequences will be if she's caught lying** about a bad decision. Thank her when she tells the truth the first time around.
- **Ask her to clarify her answer if you think she's trying to mislead you.** Explain why this is really a lie as well.
- **Use any teachable moments** to point out the pitfalls of lying seen in the world around you—TV, movies, school incidences—and the people who are hurt by the lie.

that you want to tell her about something very important that will be happening to her body. If she shuts down or seems disinterested, then set another time and make it special for her. How she reacts is out of your control, but your responsibility is to let her know she can come to you with her questions.

Should I use books or charts to illustrate the physical facts of puberty?

Pictures are worth a thousand words, and they're very helpful in explaining puberty to a child. Showing your child illustrations of his anatomy will help make an abstract issue more realistic. These books can be found at the local bookstore or in your physician's office.

How will puberty affect the personality of my son? My daughter?

"I am a lion, hear me roar!" Puberty is often a time of turmoil. Generally kids feel frustrated with what's happening to their bodies and don't have any control over their emotions. This anxiety can lead to moody behavior for both boys and girls. Your child might not be able to pinpoint what's wrong, or he may lash out, sulk, or withdraw for no apparent reason. Fortunately, his basic personality is still intact. Rest assured that it will reemerge when puberty ends and may even be present throughout. Patience and understanding are needed to survive this stage of your child's development. That doesn't mean you should put up with disrespectful behavior, but spending more time listening and asking open-ended questions without seeming to pry lets him know you still care about him and are just trying to understand his world.

Is it inappropriate for my child to see the opposite sex naked?

At this age, your child should desire privacy when in the bathroom and dressing. But it's healthy for her to see her younger siblings (that is, through the preschool years) naked in the bath. Her natural curiosity will be satisfied without embarrassing anyone.

How much roughhousing play is appropriate for a father and daughter?

Once your daughter starts to go through puberty, it's time to curb the roughhousing. In this day and age, it's easily misunderstood, and it might embarrass your daughter. Hugs and kisses are still appropriate, and it's always okay to ask what your daughter enjoys doing with you. If she doesn't mind the roughhousing, let her determine how long it should continue.

The Answers You Need & They Want

What should I tell my child about AIDS?

AIDS, or Acquired (you develop and aren't born with) Immunodeficiency (fights infection in your body; it's lacking) Syndrome (an illness with different symptoms), is a disease caused by a powerful virus that makes the body so weak that it can't fight off other germs. But it's very hard to contract the AIDS virus, and children don't do any of the things that could cause them to get AIDS. Only teenagers and adults do things that could cause them to get AIDS. The only way a child can get AIDS is if his mother has it when she's pregnant and passes it on to her child during birth. You can't catch AIDS from another child, even if you touch or hug him. The only possible way to catch AIDS from someone else as a child is if your blood (through a cut) comes in contact with the blood from someone with AIDS. So never touch anyone else's blood. If your friend is bleeding, get an adult to help stop the bleeding.

How do I encourage my child to use appropriate language rather than slang when referring to body parts or functions?

Modeling is always the best teacher. The first place to start is to make sure your language is appropriate when referring to your child's penis or vagina. If you haven't used those words in the past, now is the time to correct the terminology. If you're not embarrassed, your child also will be less likely to be embarrassed. If she uses the slang terminology, gently say, "You mean your . . ." and stress that it's best to call it what it is. This gives respect to all our body parts, which is an important principle to teach at this age.

What should I do when my child uses slang or profane language?

Many late-elementary kids try to show off profanity they've heard to their friends. Often they're uncertain about what's really being said. Kids try not to let the words slip out when an adult is around, because

Character Builders

Many kids begin to show compassion and caring for others at this age, but many others continue to see themselves as the center of the universe. Frame a proper perspective these ways:

- **Involve your child as much as possible in helping others—** taking a meal to someone in need, volunteering in a service project, or working at a soup kitchen together.
- **Have your child join a service organization** such as 4-H or the Scouts.
- **Use the media, news, or stories to comment** on people who show kindness to each other.
- **As a family, play the "random acts of kindness game"** for a week. Have each person secretly do one act of kindness to each family member, and then try to guess at the end of the week who did what to whom.

they know they'd get into trouble. If you happen to overhear an unacceptable word from your child, talk first about what he thinks that word means, and examine what he's really trying to communicate. It's best to initially keep the tone nonjudgmental. Let him know that your family follows certain rules of respect, and that includes no foul language. Ask him not to repeat it, and help him find some other, suitable expression that would be more acceptable to express his feelings. Discuss with him your expectations and the consequences for not following your rules. If your child slips up, make sure you follow through as you've promised! (Do you remember having your mouth washed out with soap?)

Should I monitor what movies, TV shows, and video games my child sees?

Absolutely! As your child starts to become more independent in the later grade-school years, you may be tempted to not monitor what she

Managing Media Influences

Television, movies, and videos bring several sets of new "friends" into a child's home. These "friends" have a profound influence in viewers' lives. Within hours or days, children, teens, and young adults across the country pick up the latest trends, styles, and products that have been promoted through a particular venue. Think of how many millions of dollars are spent on advertising during the Super Bowl. The fact is: advertising influences buying decisions. If the media can influence a three-year-old to beg his parent to purchase Scooby Snacks instead of the generic brand, why wouldn't sexually immoral and indecent content desensitize our kids beginning at an early age as well?

Most parents assume, "My kid doesn't get it." That sentiment doesn't hold water when research shows that violence and exposure to media are deeply connected. The connection is even stronger when you discuss how entertainment impacts sexual decision making.[1] Some movies with a PG rating show unmarried couples living together and having sex (just without nudity).

As a parent, you can't afford to give in just because "everyone else is watching it." If you want to curb the influence the entertainment industry has on your family, implement some of these practical tips:

- **Limit your children's TV and video exposure.** (This should include noneducational computer time.) Plenty of data links childhood obesity and TV viewing. Institute a "no-TV" week every so often—it might just bring your family closer together.
- **Be proactive in choosing TV shows and movies** the entire family can watch. Ask your kids questions about what they thought of the characters and overall message of the show or movie. Give your opinion at the end, especially if you don't agree with what you saw.
- **If you happen to turn on a raunchy movie, don't hesitate to turn it off.** Your kids might complain, but explain your reasons for turning it off and start a conversation—more likely than not your children will learn to model your behavior.
- **Use ratings only as a starting point.** Research TV shows, video games, and movies ahead of time so that if you don't approve, you'll have an alternative solution.

watches on TV, explores on the computer, plays in video games, or listens to on her headset. The influence of her friends' older siblings starts to filter down and may expose her mind to things she hasn't seen or heard before. Beware! It's important to think about and hold to what your standards are for movies, TV, and music. Now is not the time to let your child start seeing PG-13 or R-rated movies (even some PG ones are inappropriate) thinking she won't comprehend all the sex, language, and violence. Seeing sexually explicit material will arouse her curiosity and imagination. It's still best to sit down with your child and watch TV together. If you don't agree with the values, comment on them, or turn the show off altogether and state why. Check different websites that rate movies more completely. Also, check the ratings on the video games you buy.

▮▮ Are children affected by seeing sexually explicit material?

So often we think, *They don't get it.* Children, regardless of their age, are impressionable and curious. And without the facts from you, your child's mind will interpret any sexually explicit material in a distorted way. Your goal should be to get there first (which should be by now, if not sooner) when talking about relationships, sexual intercourse, and respect for other people. You should train your child to recognize inappropriate material and tell you about it. Keep asking him if he has any questions in this area so he looks to you as an authority. If you discover a magazine, book, or movie that's unacceptable, discuss why you don't think he should be exposed to it.

What types of clothing are appropriate for my child to wear?

As children reach the later years of elementary school, they're much more aware and opinionated about how they look and what they wear. Especially with girls, the latest styles are what they want. Boys also become aware of the trends, although this may occur a little later than with girls. But don't fall for fads that are inappropriate for your child's age. Let her choose as much as she can, but hold your ground on clothing that's inappropriate. Eight- to ten-year-old girls don't need to dress like models and wear clothes that don't cover enough skin. Of course, you'll get a lot of flack and complaints when you take a stand, but it can start a discussion about modesty and how the way you dress influences what people think about you.

Should I allow my child to attend a sleepover with his friends?

Sleepovers become a favorite for birthday parties and special occasions at this age. The problem is that very little sleep occurs at sleepovers, and they may wipe out your child for the rest of the weekend. Saturday nights wipe out Sundays when most families attend church and children need to get homework done. If your child does spend the night with someone, it's best to know the family well, know what their standards are for movies (this is an age when a lot of children start seeing R-rated movies that their parents don't know about), and ask about the plans for the night. Let the parents know your standards for movies and entertainment. If a pattern develops and your child is exhausted for the duration of the weekend, you may let him stay until ten o'clock and then pick him up. It's also okay to have a limit of only one overnight a month or quarter so that you're not battling a cranky child every weekend.

Fostering Friendships

This age is a time of significant emotional growth with increasing independence in day-to-day activities. Solid friendships play a crucial role in helping your child expand out into the world and develop self-confidence as well as deeper friendship skills. Be aware that . . .

- **Friendships for this age become more emotionally significant.** Your child is looking not just for a playmate but for someone to whom she can attach and with whom she can share the joys of play, fun, and growing up.
- **Play between friends at this age will be less symbolic and fantasy based** but more activity and goal directed—such as games, competition, athletics, bike riding, and creative activities. This is an age when achievement and even competition can enhance your child's sense of self and self-confidence, but she must also learn that one's worth is not based only in winning and achieving.
- **This may be an age when you feel you should back away** from your child because of her increasing independence. Resist this temptation, as this is a crucial period of time in her life before the hormones kick in. If you've been a workaholic or absent parent, this is an opportunity to make up for lost ground before puberty begins. Children this age need more opportunity for independence,

Should I worry about my son being exposed to pornography at this early age?

Yes! Most boys are first exposed to porn around age eight. Children who are savvy on the Internet frequently run into pornographic sites by accident. Since boys this age have a heightened curiosity about sex anyhow, this is the time to be diligent about what your son is being exposed to. If you discover your son with pornography, then it's time for a discussion on how beautiful sex is meant to be and how pornography is sexual abuse of the person in the photograph. Predetermine but they need the continued supervision and structure provided by their parents. You should remain committed to talking to, teaching, and playing with your child during this stage.

- **This is an age when bullying is common.** Teach your child that bullying is disrespectful and won't be tolerated. Remind her that the bully is the person with the problem. Give your child skills to deal with bullies, such as ignoring or avoiding them, asking for help from adults for dealing with troublemakers (this is not tattling), and strengthening friendships, because bullies are less likely to bother kids who have good friendships.
- **While you should remain involved in your child's life, you should not try to be her best friend.** That's what peers are for.
- **Encourage fun and productive friendship activities** while providing limits to protect your kids from dangers in their expanding world. Establish rules and give warnings about movies, the Internet, pornography, and other traps that friends can fall into.
- **It's still okay to limit your child's exposure** to inappropriate friendships.
- **Make sure you're teaching and modeling healthy sexuality** for your child. In her world, she's already hearing much about sexuality; be involved and inform her about the world around her.

consequences in case you find your son with the material again. (See pages 142, 144, and 190.)

My daughter is showing few signs of feminine behavior; what should I do?

Before you do anything, Dr. Joseph Nicolosi (a doctor who works primarily with gender-identity issues in young people) suggests answering the following questions with your spouse or with a trained counselor:

- Is your daughter markedly gender atypical?

- Does she reject her sexual anatomy?

- Does she go to her mother with questions? Does she ask her mother to do things with her? Does she show Mom her toys, games, and activities, or does she prefer to go to Dad? Does she have a comfortable relationship with her mother? Does she enjoy doing "girl things" with her mother?

- To what extent does your daughter interact and relate comfortably with other girls?

- Does your daughter adamantly reject the possibility that she'll grow up to be married and have children someday?

- Does her father encourage her feminine development?[2]

If your daughter is expressing herself in feminine ways at home—but not away from home—you should keep your eyes open, but don't panic yet. The reality of life for girls this age is harsh. It's easier for a young lady who hasn't blossomed yet to hang out with the boys, because the teasing and rejection isn't as tough. You may remember the pains of growing up; unfortunately, girls today are exposed to harsher criticism about their looks and behaviors earlier than any other generation in our society. Stay involved in your daughter's life, and remind her that she's loved for who she is and who she will be. If you're concerned, seek professional help.

What should I do if my son rejects me? (This is meant for fathers living in the same home.)

Don't give up on your son, and by all means, don't just let his mother take exclusive care of him. Pursue your son and get past his defensive detachment. Put your own feelings of rejection aside and try to find ways to identify with him. Many fathers give up on their sons because they don't want to be intrusive. Be intrusive; you matter to your son and his future. Sooner or later, he'll soften to your efforts and let you back into

The Answers You Need & They Want

his life. If you feel discouraged and want to abandon ship, seek professional help for guidance and encouragement to stay the course.

What are the signs my child is struggling with gender-conformity issues?

The American Psychiatric Association states five markers to help clinicians determine if a child has a gender-identity disorder:

1. Repeatedly stated desire to be, or insistence that he or she is, the other sex.
2. In boys, a preference for cross-dressing, or simulating female attire. In girls, insistence on wearing only stereotypical masculine clothing.
3. Strong and persistent preference for cross-sexual roles in make-believe play, or persistent fantasies of being the other sex.
4. Intense desire to participate in the stereotypical games and pastimes of the other sex.
5. Strong preference for playmates of the opposite sex.[3]

If you notice any of these behaviors in your child, it would be wise to talk with your child's physician or a professional counselor who shares your beliefs and values.

What happens to boys during puberty?

Pubertal development is a rather simple process for boys. The first physical sign of puberty in boys is the enlargement of the testicles and the thinning of the scrotum. Hair will appear on the face and chest, under the arms, and in the genital area. Also, a boy's voice will begin to deepen (during this time it may crack and squeak).

While these external changes are taking place, internally the testicles begin to produce sperm that are transported through the epididymis and then onward to the penis through the vas deferens. The prostate then begins to produce seminal fluid, which carries the sperm out of

125

the body during ejaculation. During puberty, boys also have a growth spurt and tend to experience rapid weight gain, while at the same time losing body fat.

What happens to girls during puberty?

While puberty for boys is simple to explain, girls undergo a significant amount of changes, providing an excellent excuse for their moodiness and poor behavior. The first visible sign of puberty for girls is the development of breast buds. These buds usually occur two years before a girl's first menstrual period. As her breasts continue to grow, hair will also begin to grow on her legs and genitals and under her arms. In addition, her hips will begin to grow wider, while her internal organs grow and mature. After all of this is complete, your daughter will experience her first period (known as menarche) and will be capable of having babies.

Questions Children Ask

What is puberty?

Puberty is the time of life in which boys and girls physically begin to become men and women and are able to have children. Puberty for most girls begins somewhere between ages nine and eleven. For most boys, it's a little later—on average between ages ten and thirteen.

Girls develop breasts, as well as hair in their genital area. About two years after puberty begins, a girl's period starts. She will grow a lot before her period starts and then keep growing a little more after that.

Boys also start developing hair in their genital area and eventually body and facial hair as well. Their voice begins to deepen, and their penis and testicles begin to enlarge. Muscles bulk up as well. The growth spurt in boys starts a lot later than in girls but can continue longer.

Do boys go through puberty?

All boys go through puberty, starting somewhere between ages ten and thirteen. They start to grow a lot faster, their voice gets deeper, more hair grows on their body, and new, darker hair grows around their penis and in their armpits. Their testicles and penis get much bigger over this period. They may get pimples on their face and start to like girls. It's a very normal process, and when it's finished, boys look more like men than they did before.

Do girls go through puberty?

All girls go through puberty, starting somewhere between ages nine and eleven. They begin to develop breasts, as well as new, darker hair around their labia (the lips outside their vagina) and in their armpits. They'll also grow a lot taller during this time and may develop some acne (pimples) on their face. When puberty ends, a girl will start her period.

What happens to boys when puberty begins?

Puberty is marked by the fact that testosterone (the main male hormone) is flooding through a boy's body. When this happens, he starts growing quickly, his shoulders and chest start to fill out, and his penis gets thicker and longer. His voice may also begin to get deeper. Eventually, curly, dark hair begins to grow in his pubic area and under his arms. The penis and testicles continue to grow larger, and facial and body hair also get darker and coarse. A downside of puberty is that acne may show up. Boys continue to grow throughout the teen years and some into their twenties.

What happens to girls when puberty begins?

Puberty in girls usually starts earlier than in boys; sometimes it may start as early as age nine, but it usually begins between ages nine and eleven. Most often, a breast bud (a bump under the nipple that can be a little tender) shows up first. It can appear in one side before the other; don't panic—the other side will eventually develop. Sometimes the first sign of puberty is dark, coarse hair in the pubic area on a girl's labia as well as in her armpits. A girl grows a lot before her first period starts, and she'll continue to grow for a couple of years after her period, but at a slower pace. Additionally, a young woman's hips and shoulders round out, and her breasts continue to grow. Generally, by age sixteen girls start looking more like women.

Why do some kids start puberty before others?

All kids will go through puberty, but the timing will vary from person to person. Sometimes when your mom or dad was very late in going through puberty, you'll be late also. Your genetic makeup can play a role in this process. That also means you might not follow your mom or dad at all!

What are hormones?

Hormones are amazing substances that are produced in different glands throughout the body. They flow through the bloodstream to all parts of the body, stimulating growth. During puberty, several sex hormones that start the process of changing the body from a child to an adult are released from the pituitary gland (in the brain). Testosterone is the main hormone during puberty for boys, and it's made in the testicles. Estrogen and progesterone are the main hormones for girls, and they're released from the ovaries. Hormones are responsible for pubic and underarm hair growth, breast development, testicle and penis growth, acne, moodiness, and all the other things that make puberty a unique experience.

What is a menstrual cycle?

A menstrual cycle lasts about twenty-eight days, but it can be shorter or longer. When a teen girl begins to have a regular period (the first year of her periods may not be very regular—meaning she could go several months without one), it means her body is capable of having a baby. As a young lady develops, eggs are being made in her ovaries. Those eggs are released about once a month. If a sperm from a man finds its way to the released egg and they unite in the fallopian tube (which connects the ovary to a woman's uterus), then they travel together down the fallopian tube and settle in the lining of the uterus—resulting in pregnancy.

Even if a pregnancy doesn't happen, a woman's body knows that a potential baby needs a tremendous blood supply for nutrition. So as an egg travels toward the uterus, even if it doesn't meet a sperm, the uterus gets ready. But when a sperm doesn't fertilize the egg, the uterus releases the blood that's been collected for the potential baby from the uterine lining, and it flows out the vagina.

Early on, a young woman may not experience a lot of blood flow each month. But it can vary from girl to girl. Most girls wear a maxi pad that can stick to their underwear to absorb the blood. A girl will usually experience a period two years after the onset of puberty. When you start to experience a growth spurt, hair growth, and breast development, it's a good idea to be prepared by carrying a thin pad in your backpack in a nontransparent baggie. But if you're caught off guard at school or camp, find an adult, and she'll be able to help you. It's also not unusual for the blood to overflow onto your clothes if you don't change your pad often enough. Try not to be embarrassed—it happens to every girl from time to time.

▪ What is a virgin?

A virgin is a person who has never had sexual intercourse (oral, vaginal, or rectal intercourse). Many teens falsely assume that they are virgins if they've only had oral sex. This is simply not true. Oral sex can place you at tremendous risk for physical and emotional consequences. Therefore, having oral sex does indicate that a young person is no longer a virgin.

Character Builders

During grade school, your child will build his self-confidence when he's given more responsibilities. He's also capable of carrying out tasks without messing them up. Here's how:

- **Discuss some new responsibilities** your child is interested in. Help him plan how he can accomplish them.
- **Start an allowance**—not to pay for service but to show responsibility in spending. You can use different envelopes for different categories, such as saving, spending, gifts, and donations. The purpose is to teach your child the power of money and the joy of sharing it. And once it's gone, there's no more power!
- **Help your child see the consequences when his responsibilities are neglected** and how it affects those around him. If the dishes aren't cleared at dinner, there won't be any clean ones for breakfast.
- **Read about people who fulfilled their responsibilities** and how it helped them shape their character.
- **Caring for a pet is often a wonderful teacher of responsibility**, but again—make sure your child is up for the task. Start with an easy one first!

⫘ How does a girl get pregnant?

For a girl to become pregnant, several things need to happen. First, she needs to have matured enough to be having periods (rarely a pregnancy will occur before a first period). Next, an egg needs to be released from the ovary into the fallopian tube; this generally happens during the middle of her menstrual cycle. Finally, she needs to have sexual intercourse with a man who releases sperm into her vagina, and these sperm (millions of them) make their way up through her uterus and into her fallopian tube. It only takes one sperm to unite with her egg to start a baby (this is called conception).

What is sex?

Sex includes the very broad topic of how our bodies work as male and female. Sex can also refer to "making love" or "sexual intercourse."

What is sexual intercourse? Is it the same as sex?

Sexual intercourse is the scientific name for "having sex," "making love," and a whole host of other names. What really happens during sex, or sexual intercourse? Anyone who's old enough to have gone through puberty can have sexual intercourse. But sex is an activity that's meant to involve the entire person—heart, mind, and body. Research shows that the best sex happens when two people love each other and commit to one another in marriage. Having sex before marriage not only cheapens sex, but it also can put both parties at risk for an unwanted pregnancy or a sexually transmitted infection.

When a couple loves each other so much, they want to hug and kiss as close as they can. That means they take their clothes off. When this happens, the husband's penis gets big and hard, because he's very excited to be so close to his wife. The wife's vagina gets moist, and she lets her husband put his penis inside her vagina. It feels very good for both of them. At the same time that the man feels great pleasure being inside his wife, his penis shoots out a sticky fluid that contains millions of sperm. Sex is an activity that allows couples to show one another just how much they love and care for each other—this is such an intimate activity that you won't want to share it with anyone else.

▮▮ At what age is it okay to have sex?

It's never okay to have sex if the other person doesn't want to. This is called rape or child abuse. When is it the right time to have sex? When you get married is when it's okay to have sex.

Many people say, "When you're ready, you'll know it," but there are so many things besides the physical act that you need to think about. Some girls want to be loved, so they'll have sex with a boy in hopes that the boy will love them. But often boys just want to have sex, so sex outside of marriage sets someone up for getting hurt. Emotions can fool you when you're a teen and you think you're ready for sex. Then there are the physical problems that go along with sex. A girl can get pregnant when she doesn't want to. A girl or a boy can get a sexually transmitted infection that may be hard to treat (see chapter 14). Finally, don't forget how these things can change your future—if you become a parent as a teen, will you finish high school, go to college, or be able to get a job and work while rearing a child? What will your parents think? Will you feel guilty or lose your self-respect?

The best time to start having sex is when you have found the love of your life and are married. Research shows that the best sex happens in marriage when having sex means you will love each other forever. You will never regret that you waited.

▮▮ Is sex a good thing or a bad thing?

Sex is a great thing. Sex is healthy and normal for married people. Teenagers, however, sometimes choose to be sexually active, and this isn't healthy. For teens, sexual activity can cause both emotional and physical problems. These problems include infections that may not allow them to have children in the future and teenage pregnancy—which will impact a girl's life forever.

The Answers You Need & They Want

What is a homosexual?

A homosexual is a man or woman who is sexually attracted to people of the same sex and feels little or no sexual desire for persons of the opposite sex. The word *gay* is often used for men who are homosexual. The word *lesbian* is used for women who are homosexual. All people, including homosexuals, need to be treated with respect. There are many slang words that insensitive people use to refer to others who are homosexual.

What is AIDS?

See pages 110 and 117.

Why do I have a lump growing under my nipple? Should I be worried?

Usually when puberty starts, many girls (and some boys) discover a lump under one or both nipples as the first sign of their bodies changing. When it's only under one nipple, one on the other side will usually show up in the next several months. These bumps aren't harmful, and the tenderness will go away. As you develop, these bumps will turn into breasts or (if you're a boy) will eventually go away.

What is pornography?

Pornography is books, magazines, pictures, videos, phone messages, video games, movies, or websites that show images of men, women, and children naked and in sexual situations. Pornography is usually used to help people experience an orgasm with or without a sexual partner. Being exposed to pornography can lead to a very damaging view of sex that can hurt you and others. If you find some magazines, a friend gives you a video, or you discover some sexual material on the Internet, tell an adult. It's not wrong to discover pornography by accident, but it is

Materialism & Sexuality

Many parents don't understand how teaching your children about money management relates to sex education. The bottom line is—if you can teach your child how to wait for the things she wants now, she'll be able to wait for things she wants when her hormones have kicked in. At this age, kids become more aware of what things cost.

- **Give your child an allowance** and be clear on what you will pay for (food, clothing, school supplies) and what she can use her allowance for (toys, candy, special gifts). This will teach her how to use her money wisely.
- Your kids are watching what you're spending, so **model a budget** if you have one, eliminate whimsical or impulse spending, and avoid the trap of "keeping up with the Joneses."
- **Teach spending.** If your child wants something special, encourage her to use her savings. Her investment may make a difference in how she treats the new toy or CD.

dangerous to not get rid of it right away. You can become addicted to pornography, just like drugs, tobacco, and alcohol.

What does it mean to ejaculate?

Ejaculation is when men release a burst of fluid during sex; it's accompanied by tremendous physical pleasure.

What is oral sex?

Oral sex describes the sex act of partners using their mouths on each other's genitals to physically excite one another.

Is oral sex, sex?

Yes. Oral sex is sex. Sex occurs when one person touches another person's genitals and causes that person to get sexually excited. Just as with penetrative sex (when the penis goes into the vagina), individuals can contract infections from oral sex. Some teenagers experiment with oral sex because it can be pleasurable and won't lead to pregnancy.

Are you a virgin if you've had oral sex?

The word *virgin* has two meanings. The first means inexperienced and pure. The second is more scientific and means never having had penile or vaginal sexual intercourse. Virginity refers to both boys and girls. According to the first meaning, a girl or boy who has had oral sex isn't a virgin because he or she has had a sexual experience. According to the second definition (which your doctor may use), a girl or boy would technically still be a virgin because he or she hasn't had penile or vaginal intercourse. The most important thing, though, is that a girl or boy who's had oral sex doesn't feel or think like a virgin anymore, because he or she has had a form of sex.

Tell Me More

Early Adolescents: Eleven- to Twelve-Year-Olds

Remember that song in the movie *Grease* where the girls and guys sing in high-pitched voices, "Tell me more, tell me more"? That tune likely summarizes the thoughts swirling through your preteen's mind. Puberty is just around the corner, so take advantage of this momentum and get a jump start preparing him for the turbulent times to come.

Of course, not all teens will experience turbulence. But just in case, consciously continue to develop a relationship with your child—think of it as an investment in the future. Is there a sport or hobby he excels at that you can do together? If so, get involved with him. The time you spend together will help prevent some of the headaches you may experience tomorrow.

As your child approaches puberty, remember to celebrate the changes. Whatever you do, don't make fun of your child or minimize the emotions he's feeling during this transition. If you do, you'll likely sever the trust you've developed over the years. Remember, with hormones in control, this isn't the time to poke fun of him. Be sensitive, respectful, and available. Doing so will allow you to experience the reward of watching your child blossom into a young adult.

Parents' Questions

▪▪ How do I explain the process of making love to my child?

There are many ways to approach talking with your child about the mechanics of sex, but if you want to satisfy her curiosity as well as plant seeds of expected behavior for the future, it's important to discuss this in a context that she can understand.

First, start the conversation with the question, "What do you understand making love to be?" Since many kids this age have friends who are experimenting with sexual play, you might be surprised by the answer.

Then dive in by saying, "Making love is an activity that most often happens between a husband and wife as an expression of their intense love for one another. When a person is touched by a person he or she loves, the brain releases chemicals that cause a physical response throughout the body. A person may get the tingles or become incredibly relaxed. During this process, an individual's sensory system is in full gear, and the slightest touch or kiss is completely enjoyable. As the body becomes excited, a man and woman will embrace and continue to caress, during which time the husband's penis will fit perfectly into his wife's vagina. The sensation during this process is enjoyable and causes a chain reaction known as an orgasm throughout the body.

"Making love is the greatest bonding agent of a marital relationship. Often people who aren't married will 'make love,' but outside of marriage, true intimacy is hard to maintain."

▪▪ How will my child be different now that he's going through puberty?

As mentioned before, your child's behavior will change almost daily. Some days will be great; your child will be the same person you knew prior to puberty. Other days won't be so great. Regardless of behavior, your child desperately needs your support as he transitions through this difficult stage of life. Try to remember what you felt like when you were going through puberty. Be your child's advocate during this transition.

◼ Should I be concerned about what movies, music, and other forms of entertainment my child is exposed to?

Regardless of your child's age, media and entertainment should be something you're concerned about. Since the entertainment industry portrays casual sex as normal and acceptable, this could have an impact on your child's choice to have sex. Screening the movies your preteen watches is very appropriate. Also, watching TV and listening to music with your child can provide a great springboard for communication and an opportunity to express values that you feel are important. One of your goals at this age should be to encourage your preteen to develop skills in making good media choices independently. In the long run, this will be much more important than supervising every exposure.

◼ Is it too early to promote sexual abstinence to my child?

Promoting sexual abstinence to your preteen is something that can never be done too early or too often. In fact, research shows that kids want their parents to establish what the acceptable norm of behavior will be in the home.[1] Setting realistic boundaries should be done for all risk behaviors (drinking, violence, drugs, and sexual activity) early and often.

◼ I'm divorced. How do I talk to my child about sex?

Your being divorced doesn't mean that you don't have the right to talk with your child about sex. In fact, hopefully you've learned valuable lessons from your failed relationship that you can pass on to your child in hopes that she can avoid the same mistakes. Promoting sexual abstinence until marriage is still the best advice about sex that you can

139

Character Builders

Instilling Loyalty When It Counts

As preteens enter middle school, hormones kick in and cause emotions to fluctuate. Friendships seem to suffer the most during this stage. Many preteens have trouble making and keeping friends. Here are ways you can help instill loyalty despite this:

- **Make sure you're loyal to your child** by being his biggest fan—no matter what he looks like or how he feels. Show up for his sporting events and concerts.
- **Keep your promises.** If you say you'll take him to the movies, then do it.
- **Remind him how important it is to stick by his friends** even when it's hard.
- **Don't allow your child to gossip** about friends in front of you.
- **Teach loyalty** for country, school, and family by your actions in supporting each of these as a family. Even if your child sits on the bench in a sports game, be loyal by supporting his team.

give her. As with all things, your actions will speak louder than your words. It's important for you to set a good example for your preteen. If you want her to remain abstinent, it's important that she doesn't see you "sleeping around."

How do I protect my daughter from growing up too fast—you know, being overexposed to sexual pressures, concerns, and behaviors before being developmentally ready?

It's natural to want to protect your daughter from growing up too fast. Unfortunately, you have no control over how fast your child physically develops, but you can protect her from being overexposed to sexual pressures, concerns, or behaviors before she's ready. One way of doing this is to know your daughter's friends. Make your home the place where her friends want to hang out. If her friends are inappropriate in their behaviors or speech, you'll need to intervene. Making an effort to connect with your child and staying involved will help you keep a pulse on whether she's growing up too fast. Based on your insight, you may encourage your daughter to make new friends or find new activities for her to be involved in.

How do I prepare my child for the need for physical boundaries without frightening him?

Knowledge is power. Kids in this age group deeply desire to be trusted and struggle with the desire for independence. Because of his need for trust, this is a great stage to revisit previous conversations about talking with strangers, physical boundaries, and other safety issues. Utilize stories from the news to emphasize the things you want him to do to be safe while he's not with you and to remind him that there are people in the world who want to hurt children and he's not invincible. If you feel your child is aware of these stories, use them to emphasize your point. Also, if you have the means, it might be wise to invest in a two-way radio that he can use to talk to you while he's in the neighborhood.

How can I present the facts about pubertal development and the social dangers of premature sexual experimentation without overprotecting my child?

Presenting facts about pubertal development and the dangers of premature sexual activity is in no way "overprotecting" your child. The opposite is true. If you don't give her this information, you're actually placing her at risk. There are many consequences associated with premature sexual activity, including physical (sexually transmitted infections and nonmarital pregnancies), emotional, intellectual, social, and spiritual ones. Each of these consequences should be discussed with your child throughout her development. These discussions will occur naturally if you're spending time cultivating a relationship with your child.

My daughter says she has a boyfriend; should I be concerned?

At this age, you shouldn't just shrug the boyfriend thing off. It may be her attempt to talk with you on a more "grown-up" level. During this stage of preadolescence, girls are usually much more interested in boys than the reverse. Depending on her peer group, you may want to find out more about the boy from other parents or teachers. You shouldn't get too worked up but rather realize that your daughter has started noticing the opposite sex. Depending on where you live, you might dig deeper and find out what the relationship means. In some communities, kids this age are experimenting with sexual play.

Should I be concerned about my child being exposed to pornography at this age?

Yes. Many experts believe that many kids with access to computers have their first exposure to pornography around the age of eight. If you have a computer in the home, make sure it's located in a place where your child can be monitored. Also, install filters and other software to prevent your child from accessing porn sites inadvertently. Many porn sites use popular web addresses and change the ".org" to ".net" or ".com" in hopes that a person will key in the wrong address and be pulled to their site.

Also, preteen boys may sneak copies of magazines into their rooms out of mere curiosity. If you catch your child reading porn, don't lose your temper. Rather, talk through with him why porn is so dangerous. It probably won't be the last time he views porn, but it will make him think twice the next time he does.

The Answers You Need & They Want

Should I allow my preteen to go to the mall with a group of friends without parental supervision?

Before you decide, ask yourself a few questions: Where do you live? What is the community like? Will there be adults at the mall who can watch over your child? The reality of today's world is that there's no safe place for teens to roam. It might be wise to go to the mall with your child, allow him to roam with a cell phone, and have him check in from time to time. Remind him that your decision about going has nothing to do with trust but rather your concern for safety.

Should I allow my child to attend coed parties at this age?

Coed birthday parties are one thing. But parties at a friend's house on Friday night that aren't occasion oriented should be suspect. Most kids this age aren't completely interested in the opposite sex, and in general, it's more fun to attend same-sex parties.

How can I know if my daughter is participating in oral sex with her peers?

Some preteens are participating in oral sex. If your daughter is involved, there usually is no physical evidence. It's important to realize that oral sex isn't a safe practice and can be associated with sexually transmitted infections, such as gonorrhea of the throat or genital herpes that could be transmitted from cold sores. Having an open line of communication with your daughter is important. A nonthreatening way of bringing up this topic would be to tell her that you know some kids in her age group are participating in oral sex and ask if she has heard anything about such activities around school. Also, talk with other kids' parents and administrators. Enrolling your daughter in after-school activities is a good way to keep her busy. Studies show that most sexual activity in this age group occurs during the afternoon when kids are unsupervised because parents aren't home from work.[2]

143

Porn in Your Home?
It Could Be....

The continuing boom of the communications industry has been paralleled by an explosive growth in the multibillion-dollar pornography industry—and porn is potentially accessible in every home and any neighborhood. Whether it's in print, film, television, or Internet format, porn is destructive because it promotes sexual stimulation and expression outside of the most important part of human sexuality—an intimate relationship with a real person.

This fact creates a potential destructive monster in our culture, especially for boys and young men whose sexuality is more sensory than relational. To celebrate the gift of sexuality, you must take steps to

- **Protect:** Begin at home. It's essential to keep your home free of printed pornography and set careful boundaries about movies, entertainment, and even dress. Use filters on your computers and with the Internet. Monitor email in and out. If a child has a personal computer, place it in the living room where it can be monitored too. Many children and teenagers are quite savvy about getting around Web filters, so a persistent vigilance is in order.
- **Prepare:** Educate your children about pornography's dangers. Open and honest discussions about sex, sexuality, and the risks of pornography should be a part of every parent-child relationship.

▮▮ How can I help my son avoid sexual pressures from his peers?

The best way to help your son is to stay connected with him. Most kids find out about sex and other relational issues from friends because parents are afraid to talk openly about these things. If your son is prepared with information when he joins his buddies on the playground,

This atmosphere combats the secretiveness and resulting shame inherent in pornography. Emphasize, "Pornography is the stimulation of sexual curiosity and drive outside the bounds of a healthy, nurturing marriage relationship with a real person; in effect, it can become a substitute for healthy relationships and become addictive. In fact, anything that takes the place of a healthy relationship will, by nature, become addictive." Then encourage healthy friendships, which allow exercising the human need for relationship, and activities like sports and hobbies, which allow for appropriate expression of the human need for achievement and purposeful activity. As your child grows, support from other adults and families who share your values and beliefs becomes increasingly important.

- **Nurture:** Parents are the first and foremost source of nurturing for children and teenagers—and this includes affirming and respecting the child, teaching boundaries and character, and celebrating the maleness or femaleness of each child. By its very nature, nurturing builds self-esteem, a sense of confidence, and a trust in seeking healthy relationships. This is challenging work and requires that parents make the commitment to a healthy lifestyle, including healthy relationships for themselves. Just remember: most kids genuinely seek to be loved. Meeting your child's needs for love, affection, and attention at home is the best strategy for keeping him from looking for these things in other sources.

he'll be less tempted to join the crowd. Also, spend time helping your son find activities he excels in. A confident child is more likely to be an independent thinker (and leader) who doesn't need peer approval to feel good. Research also shows that kids who are involved in religious activities and deeply committed to their faith are less likely to fall victim to peer pressure.[3]

How do I bring up the topic of opposite-sex relationships with my child?

Go to the movies with your daughter, listen to her music, take her friends on an out-of-town adventure, and listen to her conversations. More than likely, she's already talking about dating and boys she likes. All you have to do is watch a teen movie to know dating's on the brain.

It's much easier to bring up these issues with your daughter than your son. When girls start calling your son, use these phone calls as a conversation starter.

What should I do if my son is being bombarded with phone calls from girls at school?

First, ask your son what he'd like you to do. Try to find out if he likes getting the calls or not. If he's overwhelmed by the calls, let him use you as a scapegoat. Tell him to tell the girls his parents don't allow him to receive calls from girls. If he's too embarrassed to initiate this conversation, offer to tell the callers for him. Then when he's feeling pressure at school, he can shift the blame to you.

I found a porn magazine in my son's room (or I noticed that he has been accessing porn on the Internet); what should I do?

You should confront your son and explain the harmful effects of pornography. The conversation should be calm; resist the temptation to say, "How could you do this?" Inquire where and how he obtained the porn magazine. Does he have any questions about sex or anatomy? Does he understand that porn can be very harmful and addictive? Explain that the woman in the photograph was used for money and profit. You can use this opportunity to explain how wonderful and beautiful sex is at the right place and time, but pornography is humiliating and degrading for the female and harmful to the male.

The Answers You Need & They Want

Addressing Masturbation

It's an experience universal to all young men and many women, yet it's often associated with an intense amount of secrecy and shame. Simply put, masturbation is the rubbing or manipulation of genital areas—the penis in men and the clitoris and vagina in women. The activity is associated with sexual arousal and usually orgasm. Masturbation isn't inherently physically damaging unless excessive force or instruments are used; however, it can be emotionally destructive and even become a substitute for relational intimacy in marriage.

With the exception of mutual masturbation, the practice occurs in secrecy and can be accompanied by shame. This very fact tends to increase the possibility for masturbation to become addictive and a substitute for real relationships.

Masturbation is a common and predictable event—especially in the lives of young adolescent boys. Addressing the topic with your kids requires that you be honest, open, and unshaken by the topic yourself. You should start talking about masturbation in anticipation of your child entering adolescence. It should be described as a common experience that isn't fulfilling, because it's a substitute for a real sexual relationship that should occur in an intimate marital relationship. Your child should understand that masturbation can become addictive and he can lessen the risk for this addiction by having an honest sex education grounded in the values of abstinence until marriage.

Healthy friendship experiences and participation in positive peer-group activities can help keep your child from becoming obsessed. In addition, you should strongly encourage him to avoid the use of pornography, drugs, and alcohol if he wishes to avoid the consequences associated with becoming addicted to masturbation.

If you've discovered (or heard) your child masturbating, remain calm and use this situation to affirm your love for him and remind him of the dangers of pornography; obsessive, all-consuming masturbation; and group masturbation.

What should I do when I find women's clothing in my twelve-year-old son's drawer?

Be calm and find a quiet time to address this issue with your son. It isn't uncommon for young adolescent boys to stow away female undergarments in their dresser drawers. This isn't necessarily a sign of a sexual problem, but it's definitely an opportunity for you to talk with your son about the appropriate expression of sexual feelings. Boys this age experience a significant increase in their sexual curiosity and sexual drive and may develop secret ways to deal with this drive. Women's undergarments often have an attraction because of their feel and can serve as aids to masturbating and other experimental sexual behaviors. (Lingerie ads can serve as aids as well.)

Share with your son that his sexual curiosity is normal and that he'll never be punished for the normal feelings he's been given. There are, however, boundaries for sexual behavior. Anything, whether it be underwear or porn, that reinforces the opportunity for masturbation or other fantasy experiences is of some danger to the healthy development of one's sexuality. Encourage your son to ask questions, get appropriate information, and direct himself toward healthy relationships with both sexes.

My son has been pinching other kids in the genitals. What should I do?

This behavior can be the result of out-of-control playfulness, or it may be a sign of struggle with sexual impulses. Take the time to ask your son about his behavior, looking for clues as to why the behavior is occurring and other people's responses to the behavior. Talk with your son again about self-control and appropriate expression of aggression, emphasizing the inappropriateness of the behavior and the need for a sense of the effect one's behavior has on others. Encourage your son to be involved in appropriate friendships and activities. If this behavior persists, seek professional help.

The Answers You Need & They Want

How should I approach the issue of body odor with my child?

Body odor is a natural part of life, and there should be plenty of opportunities to bring up the discussion with your child. If she participates in sports and other outside activities, encourage her to shower after the event is complete. As she enters puberty, a frank discussion on the importance of deodorant and toothpaste is advised. Use your own hygiene as a conversation starter. Remind your child that taking care of her body not only benefits her but will help her show respect to others.

When should I encourage my son to start shaving?

Shaving in our culture is a milestone for young adolescents. A young man should start shaving when the hair on his face is no longer peach fuzz but dark and coarse. This will happen sometime during the adolescent years. This is a great issue for a father or positive male role model to handle.

When should I allow my daughter to begin shaving her legs?

Believe it or not, how you answer this question may impact whether or not your daughter will feel comfortable talking with you about her other developmental issues. Most girls desire to shave their legs in early junior high. Between the ages of ten and thirteen, depending on where you live, your daughter will be surrounded by peers who are already shaving. Before you make a decision about this issue, find out why your daughter wants to shave. If you determine it's appropriate for her to begin shaving, buy her a nice razor and teach her how to use it. It isn't necessary for her legs to experience unneeded bleeding.

▮▮ What goes on during the menstrual cycle?

The menstrual cycle is an intricate process that includes thousands of details and has been explained in hundreds of books. If you're looking for a fabulous explanation of this process, take a look at *Focus on the Family's The Complete Book of Baby and Child Care.*[4]

Basically, the menstrual cycle is cued to start by the hypothalamus. This structure at the base of the brain regulates basic bodily functions such as temperature. It also signals the body to start the reproductive cycle. The hypothalamus informs the pituitary gland (which tells the organs what to do) to get the ovaries in gear. The ovaries serve two functions: releasing the eggs each month and secreting estrogen and progesterone. Once an egg is released, it travels through one of the fallopian tubes to the uterus. The fallopian tube serves as a meeting place for the egg and sperm. If the egg is fertilized, the resulting embryo travels to the uterus and continues to grow there until birth. If the egg isn't fertilized and no additional hormones are released, estrogen and progesterone levels fall, resulting in a spasm of the blood vessels in the uterus. Without the necessary nutrients, the lining of the uterus dies and passes from the uterus along with blood and mucus in what is known as the menstrual flow or menses.

▮▮ What is PMS?

Premenstrual tension is experienced by 90 percent of women, while around 25 percent experience more severe symptoms known as premenstrual syndrome. This is not the same problem as menstrual cramps. (Women can have cramps with a period, and some may experience them during the middle of a cycle.) Rather this occurs during ovulation, not menstruation. The cause of PMS isn't known; however, symptoms may include bloating and fullness in the abdomen, breast tenderness, backache, fatigue, and dizziness. Some of the emotional symptoms associated with PMS may include irritability, anxiety, depression, poor concentration, and difficulty making decisions.

When should I be concerned about my daughter's irregular periods?

Your daughter should see her physician about her irregular periods if they're occurring every three to four months after more than a year has passed since her first period; if she's having more than one period in a month; if her period lasts more than eight days; or if she's experiencing heavy soaking of more than eight pads or tampons per day. There are many underlying causes for these issues, and they shouldn't be ignored. Failure to take action could result in serious long-term consequences to your daughter's health.

My daughter shows very few signs of feminine behavior. Should I be concerned?

There's a great deal of variety in how children's temperament and play preferences are expressed. Affirm your daughter for who she is (personality, temperament, and talents, including athletic ability), while encouraging comfortable relationships with girls of the same age. Keep the lines of communication open because this is how she will begin to understand herself and her relationships with boys and girls around her. Be sure to offer empathy and comfort if she experiences ridicule for her special giftedness. (See previous chapter.)

My daughter seems to be obsessed with eating issues. I think she may be anorexic. What should I do?

Eating issues seem to be of growing concern, especially for girls this age. The culture, media, and even parents themselves seem to be driven by the desire for fitness and thinness, and as a result, eating disorders are on the rise. On the other hand, it isn't uncommon for girls (and sometimes boys) this age to struggle with issues surrounding body image and to become concerned about weight and figure. Encourage a healthy eating style, where meals and eating are a positive relational event. Also teach healthy eating habits without nagging, criticizing, or worrying

Fostering Friendships

As your child ventures further into the world, friendships only increase in importance as a means for further independence and life skills. Your child will become closer to friends, and this may be the beginning of conflict with parents about friendships. Keep in mind:

- In spite of the fact that this is a time of increased involvement outside of the family, **your child still needs you to be involved** in his life. Your opinions and teaching do matter and serve as a base he can hold onto.
- While friendships will remain primarily with the same sex, **there is a growing interest in the opposite sex**—especially for girls—usually demonstrated by flirting and teasing. A little of this is to be expected and even celebrated. Don't make the mistake of embarrassing or ridiculing your child for having an interest in the opposite sex.
- **Allow your child to make more choices** for activities with friends while you still set boundaries for acceptable behaviors.
- **Teaching and explaining faith-based values and character traits is of increasing importance** and should be connected with further teaching about choosing good friends. It's still

about your daughter's body weight. If you continue to have concerns about an eating disorder, it would be wise to consult a professional. Your daughter's desire to postpone puberty also may be a reason she is struggling with food issues.

▌▌ Why are girls this age obsessed with their bodies? Is this a sign of sexual abuse?

Most likely this obsession isn't an issue of sexual abuse. Early-adolescent girls experience tremendous changes during puberty. During this

152

appropriate to have some direction in your child's choice of friends, but remember that outside your home, he may be exposed to inappropriate friendships. Use character traits to teach about these inappropriate friendships.

- **Bullying and badgering becomes an even bigger issue**, for both boys and girls. Your child will probably have times of feeling hurt, isolated, and even rejected by friends. Emphasize again the qualities of respect, care, and compassion among friends. Teach that some kids act like bullies because of family problems and their own personal insecurity, while other kids may seem to follow those bullies simply to protect themselves from bullying.

- **This age ushers in the need for your child to develop strengthening relationships with adults other than you**, his parent. Teachers, coaches, and other adults are important resources to support his growing autonomy and sense of self. Make sure your kids are exposed to other adults who share your value system.

- **Anticipate the teen years with a sense of celebration** and excitement, not doom and gloom. You will continue to be the primary source of character and family values. Don't abdicate your responsibility.

transition, most girls have questions, concerns, and outright fears about their bodies. Additionally, girls seek to connect with their peer group and in so doing usually begin to compare their bodies with those of others. Communication with trusted adults and strong friendships will minimize a young woman's "obsession" with her body.

▮▮ Should I be concerned if my child is smoking?

While some children experiment and try one or two cigarettes, if the smoking continues, this should be cause for concern. Studies show that kids who smoke are more likely to engage in other risk behaviors. If your child is smoking, this is not an issue you should ignore. Talk to his physician and monitor his activities closely.

Questions Children Ask

What is puberty?

Puberty is the time of life in which boys and girls physically begin to become men and women and are able to have children. Puberty for most girls begins somewhere between ages nine and eleven. For most boys it's a little later—starting between ages ten and thirteen.

Girls develop breasts and hair in their genital area. About two years after puberty begins, their period starts. A young woman will grow a lot before her period starts and then keep growing a little more after that.

Boys will start to develop hair in their genital area and eventually will grow body and facial hair as well. Their voice begins to deepen, and their penis and testicles begin to enlarge. Muscles bulk up as well. The growth spurt in boys starts a lot later than in girls but can continue longer.

Why do some kids start puberty before others?

All kids will go through puberty, but the timing will vary from person to person. Sometimes when a mom or dad was very late in going through puberty, his or her children will be late also. Your genetic makeup can play a role in this process. That also means you might not follow your mom or dad at all! Unfortunately, the science surrounding puberty is still a mystery, so don't be worried if you're a late bloomer.

What are hormones?

Hormones are amazing substances that are produced by different glands throughout the body. They're distributed by the bloodstream to other parts of the body where they cause some reaction. During puberty, sev-

Character Builders

Nurturing Respect in the Teen Years

Name calling and making fun of others is a big deal during this stage. Respect requires one to treat others with honor and politeness, not rudeness and meanness.

- **Show respect to those who act differently** than you.
- **Treat your preteen with respect** at all times—don't demand, but request and talk to her how you want to be spoken to. Remember, your tone is just as important as your words.
- **Use "please" and "thank you"** with her, and expect this from her.
- If she's being disrespectful in her speech or actions, **give her a chance to start over** before you punish her for her behavior.
- **Expect her to respect her body** by practicing healthy eating, exercise, and hygiene, as well as saving sexual activity for marriage.
- **Expect her to respect her own things as well as others' property.** If she breaks it, she pays for it.

eral sex hormones are released from the pituitary gland (in the brain). These start the process of changing our bodies from that of a child to that of an adult. Testosterone is the primary hormone during puberty for boys, and it's made in the testicles. Estrogen and progesterone are the primary hormones for girls, and they're released from the ovaries. Hormones are responsible for pubic and underarm hair growth, breast development, testicle and penis growth, acne, moodiness, and all the other things that make puberty a unique experience.

What is a menstrual cycle?

A menstrual cycle lasts about twenty-eight days, but it can be shorter or longer. The first year of your periods may not be very regular—meaning you could go several months without one. When a teen begins to have periods, it means her body is capable of having a baby. As a young lady develops, eggs are being made in her ovaries. An egg is then released about once a month. If a sperm finds its way to the released egg and they unite, then they travel together down the fallopian tube (which connects the ovary to a woman's uterus) and settle in the lining of the uterus—a pregnancy is begun. If the egg isn't fertilized (no sperm joins with it), the uterus releases the blood that's been collected to nourish the potential baby from the uterine lining through the vagina.

Am I supposed to have my period at the same time every month?

Older women generally have regular periods. But as your body transitions through puberty, your periods may be erratic. A mature menstrual cycle takes place every twenty-eight days. Your periods may come every twenty-eight days or every six weeks. It just depends, because every woman is different.

Can I swim or exercise during my period?

You can swim or exercise during your period if you use a tampon. Tampons collect blood within your vagina and can be removed while going to the bathroom. Unfortunately, many young women feel bloated and uncomfortable, so they don't want to swim during their periods. But if you feel healthy and don't mind wearing a tampon, feel free to swim.

How does a woman produce an egg, and how many are there?

The number of eggs a girl or woman has is actually determined at birth. Eggs are contained in the ovaries and are part of the female reproductive system. There are thought to be about two million eggs in the ovaries. A woman will never use this many eggs, and most of them will either die or just disappear. Usually the ovaries prepare and release one egg during

Character Builders

the course of each menstrual cycle in response to different hormones in the body. The release of the egg by the ovary is called ovulation.

Can you see the eggs?

The eggs are too small to be seen with the naked eye; however, they can be seen with a microscope.

How old do I have to be to use tampons?

Age really isn't a factor for tampon use. Currently tampons are made in varying sizes to fit women of all shapes and sizes. Many young women are hesitant to use tampons because they fear inserting them into the vagina. For many others, tampons are comfortable and convenient. The main problem with tampons is that they should only be used for periods of four to six hours at a time and shouldn't be used overnight. Extended tampon use can lead to toxic shock syndrome—a rare but deadly disease. Before you start using tampons, talk with your doctor or parent about proper use. It's also wise to alternate tampons and pads in an effort to avoid toxic shock syndrome.

How do I keep the blood from staining my clothes?

The proper use of tampons and sanitary pads will help you avoid ruining your clothes during your period. Fortunately, you'll learn the signs that indicate your period is coming and will be prepared. But if an accident happens, you can remove the blood from stained clothes by soaking them in cold water. If you're having your period and are worried about an accident, tuck an extra pair of shorts or pants in your backpack, so you can change if necessary.

How does a penis fit into the vagina?

When a woman is aroused, her vagina will become moist and lubricated and allow for any size penis to penetrate the vaginal cavity. People who haven't had sex often worry about this issue, but it's usually not a big deal. Just as nature allows for the penis to become erect, a woman's body changes to allow for the penis to fit in her body. However, the first few times a woman has sex can be painful until the vagina stretches.

What is the clear stuff coming out of my vagina?

Around the time of ovulation, a woman's body produces a clear discharge called mucus. This usually occurs in the middle of the menstrual cycle or roughly two weeks before the start of the menstrual blood flow. For some women, the discharge may be heavy—consider wearing a minipad to keep your underwear from becoming moist.

The Answers You Need & They Want

How does a girl get pregnant?

If a girl has sexual intercourse around the time of ovulation and if a sperm penetrates the egg, pregnancy results. When the sperm penetrates the egg, it's called fertilization. This process occurs in the fallopian tubes. The fertilized egg travels down the fallopian tube to the uterus and then implants itself in the wall of the uterus and continues to grow.

It's possible for a girl to get pregnant even if the boy's penis doesn't go inside her vagina. If the boy ejaculates (releases sperm) outside the vagina and any of the fluid gets inside, an egg could still be fertilized from the sperm in the fluid, and pregnancy could occur.

What is a wet dream?

A wet dream is another name for nocturnal emission. During the night, while sleeping, an adolescent boy may have an erection of his penis followed by the emission of semen. This is normal and happens in all boys from time to time.

What should I do if I get an erection at school?

An erection can happen when a guy just thinks about a girl or for no reason at all. Fortunately, it's unlikely anyone will notice it, and your penis should lose its hardness in a few minutes. It may seem embarrassing to you, but it's normal and nothing to worry about.

Why do I get an erection when I just think about girls?

When your body goes through puberty and grows into a young adult, the hormones traveling through your body are very sensitive and can be set off without much stimulation. As you become more interested in girls, these hormones are responsible for your erection. Fortunately, your body will get the message that it can go no further, and your penis will get soft in a few minutes. Usually nobody will notice what's happened, and you can play it cool. It happens to all boys and even men and is normal.

What is a homosexual?

A homosexual is a man or woman who's attracted sexually to people of the same sex and feels little sexual desire for people of the opposite sex. The word *gay* is used for men who are homosexual. The word *lesbian* is used for women who are homosexual. All people, including homosexuals, need to be treated with respect. There are many slang words that insensitive people use to refer to homosexuals.

What is a virgin?

A virgin is a person who has never had sexual intercourse (oral, vaginal, or rectal intercourse). Many teens falsely assume that they are virgins if they've only had oral sex. This is simply not true. Oral sex can place you at tremendous risk for physical and emotional consequences. Therefore, having oral sex does indicate that a young person is no longer a virgin.

At what age is it okay to have sex?

Having sex before you're married is a bad idea. Many people say, "When you're ready, you'll know it," but there are so many things besides the physical act that you need to think about. Some girls want to be loved, so they'll have sex in hopes that the boy will love them. Often boys just want to have sex. Sex outside of marriage sets people up for getting hurt. Emotions can fool you when you're a teen and you think you're ready for sex. Then there are the physical problems that go along with sex. A girl can get pregnant when she doesn't want to. Both girls and boys can get a sexually transmitted infection that might be very hard to treat (see chapter 14). Finally, don't forget how these things can change your future—if you become a parent as a teen, will you finish high school, go to college, or be able to get a job and work while

Character Builders

How a Purity Ring Can Be the Perfect Reminder

What is a purity ring? A purity ring is a special ring picked out by you or your child that she wears as a reminder of her commitment to be pure sexually until her wedding night. It's a gift she then gives her future spouse that says, "I waited for you!"

Why give a purity ring to my teen who might not make it until the wedding night? Research has shown that when teens make a commitment by signing a pledge to be abstinent until marriage, they're more likely to keep that commitment than peers who don't.[5] A ring is a daily reminder of that commitment.

When should I give this ring? A good time is during eighth grade, before high school (unless you think your child is maturing much earlier). It's great for the mom to take her daughter away and the dad his son, if at all possible, for a fun weekend doing something you both enjoy. Each family is different, and some would prefer to have both parents present for this occasion. The ring could even be given by the parent of the opposite sex. For example, a father could take his daughter out for a date on her thirteenth birthday and present her with her purity ring; a faith, hope, and love charm; or any other symbolic object. Plan to have some good discussions about the opposite sex, dating, and marriage. Then give your child the ring or go with her to pick it out. Tell her that your dream is for her to have the best sex possible within a marital relationship. For those families with faith, this could be an opportunity to challenge your child to begin praying for her future spouse.

rearing a child? What will your parents think? Will you feel guilty or lose your self-respect?

What is intercourse?

Intercourse is classically described as a man's penis being inserted into a woman's vagina. Anal intercourse is a penis being inserted into the

Teens & Abstinence:
Faith Works

Teenagers, especially girls, with strong religious views are less likely to engage in sexual activity than teens who aren't religious. Data gleaned from a recent study of adolescent health shows that religious commitment reduces the likelihood of adolescents engaging in early sex by shaping their attitudes and beliefs about sex. This study analyzed data from the National Longitudinal Study of Adolescent Health (ADD Health), the largest comprehensive survey of seventh through twelfth grades ever conducted.[6] The survey measured the effect of family, peer group, school, neighborhood, and religious institution on behaviors that promote good health in young people.

The teens were interviewed twice with a one-year interval between the interviews. Researchers asked the participating teens about their commitment to religious activities, the importance of religion in their lives, and their beliefs about how having sex would affect them and people close to them. In addition to this direct relationship of religious commitment to sexual restraint, the ADD Health Study found that teens who made a personal commitment (usually based on religious values) to purity, primarily shown by signing a pledge card, were much more likely to remain abstinent during the adolescent years.

The results of this study are reassuring: beliefs do affect behavior. This also reminds parents that a family atmosphere that encourages spiritual development and affirms religious participation helps teens to confront and resist the values of contemporary society.

rectum. Oral intercourse is when the penis is inserted into the mouth or the mouth covers the vagina for the purpose of stimulation.

▮▮ Is oral sex the same as sex?

Yes! Oral sex is sex, vaginal sex is sex, and anal sex is sex.

Character Builders

In middle school, kids become even more fashion conscious, and items they want—CDs, DVDs, and computer upgrades—can require a lot of cash. In addition, seeing friends with more money can lead to discontent and jealousy. Others' family vacations to exotic places can make one feel poor in comparison. This pattern, if not kept in check, may help your child become more aggressive in keeping up with his friends in an effort to be accepted. This is not the type of acceptance you want your child to seek. Instill self-control these ways:

- **Set a clothing budget** that will teach your child how to manage his money.
- **Encourage your child to use his allowance** to buy the extras.
- **Don't go overboard at birthdays and holidays!** Ask him for a small wish list, but warn him you also have a budget and to not expect everything on his list.
- **Allow him to do extra chores to earn money** for bigger items.

▮▮ What actually happens during sex?

During the process of sexual arousal when a man "gets excited," blood vessels in the penis are filled (engorged) with blood. This causes the penis to get longer and harder and is called an erection. When the penis is erect and is inserted into the woman's vagina, it can be incredibly pleasurable. At the height or climax of these pleasurable feelings (called an orgasm), the man's body releases semen (fluid containing the sperm). This is called ejaculation.

▮▮ What is "making out"?

"Making out" has no one definition. Some refer to "making out" as kissing and hugging, while others consider it to mean having sexual intercourse.

■■ When is it okay to kiss my boyfriend?

Making a choice to kiss your boyfriend shouldn't be done lightly. At your age, kissing is very popular and can lead to other sexual play. Before you decide to kiss a boy, decide what a kiss means to you. For many, kissing is no big deal. However, a kiss is just one step on the road toward intimate physical activity. It's a good idea to save your kisses for a man who's really worth it (someone who won't be kissing another girl before the end of next week).

■■ What is dry sex?

Dry sex is sexually stimulating another person with clothes on. In the early stages of a physical relationship, kissing may become boring, so a couple will decide to stimulate one another with their clothes on. (The idea is to prevent intercourse.) Even though the activity may appear to be "safe," in reality you're moving your relationship closer to crossing the line into sexual intercourse.

11

Fools Rush In

Full Bloom: Thirteen- to Fifteen-Year-Olds

Don't be worried if the only "hello" you get from your son is a grunt. You're probably even used to it by now. If you were expecting your son to be a fountain of conversation during his early teen years, you can send those dreams packing. The cute little athlete you remember from elementary school may appear more gangly than attractive, and your brilliant scientist may have found sanctuary in his bedroom.

As the parent of a young man, it may be hard to keep him talking, but don't give up. He still needs to eat and still needs you to tote him around to practice and extracurricular activities. Take advantage of the time you do have together; listen to his questions. And be careful not to be too intrusive or overtalk.

On the other hand, if you're the parent of a budding young woman, you'll be up to your ears in conversation. We've all seen the commercials of teenybopper girls talking incessantly to their friends about everything from brushing their teeth to shaving their legs. Keep this in mind: if you can keep track of her conversations, you may be able to answer all of her questions about relationships and sex without her realizing it.

Regardless of your child's gender, it's time for the big leagues. No longer will he look to you for approval (although he desperately needs it). No longer will she consult you for fashion advice (although her makeup will still scream "help"). This is the stage in your parenting journey to be diligent and involved. Keep your ears tuned in and your social calendar light, because parenting takes on a whole new meaning during this season of life. While you're no longer wiping bottoms, you will be cleaning up messes. So jump in with both feet and enjoy the process of ushering your child into a new stage of life—one where his thoughts, opinions, and ideas desperately need an audience. Tune in and keep cheering.

Parents' Questions

▪▪ What are the physical facts that a boy or girl should know by this age?

By the early teen years, both boys and girls should fully understand the events that take place during puberty. Additionally, they should understand not only the reproductive aspect of sexual intercourse, but also the relational and enjoyment aspects of sex that occur within the deep intimacy of a lifelong, committed marital relationship. Finally, you need to discuss the consequences associated with nonmarital sexual play: emotional, physical, and spiritual. Current trends for young adolescents include experimenting with mutual masturbation, oral sex, and anal intercourse. For many parents, this may be too much to stomach, but your kids have friends involved in sexual play (which may include reenacting porn flicks and other videos at coed parties). Remember, the facts are just a starting point—don't let the conversation end there.

The Purposes of Dating

- **Choose a marriage partner** and prepare for a lasting relationship.
- **Develop a sense of independence.**
- **Learn to feel more at ease in a male/female relationship** and enjoy friendship with someone of the opposite sex.
- **Get to know other people**—their likes, dislikes, values, ways of communicating—**and yourself.**

At what age is it appropriate for my daughter to start dating? My son?

There's no magical age. Some families don't belicve in dating at all. Others only allow their children to date in groups. The reality of the teen world today is that dating is no longer cool. Kids hang out and hook up. Unlike ten years ago, it's not as common to see kids in a dating relationship. Your child's maturity and your comfort level with her peer group will probably determine when she can date. Most experts would agree that solo dating at this age isn't appropriate. As your child's advocate, it may be wise for you to host activities for her and her friends. Make a mental note that coed parties at this age may be fine, but coed sleepovers are never a good idea.

Before your child starts dating, be proactive and talk about the purpose of dating, ideas for great dates, and how to keep a date from going stale. Parents often worry about the "when" of dating but rarely help their adolescent date successfully. Make sure to spend time helping your child be creative and realistic when it comes to dating. Use this time to share with her lessons you wish you would have known years ago.

What ground rules should I set in regard to dating?

First things first. When you set ground rules, it would be wise to include your child in the process. If he's ready to date, talk to him about what

The
10 Commandments of Dating

1. **Get a life of your own.** Get grounded. Get grouped. Get goal oriented. Get giving. Get growing.
2. **Use your brain.** Balance romance with common sense, reason, judgment, and discernment. Balance the head and the heart. Refrain from physical intimacy. Analyze your past relationships. Include others in the process. Never neglect opportunities to evaluate along the way.
3. **Seek similarities**. Healthy relationships and marriages are ones in which there's a strong foundation of similarities in background, temperament, goals, dreams, values, and the way in which individuals managed and ordered their physical and mental lives.
4. **Take it slow.** You do not get to know a person in a short period of time. You need time to bond. Protect yourself from getting attached too quickly.
5. **Set clear boundaries.** Draw definitive lines in the physical/sexual area of your relationship. Your body belongs to you. Communicate how you feel to your date. Own your own feelings, and be able to separate them from your date. Take ownership of your thoughts— keep them pure. Take responsibility for your own actions—don't try to change someone.
6. **Save sex for marriage.** Practice the healthy steps of intimacy. Reserve petting, heavy petting, mouth-to-breast, and oral and vaginal intercourse for marriage.

his expectations and desires are, and then set the rules according to his maturity.

Discussions surrounding dating should also include appropriate boundaries, curfew, attire, group dating, and financial responsibilities. All dating relationships must address expectations regarding family time and what to do in an uncomfortable or dangerous situation.

7. **Living together before marriage doesn't promote a healthier marriage.** Research shows that couples that live together first have a far greater chance of getting a divorce than those who don't. Women who cohabitate are more likely to experience domestic violence than married women.[1]

8. **Engage in healthy responses to conflict.** Avoid "avoidance," "defensiveness," "invalidation," and "intensification." Fight fair: take a time-out to consider what you really need to express, and be respectful to your partner. Be quiet and listen—seek to understand, then to be understood. Use "I" statements. Negotiate and compromise. Reevaluate your solution at a later time.

9. **Notice danger signs and end the relationship.** Any form of abuse: physical, verbal, emotional, or sexual. Addictions. Untruthfulness in the relationship. Irresponsibility and immaturity. No physical/sexual attraction. Emotional baggage. Denial—you can't admit that this relationship isn't healthy for you.

10. **Choose your dating and marriage partner wisely.** If you date and then marry the wrong person, you'll live with significant, negative, and lasting consequences of that decision for the rest of your life. Discern his or her character. Character is who you are when no one is looking. Look back at prior relationships to determine patterns of behavior. Crisis reveals someone's true character. Give your relationship lots of time. Do you feel encouraged, affirmed, inspired, and challenged to grow and be a better person when you are with him or her?

In every case, it's important to remind your child that you'll always be available to help find a way out of a bad situation—even if it means picking him up anywhere, anytime.

Next, here are nine dating standards you—and your child—will find helpful for the healthiest early dating relationships:

1. Set your physical intimacy boundary before you go on the date.
2. Boys and girls are jointly responsible for setting and maintaining limits.
3. Verbally communicate your boundary to your partner.
4. You can stop at any step of intimacy—physical intimacy does not have to progress.
5. Have self-control.
6. Consider your manner of dress.
7. Stay sober.
8. Use nonverbal and verbal refusal skills if needed.
9. Avoid dangerous or tempting situations like being alone in a house.

▮▮ What practical advice can I best give on planning a great date?

Here are seventeen starting areas where you can be a helpful coach:

1. Determine what your date likes and dislikes. Before planning your date, ask, What interests him? Does he like the outdoors or performing arts? Eliminate the things you know he won't like to do.
2. Count your money. This will often narrow down the choice. If you don't have a lot of money, spend it wisely or not at all. Many fun dates require no money. Did you know imagination and creative ideas can impress someone way more than money?
3. Maximize conversation. One of the main reasons for dating is to grow in your friendship. Always try to structure as much time to talk as possible.
4. Ensure a fun time. Take time to thoroughly plan fun dates. Go over all the details. The more your date enjoys the time, the longer she will remember it and you.
5. Keep dates out of a rut. Try not to plan the same date twice. When it's a big hit with him, do it again later, but wait a while. Add variety.

The Answers You Need & They Want

6. Include others. Group dating takes the social pressure off you and helps to keep the conversation going. In addition, you build other relationships, and it keeps you out of tempting situations.

7. Pick different times. Plan dates for the morning and afternoon as well as in the evening. You'll see different sides to your date's personality and keep the dates interesting.

8. Avoid tempting situations. Avoid places or people that put compromising thoughts in your head. Your date is special to you and her parents, so take good care of her!

9. Set your standards and limits. Know what is best for you and the other person, now and in the future; if you have different standards than your date, go with the more conservative limit.

10. Put friendship as your top priority. Your main goal for the relationship should be to be best friends.

11. Only date people who have the same values as you. If he has a "reputation," avoid dating him!

12. Find pressure-free friends. True friends want what's best for you. If a date or friend pressures you to do something you know is wrong, then she isn't thinking of you but herself.

13. Be aware of temptation. What's tempting for you? Romantic movies, dark environments, dress, alcohol?

14. Avoid drugs and alcohol. They decrease your ability to think clearly and make good decisions.

15. Know the consequences associated with being sexually active. Education is the key; realize the media doesn't give you a realistic view of the consequences.

16. Let your parents be a valuable part of your relationship, or ask another adult mentor to encourage you and hold you accountable.

17. Focus on other areas of intimacy instead of physical intimacy. Share emotional, intellectual, relational, and spiritual values and beliefs.

The Dating Bill of Rights

I have the right:

- To ask for a date.
- To refuse a date offer.
- To suggest activities on the date.
- To say what I think.
- To have my own feelings and express them freely.
- To tell someone when he or she is being impolite.
- To tell someone I'm uncomfortable.
- To have my limits and values be respected.
- To tell my date when I need affection.
- To refuse affection.
- To be heard.
- To refuse to lend money.
- To refuse sex with anyone just because some money was spent on me.
- To refuse sex at any time for any reason.
- To have friends and space aside from my boyfriend or girlfriend.

I have the responsibility:

- To communicate clearly and honestly.
- To determine my limits and values.
- To ask for help when I need it.
- To be considerate.
- To set high expectations for myself and others I choose to be with.
- To not put myself and others in situations that would lead to something we might regret.

Why should my daughter wait until marriage to become sexually active?

Simply put, for the sake of her marriage. The obvious physical consequences are pregnancy and sexually transmitted infections, but long-term, there may be consequences such as infertility or cervical cancer. Sexual intercourse isn't just a physical act; it involves the whole person. Emotional damage is likely to occur from sexual activity at this age as well, especially when the person goes from one relationship to another after a painful breakup.

The social cost to individuals and society for nonmarital births and STIs is tremendous. Teen girls who have babies at this age are more likely not to finish high school and are more likely to live in poverty. While it's hard to know what comes first, teenagers who are sexually active are more likely to smoke, use alcohol or drugs, have trouble with the law (even serve time in jail), and experience depression or suicide. Teens who have faith are likely to experience guilt or withdraw from their faith if they are sexually active.

Additionally, when your daughter marries, the baggage of multiple sexual partners may prevent her from experiencing a truly intimate and satisfying marriage. The purpose of encouraging her to wait for sex is not just to help her avoid STIs or nonmarital pregnancy, but also to provide her with the skills to enjoy marriage and have a great sex life in the future, free of guilt, scars, and memories of past broken relationships.

How can I teach my daughter about what to expect from a date?

Sometimes it's useful for a father (or male role model) to take his daughter on a date. This could start with sending your daughter some flowers, ringing the doorbell, escorting her to the car, and going out to dinner or a movie. This will be not only a fun time, but one of meaningful conversation and a chance to talk about the pitfalls of not being in control on a date. A mom could have her son pick her up for a date. (Dad could slip his son a few bills for dinner.) Be creative, and let your children accompany you on a date with your spouse. Also, help your kids think of great things to do on a date. If you're a single parent, enlist the help of your family and friends.

How should I handle curfews in my home?

During the early teen years, which correspond to middle school, it's relatively easy to set curfews since teens don't drive. The bottom line is that you the parent should be in charge of curfews and not your teen, his friends, or his friends' parents. While you're ultimately in charge of this decision, take the time to listen to your teen. He may actually prefer an earlier curfew than you would set on your own. So many parents worry about curfews but forget to be concerned about their child's whereabouts after school—the primary time when sexual activity occurs. Be careful to set appropriate curfews for the evenings and expected behavior for the afternoons.

What can I do to encourage healthy peer relations without exposing my child to compromising situations or overwhelming temptation?

In a nutshell, know your child's friends and if their parents share your value system. And even if you approve of her friends and their parents share your values, you need to investigate whether they have an older child in their home who might influence your child. Healthy peer relations with the same sex or the opposite sex are a necessary part of this developmental period, but you need to be involved. Needless to say, peers of the opposite sex shouldn't be allowed to be home alone or in each other's bedrooms. If your young teen is running with the wrong crowd, you need to somehow change her mix of friends, even if it takes a drastic measure such as changing schools or church youth groups or moving to a new neighborhood.

Date Nights Can Start Early

Since just about every child thinks about being married, it's never too early to start talking about and modeling how to treat the opposite sex. When your kids are in grade school, it's good for each parent to institute a "date night" with each child of the opposite sex. It could be once every few months or on special occasions. One family had each child take his or her parent somewhere special on the parent's birthday—at the parent's expense. (This could be expensive, so set your parameters carefully!) The point is to show your children how to treat their date and teach them the ropes of courtesy and conversation.

If this starts in grade school and has been fun, when your child hits preadolescence, he or she will still want to have a date night—even if it means being seen with a dreaded parent.

An encouraging aside: research shows that if a girl's father is involved in her life, she's less likely to initiate sexual activity during high school.[2] Since girls have more issues with self-esteem, weight, and friendships than boys do, an attentive dad can do wonders in building up his daughter to be a beautiful young woman on the inside. A dad can also provide cautionary insight on how certain clothes turn on boys.

It's equally important for boys and moms to have good discussions about what girls are looking for in a guy as the boys get more interested in the opposite sex.[3]

What should I say about my past sexual history to my child?

This is a tough question if you were sexually active prior to marriage. Every person will have to decide how to answer the question if and when your child asks, "Mom (or Dad), what did you do when you were my age?" If you were a virgin when you married, you can tell your child that you're happy you made that decision and encourage him to do the same. If you were sexually active prior to marriage, you must then decide how to answer.

Sharing your story can be a powerful teaching tool. You don't have to go into details, and it can be very short. "You know, I made a mistake when I was your age. I'd like to turn back the clock, but I can't. I hope you won't make the same mistakes I made." This can open the door for a very meaningful dialogue between you and your child. Even if the question isn't asked, if you feel he's heading for deep trouble, you could voluntarily share sensitive information with him. Sharing your painful past could avert a disaster for your teenager. Even if you had sex before marriage and didn't experience negative consequences, remember, the world is a different place today.

When should a young woman have her first pelvic exam?

There's much debate about this subject. In general, a pelvic exam is needed at any age after a girl has become sexually active. If a girl is a virgin, a pelvic exam isn't needed until sometime between the ages of eighteen and twenty-one. If a young woman is experiencing medical problems such as vaginal discharge, menstrual problems, or pelvic pain, a pelvic exam may be needed. Ultimately this issue should be discussed with her physician.

What should I do if I walk in on my child in a compromising situation?

If you should walk in on your child while he's masturbating, it would be appropriate to excuse yourself at that moment and talk to your child about the issue at a later time if it hasn't been previously discussed. Even if you've discussed masturbation in the past, it might be good to broach the subject again and acknowledge what happened. Most teens will be mortified by the experience and would probably prefer to let the incident be forgotten.

Abstinence Is Attainable

To encourage your teen to wait until marriage to have sex gives her the best chance for the best sex. Let her know at every available opportunity how you feel about saving sex for marriage, because it will influence her decision. Here's how:

- **Model fidelity in your marriage**, and if you're single and in a romantic relationship, practice abstinence.
- **Talk with your teen about appropriate public displays of affection** (holding hands and simple kisses), and discuss your expectations for her physical boundaries if she finds herself alone and in private with the opposite sex.
- **Don't let your teen be home alone with the opposite sex**— after school or anytime!
- **Remind your daughter that how she dresses will communicate to guys the type of girl she is.** Teach modesty by example, but also set guidelines as to what's appropriate to wear out of the house.
- **Have a man** (dad, uncle, grandpa) **discuss with your daughter what turns on guys** (that is, provocative clothing).
- **Model how one treats and respects the opposite sex.** Dads, "date" your daughter. Moms, "date" your son.
- **Set dating rules early** so your teen knows when she can start group dating and couple dating. Clarify curfew rules and their consequences when broken.
- **Be generous with your physical affection** for your teen— whatever she feels comfortable with. Read *The Five Love Languages of Teenagers* by Gary Chapman.[4]

If you should walk in on your child having sexual intercourse in your home, it would be appropriate to ask him to get dressed. A brief discussion about your disappointment may also be in order. Inform the partner that you will have to tell her parents what happened. When the other child has left and both of you have had a chance to settle down, you need to talk to your child about the situation. Love for your child must prevail over your disappointment, hurt, and anger. Your child should also be seen by a physician to be evaluated for pregnancy and sexually transmitted infections. Some of the questions you may want to ask include: How long has this been going on? Is this your first sexual experience? Do you know if you're at risk of pregnancy or contracting an STI?

The key point to remember is not to be angry. It's possible your child let a situation get out of control and is as disappointed as you are. However, if he shows no remorse for disrespecting you and your home, a fair punishment should be in line. Another thought to keep in mind: Have you been clear about what you expect from your child when it comes to nonmarital sexual activity? Does he know that this is something you disapprove of? If not, it's time to communicate clearly with your adolescent about your hopes and dreams regarding his future.

Should I be concerned about the clothes my daughter is wearing?

Absolutely! First of all, it's important to explain to your daughter how men and women are different. Explain that women are generally turned on by relationships, courtship, and romance. Men, on the other hand, are visual and are turned on by what they see. This explains why models sell products on TV to men. In short, men are visually stimulated, and women are relationally stimulated.

The discussion of how men are visually turned on allows you to explain to your daughter that wearing very revealing, sexy clothing turns boys on. It could lead to date rape or sexual involvement for your daughter. Even if your daughter isn't raped and doesn't become sexually active, she may have caused sexual frustration for the guys she's turned on with her skimpy dress or partially exposed breasts.

What should I tell my son about the way girls dress?

Educate him on the differences between males and females, and help him control his hormones that are kicking in during the early adolescent years. Explain why it's so easy for guys to get hooked on pornography, even the so-called "soft" pornography. Help him understand that he often can't help the first look at a pretty girl wearing provocative clothing, but he can control his actions by avoiding the second look that could lead to trouble. This is a great topic for a father or other trusted male role model to cover.

Why should I be concerned about the movies, music, and entertainment my child is exposed to?

Most movies, music, and entertainment don't reflect the values and character traits most parents want modeled for their teenagers. You need to be involved in your teen's life. You need to know not only what movies, entertainment, and music she's looking at or listening to, but also what's being viewed at the homes of her friends. Remember, your ultimate goal is not to control her media consumption but rather to train her to think for herself and make wise choices about media use.

When should I be concerned about my child's delayed sexual development?

While most girls will start puberty between ages nine and eleven, it can be delayed until they're fifteen or sixteen. It's important to know when her mother, older sisters, aunts, and grandmothers started their periods. Some families tend to have late bloomers. Boys also can come from families who tend to develop late. In fact, many men don't reach their adult height until college. If you're worried, do your homework and ask your child's doctor. This is another good reason for yearly checkups with your physician. One of the tasks of a physician during a yearly well check is to see how puberty is progressing. At some point, if puberty hasn't begun, some medical tests will need to be done.

Should I allow my child to attend coed sleepovers?

No. At this age (and perhaps any age), they're an invitation to disaster. Coed sleepovers are a dangerous trend. There's no reason for boys and girls at this age to be out and up all night together. If your child is invited to a party, allow him to attend the supervised activities, and tell him you'll pick him up at midnight.

What should I tell my child about her father's live-in girlfriend?

It's important not to negatively influence your teenager's relationship with her father, but also you need to explain why you don't approve of this living arrangement. By this age, most kids are aware of what their divorced parents are doing. While your ex may have a live-in girlfriend, make sure that you don't have your boyfriend spending the night while the kids are away.

Children from divorced homes are very perceptive and realize that their parents compete for their affection and this sometimes will happen by trashing the other parent. The best thing you can do for your child is realize she did not choose to have her parents divorce. It's up to you and her father (or mother) to make her life less complicated by avoiding situations that may cause unnecessary questioning.

I found a porn magazine in my son's room (or noticed that he's been accessing porn on the Internet); what should I do?

You should talk about the harmful effects of pornography with your son. Inquire where and how he obtained the porn magazine. Does he have any questions about sex or anatomy? Does he understand that porn can be very harmful and addictive? You can use this opportunity to explain how wonderful and beautiful sex is at the right place and time but that pornography is humiliating and degrading for the female and harmful to the male.

What am I to make of my child's physician who asks me to leave the room during an exam?

First, there's no need to worry or be overly concerned. The reality is that most teens don't want their parents present during the exam. Most physicians at some point during the visit, even if the parent is in the room during the exam, will want to talk to your teen alone. This is normal and healthy, and it's to be encouraged. The time alone with your child will allow the physician to possibly uncover some risk factors that you might not know about. Some physicians may support your family's value system, even if it's different from their personal viewpoint. A physician who supports your value system can be a big support to you as a parent. It's also appropriate to ask your physician how she'll handle certain situations if they arise.

Can a doctor prescribe contraceptives to my teen without advising me?

Yes. Both federal and state laws protect physicians who screen and treat minors for sexually transmitted infections as well as prescribe or dispense contraceptives. This is why it's extremely important to choose a physician who shares your values and believes that abstinence before marriage is the healthiest choice for youth.

Is a doctor legally bound to keep his conversation with my teen confidential?

No, but there are moral and ethical considerations if the physician has previously established teen confidentiality. Many physicians will advise both the adolescent and the parent as the youth approaches puberty that there will be a time during at least the annual physical when the physician will talk to the youth without the parent being around and what they talk about will be confidential. Most physicians will explain that they can break that confidentiality if a matter is discussed that has major health implications for the teen or for society.

Should I allow my teen to attend the school's sex-ed program?

See pages 101 and 218.

I'm a single parent with a child of the opposite sex; should I seek a positive same-sex role model for my child?

Yes, if at all possible. This might be an aunt or uncle, coach, teacher, or even a friend's parent. Make sure the individual shares your values. Even if you're not single, an older friend or relative who shares your values can be a valuable tool in your child's development. Reflect on your life. Who were the people you trusted and looked to for advice? You can't be all things to your child. Look for others in your life who can encourage him to reach his full potential.

Should I encourage my child to do volunteer service?

Part of your job as a parent is to make sure that your child learns and appreciates the importance of thinking of others rather than just herself. Volunteer service can be done through her school, faith-based organizations, community organizations, or even just your family. Volunteering together will help you model your compassion for others as well as provide a time to just be with your teenager. Studies show that adolescents involved in volunteer activities have less time to be involved in high-risk behaviors, such as drinking, drug use, and sexual activity.

How do I address sexual experimentation among same-sex peers in a culture that encourages experimentation with no boundaries?

Adolescents experience media and peer exposure to a culture that says your sexuality can be fluid and it's safe to experiment with sexually directed behavior. This is especially true in light of the mainstream media popularizing gay entertainment and highlighting celebrities who claim to be "out of the closet." Additionally, at some schools, experimenting with lesbian relationships is considered just a rite of passage for many girls. Same-sex relationships are portrayed through the media as exciting and hip, and because of this, teens are curious and feel no shame in experimentation with sexual feelings and behaviors with the same sex.

As a parent, you need to be able to engage in frank but comfortable discussions about sexual curiosity while strongly stating that sexual experimentation among same-sex peers is inappropriate. Don't be embarrassed to discuss these issues with your child, and don't be shocked when he tells you about the presence of these events in his world. You can always offer the best information and protection for your teen, if you do so in a positive, affirming, and educated fashion.

What should I do if I walk in on my daughter experiencing same-sex sexual play?

Don't panic. Stop the behavior in a firm and nonemotional way, and talk to your daughter when things have cooled down. Ask your daughter to explain what was happening and how she got herself into the situation. Try to understand the power of sexual curiosity, as well as the temptation to experiment that goes with this age. Lovingly address the inappropriateness of the behavior and the potential dangers—physical and emotional—that go along with persistent same-sex behavior. It's also appropriate to speak with the parents of the other teen involved.

Does curiosity equate to healthy sexual experimentation at this age?

Curiosity and questions about all kinds of sexual activity are predictable and healthy at this age. The key is to be an approachable parent. You shouldn't be afraid to use the support of good materials and other adults whose value system agrees with yours. Questions and curiosity should always be encouraged and serve as opportunities to affirm a teenager as well as describe boundaries for behaviors. Any sexual experimentation that involves excessive physical contact (petting, oral sex, mutual

Fostering Friendships

With puberty nearly complete and adolescence in full swing, your child needs friends! Friends serve as a connection to the outside world. Friendships act as a buffer for your kids to unload much of their stress of growing up and dealing with siblings, parents, school, and other frustrations. Keep in mind:

- **Same-sex friendships deepen but may wax and wane** along with adolescent moods. Be a supportive parent who listens to the excitement and pain that will come with friendships.
- **You'll have less opportunity to be involved in your child's choice of friends, but don't hesitate to continue to talk** about appropriate friendships, emphasizing that good friendships are positive and supportive. Also, remind your child that a good friend will not set him up to break your rules or the laws of the land.
- **Peer pressure is in full swing** during this age. Give your child the opportunity to blame you for his not participating in inappropriate behaviors, while reaffirming him for the good character and behavior choices he makes.
- **Encourage your child to be involved in healthy groups** of peers. Connections with a peer group are of absolute importance for this age, so don't ridicule him for the peer pressure he feels, but help provide an appropriate peer group for him.
- **A child this age will often attach to a "significant other adult."** This is a temporary, admiring friendship with an adult

masturbation, intercourse) and the need for secrecy and shame (excessive masturbation, pornography of all types, sexual abuse) is dangerous. Sexuality is kept healthy by strong, sensible, and correct information; strong relationships with appropriate adults; satisfying friendships; and other than his parents. This is a necessary step in growing up and becoming more independent from the family. Don't be upset that he seems to value this other adult more than you. You're still the most important influence in your child's life.

- **Make yourself available** to be a "significant other adult" to kids other than your own.
- **Remember that silliness between friends is common** to this age. Be tolerant of innocent silliness while having boundaries for inappropriate silliness.
- **Your child will probably develop a "crush" friendship** with someone of the opposite sex during this time. Celebrate these crushes, but set standards of behavior that will protect him from inappropriate choices.
- **Continue to keep yourself strong in your marriage and your own friendships.** Every child needs a best friend, and every child needs a parent. The two roles aren't interchangeable.
- If your child gets into trouble because of peer influence, **don't preach and don't blame the friend for the misbehavior.** Allow your child to experience consequences for mistakes. You certainly can make the observation, however, that good friendships won't encourage behaviors that are against the rules.
- If your child is consistently having difficulties with friendships, it may be wise to **seek outside counsel.**

healthy activities. Healthy, integrated sexuality education that focuses on the entire person (physical, emotional, social, spiritual), friendships with both sexes, and healthy group activities offer the opportunity to grow up.

Questions Teens Ask

▎ What does it mean to be sexually active?

Being sexually active with another person means to be involved in any activity that stimulates the genitals, rectum, and breasts. This activity can involve touching, mutual masturbation, and vaginal, oral, and anal intercourse.

▎ Is it normal for teens to have sex?

Most teens, especially young adolescents, aren't sexually active—some may experiment with sexual contact, but penetrative sex is uncommon. Studies have shown that over 50 percent of all high schoolers are virgins. While most teens have gone through puberty and are capable of sexual intercourse, being sexually active isn't an accepted norm. In a national survey conducted by Nickelodeon and the National Campaign to Prevent Teen Pregnancy, the majority of teens and adults thought it was important for teens to be given a strong message from society that they shouldn't have sex until they're at least out of high school.[5]

▎ What does promiscuous mean? Is there anything wrong with this?

Webster's Dictionary defines *promiscuous* as "indiscriminate." Another definition for promiscuous is having more than one sexual partner. Today, being promiscuous suggests that one has had or has multiple sexual partners. The more sexual partners someone has, the more likely that person is to get a sexually transmitted infection. Also, being promiscuous increases the risk of pregnancy. Remember, you can get an STI or get pregnant from your first sexual encounter. Apart from these physical consequences, there are emotional consequences as well.

The Answers You Need & They Want

I don't want to have sex now, but I feel pressure to do so. How can I handle this?

Perhaps you feel pressured because your friends are already sexually active. You can also feel pressure from someone you're dating. As hard as it is to resist peer pressure, there are certain areas, such as smoking, drugs, alcohol, and sex, that are simply worth your time and effort to buck the crowd for your future health, hope, and happiness. It's important to pick and choose friends who share your values. You can resist peer pressure more easily when you have friends who will stand with you. The right friends can help keep you out of trouble, but wrong friends over time will likely entice you to join them in unhealthy risk behaviors, such as sex, smoking, drugs, and alcohol.

If you're being pressured by your girlfriend to have sex, she doesn't have your best interest at heart. Rather, she's being selfish and seeking to gratify her own desires for intimacy.

If your boyfriend is more than two years older than you, you're at a disadvantage for being pressured into having sex. It's a known fact that most teenage pregnancies occur in girls whose boyfriends are older than them. You should know that if you have an older boyfriend who's pressuring you to have sex, and if sex occurs, this is actually a crime in many states. The best way to handle being pressured by an older man is to quickly get out of the relationship for your own health and well-being. (For boys, it's also a crime for older women to have sex with you.)

If you're dating someone your age and feel pressured to have sex, you need to clearly let your desires not to have sex be known. If this wish isn't respected and you still feel pressured, the relationship should end.

There are many ways to avoid putting yourself in a tempting situation. Group dating actually relieves a lot of this pressure. You can also avoid temptation by spending time with family and friends, not being home alone with your boyfriend, and not watching sexually suggestive movies together. It's very important that you are able to talk about your decisions to remain abstinent with a friend, parent, or trusted adult.

If you discover that most of the friends in your inner circle are sexually active, you should find new friends who have similar values to yours.

▮▮ Is it true that hardly any girls go to college without having had sex?

This is simply not true. Over 50 percent of high school girls (grades nine through twelve) have never had sex.[6] "Everybody's doing it" is a myth. Repeated surveys show that teens think more of their peers are sexually active than actually are.[7] Sexual activity, especially in guys, tends to be exaggerated.[8] Surveys show that the majority of sexually experienced high school students wish they had waited longer to have sex.[9]

▮▮ Why should I stay a virgin?

There are a number of good reasons for you to remain a virgin:

1. You could get pregnant or father a pregnancy.
2. Sexually transmitted infections are rampant and are at epidemic levels in this country. Most STIs occur in teenagers and young adults.[10]
3. Abstinence is the only 100 percent effective method of preventing pregnancy or an STI. Condoms and birth control are not nearly 100 percent protective.
4. Some sexually transmitted diseases (particularly pelvic inflammatory disease from chlamydia or gonorrhea) can cause infertility by scarring the fallopian tubes. This means that later in life when a woman wants to get pregnant, it may be impossible for her because of the damage caused by an STI.
5. One STI, human papillomavirus (HPV), can lead to cancer of the cervix.
6. "Emotional baggage" generally comes along with having sex at this age. Who needs emotional baggage at this age or at any age?
7. Sex doesn't enhance a teenage relationship. Actually, sex frequently speeds up the breakup of a relationship.
8. Two-thirds of teenagers who have already had sex say they wish that they had waited.[11]

The Answers You Need & They Want

9. Having sex "casually" could affect your marriage relationship later in life.
10. Many teens, especially girls, don't feel good about themselves after engaging in sexual activity.
11. Teens who are sexually active are more likely to experience depression.[12]
12. Teens who are sexually active are more likely to drink, smoke, and use drugs.[13]
13. Having sex can affect your reputation.
14. Having sex can impact your relationship with your parents.
15. For teens who are spiritual, having sex is a roadblock to a vibrant spiritual journey.

If these reasons don't convince you, talk to a friend who has been sexually active and ask her whether she would wait if she could do it over. Most teens say that given the chance to make the decision again, they'd have waited to become sexually active.[14]

What is date rape?

Date rape is being forced to have sex against your will in the context of being on a date or being in a dating relationship.

How can a girl avoid date rape?

There are several ways to avoid date rape:

- Go on group dates.
- Don't date anyone you or your friends don't know anything about.
- Don't drink. Many teenage girls report that their first sexual experience was associated with alcohol. Alcohol dulls the senses and lowers your inhibitions.[15] You will be more likely to do things under the influence of alcohol that you wouldn't normally do.

- Don't use drugs. Being high lowers your inhibitions and makes you more likely to be taken advantage of.
- Be careful with your drinks at parties and other places—only drink from unopened cans, and never set your drink down unless you've finished it. This way, you leave no opportunity for drugs such as the "date rape" drug (rohypnol) to be slipped into your drink without you knowing it.
- Never leave a party with someone whom you don't know or just met.
- Always have money with you on a date in case you need to go home by yourself.
- Carry a cell phone.

What's wrong with using pornography?

Pornography devalues sex, and it can be very seductive and habit forming, with increasing needs for more sensational material. Exposure to pornography can also lead to unrealistic sexual expectations later in life. Watching or using pornography detaches you from the "real world" and real relationships with people. Boys who routinely use pornography have to eventually get more and more increasingly hard-core pornography to get sexually stimulated. While pornography is harmful to single men, for married men, it's a marriage killer. Simply put, pornography destroys an individual's ability to be satisfied with sex with a real person and puts a spouse in an unfair competition.

Is there anything wrong with watching X-rated videos?

X-rated videos are pornography, and the same concerns are present.

What is oral sex?

Oral sex is stimulating the sex organs with the mouth and the tongue. Even though you can't get pregnant from oral sex, oral sex isn't "safe sex" because you can still get sexually transmitted infections. Contrary to popular opinion, oral sex is sex. On the streets, teens refer to it as "going down" on a girl or giving a guy a "blow job" or "head."

Can you get pregnant from oral sex?

You can't get pregnant from oral sex, but oral sex is a very intimate sexual act. Most individuals who engage in oral sex soon proceed to vaginal intercourse, where pregnancy may occur. Oral sex, however, is sex, and most of the common sexually transmitted infections can be acquired from oral sex. One problem with oral sex is that some teens today have taken the intimacy out of sex by making oral sex a group activity. Oral sex should be seen as an extremely intimate activity reserved for marriage (only if both spouses are willing).

What is anal sex?

Anal sex is penetration of the anus with a penis. The rectum wasn't designed for sexual intercourse, and physical problems can result, including acquiring a disease such as AIDS. Anal sex is never a healthy behavior, not even in marriage.

Can you get pregnant from anal sex?

With any kind of sexual activity, if sperm is near the anus, it could be near the vaginal cavity. However, it would be highly unlikely for sperm to swim over or somehow get from the rectal area to the vagina and then up into the uterus and fallopian tubes. You can, however, acquire most sexually transmitted infections from anal intercourse, especially HIV/AIDS.

▮▮ Can you get pregnant if you have sex during your period?

You can't get pregnant during your period if it's that time of your menstrual cycle when your body is shedding the unfertilized egg. Some girls have bleeding or spotting at the time of ovulation (when the egg is released during the menstrual cycle), and it's possible to get pregnant during this time of menstrual bleeding.

▮▮ Can you get pregnant if you haven't started having periods yet?

Yes! It's possible that a girl may ovulate (have an egg released from one of her ovaries) before menstrual bleeding occurs for the first time.

▮▮ Can a girl get pregnant if she's never had a penis in her vagina?

It's highly unlikely but not impossible. If any semen gets in the vagina, even though you haven't had penetrative sex, you can still get pregnant. This could occur during mutual masturbation when the sperm is near the vagina. Also, if semen is on the hand and it's introduced to the genital area, pregnancy becomes a possibility.

▮▮ Can you get pregnant the first time you have sex?

Contrary to popular belief, it's possible to get pregnant the very first time you have sex. Many other myths out there simply aren't true. You can get pregnant if you have sex standing on your head or in the shower or if you douche with Coke. In reality, a girl can get pregnant if a man ejaculates during intercourse (or even outercourse) and a sperm makes its way into her vagina and up into one of her fallopian tubes.

The Answers You Need & They Want

How does a woman know if she's pregnant?

The most common way is by missing a period. Other symptoms include breast tenderness, morning nausea, abdominal fullness, and weight gain.

How many days a month can you get pregnant?

An egg that has been released from a woman's ovary lives for about twenty-four hours before it breaks up and can't be fertilized. This means that a woman can become pregnant for three to four days in each menstrual cycle, since sperm live between one and three days.

How many sperm does it take to cause a pregnancy?

It only takes one sperm out of the millions of sperm released with each ejaculation to reach the egg, clean the lining around it, penetrate a ripe egg, and start a pregnancy.

Can a person tell if another person has had sex?

You can't tell from simply looking at a guy's penis if he's ever had sex (unless you happen to see lesions, sores, or penile discharge that are generally associated with sexually transmitted infections). Women have a covering to the vagina called a hymen. When a woman has sex for the first time, the hymen is torn or broken away. Sometimes it's difficult even for a physician to determine if a female is a virgin or has had a very limited number of sexual contacts. In many virginal women, the hymen is torn because of the repeated use of tampons.

How do you know if you're sexually compatible with another person?

Even though some may claim this as a concern, it's not an authentic physical issue. Sometimes this concept is used when a person is putting pressure on another person for sex within a relationship. ("We have to know if we're sexually compatible.") It's more important to develop a relationship with a person that you're interested in, as opposed to sexual compatibility. Talking and getting to know the other person (his goals, dreams, and desires) and having him get to know you is a far greater marker of compatibility in a relationship. What's important is that the relationship is healthy. Sexual problems or sexual dysfunction are often the result of past sexual abuse or sexual promiscuity and can be solved by counseling and time, not by "trying it on for size." Besides, the first few times a woman has sex, it may be painful.

Do both men and women have orgasms?

Yes, both men and women have orgasms. They tend to be different in males and females, but both sexes experience orgasms. Some sexually active adolescent women admit not experiencing orgasms during sexual intercourse.

What does an orgasm feel like?

Some may describe an orgasm as an explosive release after a buildup of immense pleasure. Others have even compared it to a sneeze, where there's a buildup of the sensation of the sneeze coming on and then there's a release. While orgasm is hard to describe, it's very pleasurable to both partners, even though the orgasm for each sex is different not only in feelings but even the duration of the experience.

What is foreplay?

Foreplay is classically described as sexual activity prior to actual intercourse. This could include a range of sexual activities, such as deep and prolonged kissing, hands to the breasts or genitalia, and the mouth to the breasts or genitalia. A modern term that essentially means the same thing is "outercourse," when a couple doesn't intend to have penetrative sex but lie next to each other with no clothes on or with clothing partially

Character Builders

As teens enter high school, responsibilities increase and more independence is desired. The two should be closely linked. Freedom should increase as your teen shows he can handle the responsibilities of school, sports, driving, drugs, and sex. It takes self-discipline to accomplish these tasks. Remember:

- **Demonstrate your own self-discipline** by having good habits of exercise and eating. Develop a habit of being on time.
- **Losing your temper is a lack of self-discipline** in your emotions—so before you explode at your teen, take a deep breath, count to five, and lower your tone of voice to a whisper. This is powerful in helping both of you deal with anger.
- **Self-discipline in schoolwork is critical.** You should no longer be bailing your teen out. Help him come up with a plan and schedule that gets his homework done on time.
- **Praise him whenever he's accomplished something** on his own, without a specific request from you to do so.
- **Any opportunity to teach delayed gratification will apply to waiting for sex.** If there's something special your teen wants to purchase, help him find ways to earn it. The anticipation of future ownership is half the excitement.
- **Encourage involvement** in sports, music, or Scouting activities, since these require a lot of self-discipline.
- **Abstaining from alcohol, drugs, and sex requires self-discipline** when peers are "enjoying" these activities. (They frequently are associated.) Discuss how self-discipline is needed to avoid them.
- **Allow your teen to have more independence** as he shows you he's capable of owning his own responsibilities.

removed. Some believe that this is a "safe" and "healthy" alternative to penetrative intercourse. This isn't true, for a few reasons. Although uncommon, it's possible to get pregnant from foreplay or outercourse. You can also catch sexually transmitted infections. Last, sex tends to be progressive. Foreplay is intended to prepare the body for sexual intercourse. Most adolescents who start with foreplay or outercourse usually proceed to having vaginal intercourse after weeks or months.

What is masturbation?

Masturbation is the manual stimulation of the genitalia. This can be done to oneself or performed simultaneously with another person (mutual masturbation).

Is it harmful to masturbate?

In general, it isn't physically harmful to masturbate, though in girls it's possible that masturbation can be associated with an increase in urinary tract infections. Masturbation can become an emotional problem if it replaces normal (nonsexual) peer relationships in order to live in a "fantasy world" (which is common when pornography is involved). While the subject of occasional solo masturbation may be a source of disagreement between some people, almost every adult will agree that masturbation with another person outside of marriage, the use of pornography with masturbation, or compulsive masturbation that is "all consuming," is harmful.

Is it normal to have wet dreams?

Yes. A wet dream is another name for a nocturnal emission. During the night, while sleeping, an adolescent boy may have an erection followed by the emission of semen. This is normal and happens in all boys from time to time.

What does jerking off mean?

This phrase typically refers to male masturbation.

What is an aphrodisiac?

An aphrodisiac is something that's thought to enhance sexual arousal.

What's the normal size for a penis? Can a penis be too big? Too small?

The "normal" size for a penis varies. It can depend on the age and sexual development level of the teenager. The penis in the erect position becomes much longer. The concept of a penis being "too big" is a myth. With very rare exceptions, a penis is never too small. In reality, the size of the penis doesn't matter. What matters is having sexual intercourse within the context of a loving, committed, lifelong relationship (marriage). When this occurs, sex can be wonderful and fulfilling to both the male and female regardless of the size of the penis.

How much body hair is normal?

This varies and has to do with age as well as genetics. To have no body hair is abnormal. Some people have a small amount of body hair, whereas others have lots of hair. Both are normal. Today it's trendy for both boys and girls to shave their body hair, especially in the pubic region.

Are you supposed to shave your pubic hair?

The majority of women don't shave their pubic hair. Some women shave around the edges during the summer so that their hair doesn't show when they're wearing a bathing suit. Shaving pubic hair causes the skin to be itchy. Sometimes women can get minor skin infections or irritation after shaving. That's why most women shave only around the edges when necessary.

I sweat a lot; is that normal?

It's not abnormal to sweat a lot during physical activity or when you're under pressure, like taking a test or giving a speech in front of a large crowd. Excessive sweating outside of physical activity may be a concern. If you're consistently wet with sweat and have dripping palms, this is a condition known as hyperhidrosis. You should discuss this with your physician.

Why are my breasts different sizes?

It isn't unusual to have different-size breasts. Occasionally this may be extreme, but usually it's subtle with only minor differences.

Is a lump in my breast normal (males)?

It's not unusual for teen boys to have some initial breast development. This may start as a lump under the nipple and may occur just on one side. It's a normal part of adolescence and almost always goes away.

Why do some boys have some breast development?

Adolescent boys, particularly younger ones, may have some initial breast development that usually resolves on its own over a period of several years. This is a normal part of pubertal development. For most males, the breast enlargement is rather small and may be limited to a lump that others can't see but the individual can feel. It may even be tender. Rarely, boys will have rather large breasts; this is called gynecomastia. Generally, gynecomastia resolves without intervention; occasionally surgery is performed to remove the excessive breast tissue. Some boys who are significantly obese appear to have increased breast tissue—it's actually fat.

Why aren't my testicles the same size?

It's normal for testes to vary in size, with the left testicle hanging lower than the right. Young men, starting in the teen years, should do testicular self-exams to look for any new or unusual lumps or bumps. This screens for testicular cancer, and if you feel new lumps or something that doesn't seem right, let your parents know so you can be seen by a physician.

Why shouldn't I get a tattoo?

Getting a tattoo with dirty equipment can expose you to hepatitis B or C or HIV. Many teenagers get tattoos on a whim and wish they hadn't done so as they get older. Even though dermatologists can perform some procedures to help remove a tattoo, these can be expensive and painful and often leave the skin somewhat scarred.

Why do people get body piercings?

Body piercing is a form of body art, and people get this done for a number of reasons. Some actually like the cosmetic effect. Others get piercings because many of their friends have done so. Some people describe a sense of increased euphoria or happiness at the time of piercing. Still others get piercings to enhance their sexual pleasure. Body piercing can be associated with infection and scarring, and in some people, keloids (large scars) may develop. People have all sorts of body parts pierced, including lips, eyelids, belly button, breast nipples, labia, and penis. All of these piercings can put an individual at risk for unnecessary infection.

What is a condom?

A condom is a temporary cover for an erect penis and is usually made out of latex (rubber). The purpose of the condom is to collect ejaculated sperm so that they don't go into the vagina and potentially start a pregnancy. A condom may also be used in an attempt to reduce the chance of transmission of a sexually transmitted infection. In no case does a condom eliminate the risk of pregnancy or totally protect you from catching an STI, even if used correctly every single time. (See chapter 15.)

■ What is a douche for?

A douche is a solution used to rinse the vagina. In nearly all cases, douching is unnecessary because the vagina cleanses itself. Frequent douching can change the pH balance of the vagina and cause problems. For this reason, douching is almost never recommended by physicians.

■ What is birth control?

Birth control is a method to eliminate or reduce the risk of pregnancy. Abstinence is the only 100 percent effective birth control method for a teenager. Other forms of birth control include oral contraceptive pills, patches, condoms, spermicides, diaphragms, cervical caps along with a spermicide, periodic injections of hormones, and IUDs (intrauterine devices). Natural family planning is attempting to avoid pregnancy without using chemicals, birth control pills, or condoms. It's based on the woman's menstrual cycle and avoiding sexual intercourse during times when a pregnancy could occur. While this form of birth control can be very successful with highly motivated married couples, it's never recommended for adolescents. (See chapter 15.)

■ What is circumcision? What's the difference between a circumcised and an uncircumcised penis?

Circumcision is a procedure in which the loose foreskin around the tip of the penis is removed. In most cases, this is done in infancy. Circumcision is rarely medically necessary, but it's frequently performed on boys for cultural or religious reasons. In a circumcised male, the tip (called the glans) of the penis is visible. You don't see the tip of the uncircumcised penis because it's covered by the foreskin. The tip can be seen if the foreskin is retracted or if the penis is erect and the foreskin retracts on its own. There's some evidence that being circumcised may reduce a person's chance of acquiring certain sexually transmitted infections (particularly HIV).

Why am I developing slower than my friends?

Developmental pace is something that's genetically programmed. You have no control over it. Just because you're developing slower than your friends doesn't mean you're abnormal. If you have concerns in this area, discuss your level or rate of development with your physician.

How do I know if I'm a homosexual?

Homosexual feelings and curiosities are normal, passing feelings that many teenagers this age experience. Almost all teenagers have had a concern about homosexual tendencies. Homosexuality means the consistent feeling of sexual attraction to a person of the same sex while feeling no attraction to the opposite sex. The exact origins of homosexual feelings are still unknown, but the dangers of homosexual behavior, both physical and emotional, are well-known. Homosexuality doesn't occur because someone tells you that you're homosexual or because you've experimented with same-sex relationships (see chapter 6).

What should I do if I think I'm a homosexual?

Remember, homosexual curiosity doesn't mean you're homosexual. Feelings and attractions aren't always under one's control. Behavior choices are controllable. Choosing to engage in homosexual behavior can be physically and emotionally dangerous. If you think you're a homosexual, it's important to share this with a trusted adult who can help you think and talk through the many feelings and emotions you may have. It's only through support and accountability that you can discover the truth about your sexuality and plan behaviors that won't cause physical and emotional harm.

If you're concerned about your sexual preferences, guard yourself from the temptation for homosexual behavior, and protect yourself especially from those who would overly sympathize with you, offer inaccurate rationalizations affirming homosexuality as just an alternative lifestyle, or tempt you into homosexual relationships. Finally, seek professional counseling.

12

Free Falling

Late Teens: Sixteen- to Eighteen-Year-Olds

Hollywood and other pop-culture icons would like you to believe that your work with your teen is finished and that you're no longer an influential factor in his life. Nothing could be further from the truth. Your teen needs you more than ever. He doesn't need you to make his decisions, but he does need you to listen as he processes his decisions.

Even though your teen may be heading off to college shortly, your parenting responsibilities aren't finished, especially when it comes to the issue of sexuality. If he's involved in a serious relationship, make an effort to get to know his girlfriend (even if you think she's not the girl for him). Now is the time to engage him in discussions about his dreams and desires for his future. It's also the right time to remind him how casual sexual relationships can impact his future dreams of having a family.

Don't make the mistake of thinking your teen doesn't care what you think—he does. Just remember that he desperately wants to be heard. Make an effort to listen and understand the world from his perspective, because it's tremendously different from the one you grew up in. Finally, get involved in his life, and if you haven't done so already, make your home a place where he and his friends want to hang out.

Parents' Questions

■■■ **Should I be concerned if my teen's involved in a long-term relationship?**

Some teens are involved in long-term relationships, and it's important for parents to have a realistic sense of what the relationship is about. You can do this by getting to know your teen's boyfriend. Invite him to your home and include him in family activities so that you can see how he treats your teen and how she responds to him. If they have a healthy relationship, treat each other with respect, and seem to have a healthy friendship beneath the romance, the two may certainly be in love.

This can be a good experience, but it can also pose some problems. Research indicates that teens in long-term relationships are strongly tempted to be sexually active (this is especially true for girls dating boys two or more years older).[1] Parents need to be involved and help their teens avoid sexual activity because of the negative consequences associated with nonmarital sexual activity (including sexually transmitted infections, pregnancy, and emotional distress).

Some teens will stay in unhealthy long-term relationships because the teen won't see how bad the relationship is. That's why she needs you to help get her out of it. How do you know if the relationship is unhealthy? Here are some questions to help you decide:

1. What is your teen like around her boyfriend? Is she irritable, or does she act more immature than usual?
2. Does the boyfriend allow her space and free time, or is he possessive and domineering?
3. Has your teen ever tried to break up with him, and the boyfriend refused to let her go?

Many times teens will stay in long-term relationships simply because they can't get out. Help your teen periodically evaluate the health of her relationship. Keep the lines of communication open by asking the questions, then staying quiet long enough to hear the answers. If you're sincere in your quest to help your teen negotiate intense relationships, she'll respond to you. If you simply preach and fail to listen, she'll shut you out.

How do I protect my child from compromising situations?

Think ahead! Talk to your teen long before he's in a compromising situation about what it means to be into something over his head. Help him develop a game plan to remain abstinent until he's married. Following are some ideas to help you get started with your teen:

- Think through possible scenarios where a teen would be drawn into temptation that might be overwhelming. Long periods of time alone together shouldn't be an option; neither should babysitting other children together (particularly when the kids are asleep and the house is quiet). Encourage your teen to think through situations where he might find himself wanting to do something he's committed to not doing; don't simply lay down the rules about time alone with a girlfriend without his input.

- Help him purposefully choose to spend time with his girlfriend while others are present. Make sure they date in public places—restaurants, malls, movies, and so on.

- Encourage your teen to have a close friend or two commit to helping him stay abstinent. They can talk to one another and confide in each other about their struggles; this will lend him tremendous support.

- Encourage your teen to carry a visible symbol as a reminder of his commitment. Some teens wear a ring, bracelet, or necklace to remind them of the commitment they've made to remain abstinent until they're married.

- Address the issue of trust up front. Many teens complain to parents that the reason parents don't want them alone with a girlfriend is because the parents don't trust them. Clarify for your teen that helping him avoid periods of being alone with a girlfriend isn't an issue of trust. It's about helping him avoid situations where he's tempted to do something that he may regret.

▐▇ Should I give my child condoms or birth control, since she may have sex anyway?

No! Never assume that your child will "have sex anyway." In fact, most healthy teens take cues about their sexual behavior from their parents. If your teen feels that you think she's going to be sexually active, she probably will be. If you think your teen is going to be (or is) sexually active, sit down with her at a time when the two of you are relaxed, rested, and not in the midst of a fight. It's important to listen first and then respond in love; resist the temptation to lose your cool or raise your voice if she says something you disagree with.

At the appropriate time, ask her questions such as: Why do you want to be sexually active? (This would also be a great time to discuss how beautiful and wonderful sex is at the right time in her life [marriage] when she won't have to worry about having a baby outside of marriage or getting a sexually transmitted infection.) Do you understand the risk? Do you think sex will make you feel better? This would also be a good time to talk about the social, emotional, and spiritual aspects of sex outside of marriage. The truth is, most kids will respond very well if you take the time to listen and talk patiently with them and give them good reasons to stay away from sex until they find the person with whom they want to spend the rest of their life.

Explain that no method of contraception is perfect. The condom has approximately a 15 percent failure rate during the first year of use, and even the pill has around an 8 percent failure rate during the first year, since many teen girls don't take the pill consistently and correctly.[2]

Additionally, condoms never eliminate the risk of any STI. At best, they reduce the risk if they're used every single time, but even then the chance of infection for most STIs is about 50 percent if you have sexual intercourse with an infected partner over time. The chance of HIV infection with 100 percent condom use is less, but HIV is a disease that often leads to death (so even reduced risk is a concern). With the exception of HIV and genital herpes, there's little or no benefit from inconsistent use of condoms. Consistent and correct use of condoms over time is uncommon.[3]

How do I stay involved in my child's life when he wants me out?

Remind yourself frequently that while your teen appears to want you "out" on the outside, inwardly he needs you very much. He's simply uncomfortable with the fact that he still needs you but in a very different way. He's like a toddler—confused, wanting independence, but struggling to get that independence. Know and believe that no matter what you see, he desperately needs your approval, your love, and your commitment to stick by him no matter what. (This doesn't give you a license to micromanage his life.)

Find areas of common interest where you and your teen can spend time together. This should be fun, "connecting" time when the two of you can just try to enjoy each other. Going out to lunch or dinner alone is a great place to start. Spending small periods of time together will help smooth those tough conversations that need to take place and will provide the groundwork for the beginnings of your adult relationship.

What do I do if I find birth control pills in my daughter's room?

First, allow yourself some reaction time before you talk to your daughter. If you're angry, sad, or disappointed, call a close friend and work through your feelings. You might feel like a failure or consider yourself a terrible parent. Don't wallow in those feelings. Remember, teens are growing up in a culture that's seducing them everywhere they go to be sexually active. All good parents have a lot working against them

Character Builders

This is the age when your teen is preparing to leave home. It's time to reevaluate strict rules and teach her to make decisions on her own. If she still has lots of rules to live by until she leaves home, disaster will await her at her new destination. Giving your teen more responsibility now, as well as more freedom, will give you some idea of how she'll handle the world when she leaves home.

- **Show your teen how important your own responsibilities are** in your life and who would be let down if you didn't keep them.
- **Encourage your teen to get a job.** This is the best teacher of responsibility and is connected to a financial reward.
- **Talk about what it means to be responsible** in the areas of sex, drugs, and alcohol. Let her know your standard of zero tolerance, and brainstorm ways to avoid or get out of uncomfortable situations.
- **Show your trust** (if she's trustworthy!) by giving your teen a later curfew each year.
- **Let school be her responsibility**, so that she understands her future for college and career is up to her own effort.

where their teens are concerned, and your family is no exception. Get over the guilt and move ahead.

After the shock, tell your daughter that the two of you need to make time to talk about some important things. Agree on a time, then WAIT until then to tell her what you found. She'll accuse you of having "no right to get into her belongings," but don't get into that argument. If you've discovered the birth control pills, you'd be negligent as a parent if you didn't confront your daughter.

Ask when she got the pills, where, and who gave them to her. Ask her if she's been sexually active; if so, ask her how long she has been.

Then listen. Ask why she's sexually active. Then listen. Ask with whom she's been sexually active. Watch her response very closely—even if there's silence on her part. Remind her that you love and care about her and don't want her to get hurt.

When she's finished talking, let her know that while everyone around her may feel that sex isn't a "big deal," it is. Emotionally, psychologically, and physically, sex can have very painful consequences at her age, and your job is to help her avoid getting hurt. Explain that sex is an incredible gift, and if she continues to be sexually active, she risks ruining this gift for the rest of her life. You don't want that for her. You want her to have a great sex life, and the best way to ensure this is to wait until marriage, or if she's already been sexually active, to make the decision to remain abstinent from this time forward until marriage. If she listens, keep going. If she balks and storms off, reopen the issue in a day or two, but don't let up. Remember, if you don't fight for her, who will?

Find a physician who is like-minded, believes that it's unhealthy for unmarried teens to be sexually active, and will do everything possible to keep your daughter as safe and healthy as possible. Remember, however, that even if her physician feels as strongly as you do about sexual activity at this age, it often takes time to encourage adolescents toward the healthiest choice—abstinence. Call the doctor ahead of time, tell her what's up, and ask if you can schedule an appointment for your daughter. If your daughter is already sexually experienced, she'll need to be examined for pregnancy and sexually transmitted infections.

Outside support, such as family, friends, and your faith community, can make a world of difference for both of you. Remember, most teenagers at one time or another will make a wrong choice—and certainly sexual activity is an unhealthy choice. When that happens, it's your job to continue loving her even though you disapprove of her action or lifestyle. Over time, if you continue to love and support your daughter and keep open the lines of communication, you're likely to powerfully influence her future choices.

I found condoms in my son's jeans. What should I do?

(See the previous question.) Be prepared to talk about his friends, what they are doing, and why. Also, recognize that he indeed has very strong physiological urges and the urges are good and normal, but encourage him that he has (contrary to what friends tell him) the ability to control his actions and that learning self-control is a very masculine trait. Ask him what he knows about condoms. What can he expect from condoms and under what circumstances? Does he know how to use a condom correctly? Does he know that condoms at best only reduce the chance of infection, but they never totally eliminate risk? Realistically, condoms don't have much chance of helping unless they're used perfectly every time—which seldom happens. By educating your son about condoms, hopefully he'll see that they really aren't the answer—at best they may minimize damage.

If my teen is drinking or smoking, is she more likely to be sexually active?

Yes. Studies show that teens involved in alcohol and drugs are more likely to be sexually active.[4] This stands to reason. Whenever a teen is drunk or high, her inhibitions lower, and she's more likely to lose self-control. So if your teen smokes or drinks, make sure to ask about her sexual activity. Remind your son that if he drinks and is sexually active with his date, he could be accused of rape. Remind your daughter that drinking places her at risk for being raped.

My child wants to attend an all-night party with friends at school; is that okay?

All-night parties have become very popular. They originated from concerns that teens would drink and then drive. To avoid that, parents and teachers offered all-night parties as a means to keep teens off the roads. While the idea is well intentioned, these parties also carry risks.

The Answers You Need & They Want

First, many teens still drink, but within the confines of the party. Second, many teens still have sex, but at the party instead of off privately somewhere. The parties may reduce drunk driving, but not necessarily anything else. Some parties have adult "chaperones," but usually this is nothing more than a parent asleep upstairs somewhere. The best advice: know where the party is, who is chaperoning, and what kids will be there. If you don't like any of the above or you don't know the parents—don't let your teen go. Even if they're "good" kids and "good" parents, too much of a good thing can turn bad.

My daughter has told me she's a lesbian; what should I do?

It may be hard, but try not to overreact. This is important because you want to keep solid lines of communication open with her. If she senses that you're very upset, she's likely to shut down and not trust you. So if you feel angry, confused, or hurt, try not to show it to her at first. Talk to a trusted friend who can help you.

It's important to ask your daughter why she feels this way and how long she has felt it. Depending on her age, you may find that she thinks she's a lesbian because she has strong emotional attachments to some of her girlfriends. For instance, some girls in their early teen years feel comfortable around other girls and not around boys. A young girl may feel that since she doesn't like being around boys, she must be a lesbian. This, of course, isn't true.

Additionally, many girls in early adolescence may experiment with homosexual play (boys may do this as well). Again, simply because she has fondled another girl's genitalia or breasts or has been the recipient of such behavior doesn't make her a lesbian, even though she may think that she is. The sexual identity of girls is still in formation during the early adolescent and teen years, and many times girls feel like they're lesbians because they have emotional or sexual feelings toward another girl. Understanding that these feelings sometimes occur and that they can be confusing may help your daughter see that she really is a heterosexual experiencing some mixed feelings common at her stage of development. (Same-sex relationships are very trendy in some communities, and your daughter may just want to fit in.)

If, on the other hand, your daughter comes to you when she's an older teen and tells you she's a lesbian, you'll face different issues. Again, you want to be sure not to overreact. Calmly ask her why she believes this to be true. She may tell you that she's only attracted to women and has never had romantic feelings for a man. She'll probably be very defensive when talking with you and may be waiting for you to be critical, angry, and disappointed. Rather than react to her with any of these feelings, show her that you are concerned about her and her emotional health. Continue to reach out to her in love and acceptance. Over time, after her defensiveness breaks down, ask her if she would be willing to talk with a counselor about her feelings.

Many gay teens struggle with emotional turmoil, depression, and even a history of sexual abuse. Your daughter needs help untangling a web of complex feelings. If you genuinely show her that first and foremost you're concerned about her emotional health (not her sexual orientation) and you want to help her see her way toward feeling good about herself and life, she'll be more willing to accept your advice. Then, if she accepts the idea of counseling, be sure to do some research and find a counselor who will help your daughter with her identity and depression issues, as well as be willing to offer help and encouragement to her if she desires to leave her current lifestyle.

The decision to change a lifestyle must come from within. It's possible, however, if the individual truly desires to change. It's not easy and may take years of counseling. The success rate of leaving the gay lifestyle is similar to overcoming alcoholism. Neither is easy, but both are possible. Your role at this juncture is to unconditionally love and support your daughter and help arrange and finance counseling if this offer is accepted.

▮▮ My daughter wants to date a college boy; should I let her?

It depends on how old your daughter is. If she's a senior in high school, he's a freshman in college, and the two are about one year apart in age, dating can be fine. But she'll probably want to visit him at college for the weekend—this should be off-limits. If, on the other hand, your daughter is sixteen and she wants to date a man who's in his twenties, this isn't appropriate. A good rule of thumb about dating is to keep girls dating boys the same age, or at most one year apart in age. Girls often want to date boys who are older because most boys lag behind girls in their physical and emotional development in high school.

When a girl dates a much older boy, she places herself in a situation where she can be physically, intellectually, or emotionally outmaneuvered. He has an immediate psychological advantage over her because she looks up to him and considers him (usually subconsciously) as older, wiser, cooler, stronger, and so on. When this happens, she'll defer to him on many different levels and in different situations, and this can be dangerous when it comes to sexual issues. So keep your daughter on even ground when it comes to dating boys. In general, college boys and high school girls don't mix.

My son has gotten his girlfriend pregnant. What should I do?

When you first find out about the situation, you'll probably feel angry, disappointed, hurt, and like a failure as a parent, all at the same time. To make matters worse, you'll feel this in the presence of a son who, depending on his age, may feel scared to death. So take a deep breath, give both you and your son some breathing space, and then try to sort things out and help him make the best decisions possible.

First, encourage him to be responsible. While neither of you can control what his girlfriend does with the pregnancy, you can encourage your son to help her. He can encourage his girlfriend to get good medical care as soon as possible to ensure the health of the baby. Help them find a good physician, and offer to take her to her appointments if her parents are unwilling or unable.

Then you might want to encourage them to seek the help of a local pregnancy resource center where they can help your son and his girlfriend with decisions about whether to keep the baby or offer it for adoption.

If his girlfriend decides to keep the baby, your son will be financially responsible for the child even if they don't decide to marry.

▮▮ My daughter is pregnant. What should I do?

Your first and most important reaction must be to unconditionally love your daughter. Resist the temptation to say, "How could you do this?" or, "I'm so disappointed." Initially, your daughter needs to be held and loved and told that you will stand with her as decisions are made in the coming days for her baby's future. Thank her for coming to you for advice.

After a period of time, perhaps after a good night's sleep, you'll need to sit down with her and help her work through her options. None of the options your daughter must consider are easy, and all will involve a measure of pain and heartache. As parents, you should offer your best advice in a nonjudgmental way, knowing that ultimately she may make a decision that's contrary to what you think is best. Since this is such an emotional issue, consider writing your thoughts in a letter to your daughter. Below is a sample letter.

Dear Daughter:

Thank you for letting us help you during this difficult time in your life. Your mother and I would be less than honest if we didn't tell you that, like yourself, we are hurting. Know that our love for you has not diminished because of your pregnancy.

There are many options available to you. The first option is presenting the baby for adoption. Releasing your baby for adoption will bring great joy to a married couple unable to have children of their own. There will be pain, however, in carrying your baby nine months and then having to hand over your baby to the adopting parents. The joy, however, will be knowing that a loving, married couple will rear your baby in a two-parent home.

The next option is keeping the baby as a single parent. It's difficult at times for a stable, two-parent family, much less a single teenager. Your mother and I aren't saying it's impossible but only that it will be extremely difficult.

The Answers You Need & They Want

Another option is marrying the father of your child, but many teen marriages end in early divorce. If you choose to marry, you and your husband will have to work hard to create a lasting marriage.

The last option is abortion. You know that for your mother and me it isn't an option. We believe that life begins when the sperm from a male fertilizes the egg of a female. The new life has inherited twenty-three chromosomes from each parent, forty-six in all. This one cell contains the complex genetic blueprint for every detail of human development—the child's sex, hair and eye color, athletic ability, musical ability, and personality. Then only food and oxygen are needed for the baby to grow from one cell to a seven-pound baby nine months later.

The baby's heart begins to beat on day twenty-one. By day twenty-two, the foundation for every organ system is established and developing. At nine weeks, the baby is unmistakably recognized as a human being.

While the pregnancy can be terminated by an abortion, the memory of the pregnancy will last a lifetime. Some women will experience post-abortion syndrome. Abortion isn't without risks, and complications can and do occur. Some women are never able to get pregnant in the future, and then you must live with the fact that you ended your one and only pregnancy.

I would encourage you to see your physician and let her be a resource to help answer your questions. I would also urge you to visit our local pregnancy resource center. Your mother and I will be praying for your decision, but also know that we love you no matter what happens and we will always be here for you.

Love, Dad

My son wants to stay at a hotel on prom night; how should I respond?

First, ask him why he wants to spend the night at a hotel. Who will be there, and why does he think this would be a good idea? Then tell him that the only "benefit" to staying at a hotel would be either to continue to party with friends after the prom or to keep him from driving if he's been drinking. These are the common reasons teens use to defend wanting to stay at a hotel after a party or prom.

What Is Post-Abortion Syndrome?

Post-abortion syndrome (PAS) is a form of post-traumatic stress syndrome (PTSD). PTSD is the result of having suffered an event so stressful and so traumatic (usually a life-threatening event or being a witness to death) that the person's normal ability to process the event is shut down. A variety of substitute coping mechanisms (e.g., repression or outright denial) help the person to numbly keep moving forward in life, but eventually a variety of reactions begin to surface that are outside the person's ability to control.

The path to healing after an abortion includes (1) the willingness to identify and name the trauma, (2) finally processing the strong emotions that have been frozen in time (guilt, anger, grief), (3) mourning the loss, and (4) reintegrating back into one's life.

Following are some of the symptoms of post-abortion syndrome:

- Depression and thoughts of suicide
- Deterioration of self-esteem
- Disruption in interpersonal relationships (psychological numbing)

Concerning his first answer, tell him that all fun must end sometime, and two o'clock in the morning is a better time than eight o'clock. This isn't a trust issue; you want to help him stay away from situations where he'll be tempted to do things he'll regret later. He must avoid those situations in the same manner that you as an adult would avoid tempting situations. Healthy maturation requires him to develop this skill; tell him that he needs to start making those tough decisions now.

Second, if he says he wants to stay at a hotel to avoid driving drunk, don't ignore the fact that he wants to drink. In no way should you encourage him to drink alcohol even in a "safe" place. Besides, he may be breaking the law.

- Sleep, appetite, and sexual disturbances
- "Anniversary syndrome" (an increase of symptoms around the time of the anniversary of the abortion and/or the due date of the aborted child)
- Survival guilt
- Reexperiencing the abortion (while awake or through nightmares)
- Preoccupation with becoming pregnant again
- Anxiety over fertility and childbearing issues
- Disruption of the bonding process with present or future children
- Development of eating disorders
- Alcohol and drug abuse
- Other self-punishing or self-degrading behaviors (abusive relationships, promiscuity, avoiding medical care, deliberately hurting one's self)
- Brief reactive psychosis (an episode of drastically distorted reality within two weeks of the abortion without subsequent psychotic break)

For more information, see *A Solitary Sorrow* by Teri Reisser, M.F.T., and Paul Reisser, M.D.[5]

■■ My daughter (a high school senior) has been invited to go on a graduation trip to Cancún without adults. Should I allow her to go?

No! First of all, teens can drink whenever they want in Cancún, and alcohol and teens are a bad mix. Second, it's not uncommon for alcoholic drinks to be laced with illegal drugs in countries like Mexico, and teens can get into a lot of trouble even if they have their guard up. If your daughter wants to go to Cancún, go with her, have another parent go with her and her friends, or don't let her go. If she says that she doesn't want adults along, red flags should appear in your mind.

Should I allow my teen to attend the school's sex-ed program?

Before your teen attends the sex-ed class, do your homework. Ask the teacher if you can review the curriculum. Ask to look at books, and if a video is shown, ask to see it ahead of time. It's ideal if you can do this long before your teen has the class, because if you ask to review the material right before it's presented, he'll be embarrassed. Then, if the material isn't offensive to you, let your teen attend the class, and be sure that the two of you discuss what was taught. He may be hesitant to discuss it, but you must be bold enough to talk about it in spite of his hesitation. If there was material that you liked, say so. If there was material that was bothersome to you or that you disagreed with from an ethical or religious vantage point, tell your teen how you feel. But remember, before you state your feelings, ask him to tell you his feelings. This keeps the channels of communication open.

If you found the material completely offensive after you reviewed it, tell the principal of your school. Also, there's an enormous variation in material presented in schools, and even if the curriculum is good, each teacher naturally presents it from his own bias. So don't hesitate to ask the teacher what he intends to communicate to the class regarding condoms, abstinence, birth control, and so on. Find out his views. If you strongly disagree or you find the curriculum itself offensive, have your teen bow out.

Should I be concerned about who my teen's friends are?

Yes. Teens are highly impressionable, and while they universally want to be "different," they remarkably gravitate toward imitating their friends' behaviors. In general, whatever your teen's friends are doing, she's doing as well. You may want to believe that she's strong enough to resist temptation to engage in bad behaviors, but the truth is, most average, healthy, American kids just aren't able to do so—at least consistently. There are sound psychological reasons why this is so, but suffice it to say that most teens want to go along with their friends' behaviors because they desperately want to be accepted. If the kids are responsible and respect one another, that's what your teen will do. But if they engage in high-risk behaviors, that too is exactly what she'll do.

Why is teen sex so risky?

Teen sex is risky for several reasons. For teen girls, sex is much riskier than for women in their twenties because of anatomical differences. The cervix of a seventeen-year-old girl, for instance, has a different lining than the cervix of a twenty-five-year-old woman.[6] The cells in the lining covering the teen cervix are more vulnerable to bacteria and viruses that come in contact with it during sexual intercourse.[7]

Teen sex is risky because of the ways in which teens behave sexually. For instance, the popularity of oral sex has increased among teens in recent years for two reasons: many believe that they can engage in oral sex and stay disease free and remain virgins. Teens need to understand that almost any sexually transmitted infection that they can acquire through vaginal intercourse can be acquired through oral sex. And while physically teens are virgins after oral sex, many don't feel emotionally that they are virgins.

Other sexual behaviors that place teens at higher risk are an increased number of partners, drinking alcohol or using drugs before sex, and engaging in sexual behaviors such as anal and oral sex, which lead teens to feel "safe" regarding their vulnerability to contracting STIs.

A teen who begins sexual activity at an early age, say at thirteen, is more likely to have a greater number of lifetime partners, and the more partners, the greater the risk of infection. If you can help a teen postpone the initiation of sexual activity, he's more likely to have fewer sexual partners and therefore will be less likely to contract an STI.

If you look at a teen's mental and emotional development, it makes sense that teens would be at higher risk for developing STIs. Most teens' abstract-thinking skills aren't developed until they're close to twenty years old—new research suggests it may be closer to twenty-five.[8] Abstract thinking allows them to grasp the future in a meaningful way—the understanding that action A today leads to consequence B tomorrow or

Fostering Friendships

Strong friendships are essential to this stage of adolescence. Peer friendships serve as a solid bridge for crossing into adulthood. Remember:

- **Same-sex friendships will be strong.** It isn't uncommon for teens this age to change friendships as they mature and deepen in their understandings of themselves. These friendships are important forces in developing self-confidence and a sense of direction for the future.
- **Friendships are less dependent on your input or opinions.** Don't give up on appropriate boundaries, but allow your teen some flexibility in his thinking and opinions.
- **Remind your teen that a few close friendships are more productive** than superficial relationships with lots of peers.
- **Strong friendships with the same sex are necessary to prevent overdependent and controlling relationships** with the opposite sex.
- **Dating relationships are most likely to begin** during this age. Emphasize with your teen that friendship skills with the opposite sex are more important than romantic feelings. True intimacy in later years will require friendship skills more than just romantic feelings. Couples married thirty, forty, and fifty years are truly each other's best friend.
- **Maintain family standards, but don't police your teen.** Give him room to make decisions for himself, even if those decisions may bring unexpected or unwanted consequences. This age is the last time to "experiment" with freedom before total freedom actually exists.
- **Instruct your teen about passionate feelings** that will come with opposite-sex relationships. Teaching and encouraging self-control will never be more appropriate than during this time of heightened passions.
- **Begin to prepare yourself for the day your teen will leave home.** Strengthen and maintain your own friendships and marriage as well as your identity outside of being the parent of your teenager.

in ten years. Until this form of thought is completed, teens are limited in their beliefs about what can actually happen to them. They're not stupid but are intellectually living out what psychologists refer to as the "personal fable." This thinking transfers into their sexual activity, leading them to believe that they'll never become pregnant, contract an STI, or experience any other serious consequences of sexual activity.

▪ Should my teen have a regular checkup at the doctor?

Yes, all teens should ideally have physical exams once a year with an established family doctor, pediatrician, or internist. Many teens (and their parents) feel that it's unnecessary to go this frequently to the doctor's office, but teens face many serious health issues, and they need a place to go and have these issues reviewed and their overall health examined. Girls who are or have been sexually active (even once) should have a pelvic examination, a Pap smear, and screening for sexually transmitted infections if indicated. If a teen girl has never been sexually active, she should have her first pelvic exam between ages eighteen and twenty-one, then regularly from that point forward. The frequency of Pap smears is currently being debated; the best bet is to follow your physician's guidelines.

Teen boys should be encouraged to see their physician yearly as well. They need to be frank with their doctor about their sexual activity so that they can be checked for any STIs. Remember, many STIs have no symptoms, and simply because a teen feels fine, this doesn't mean that he doesn't have an STI.

▪ How do I prepare my adolescent for the sexually saturated environment that exists on college campuses today?

There's no way around it—sex and alcohol are prevalent on college campuses across the nation. It doesn't matter whether your young adult is involved in the Greek system or just hanging out in the dorm; reckless abandon is often the attitude that rules, especially during the first two years.

221

In order to help your child succeed in this environment, it's important that you develop an incredible rapport with him during high school. If he knows you're willing to listen to him, he'll be open and honest about the peer pressure he's facing. If he fears you, the opportunity for openness will evaporate, and you won't know whether he's prepared to resist the temptations he'll encounter or not.

Find some young adults who have experienced negative consequences associated with the party scene, and have them talk with your teen. If you've made mistakes, it may be beneficial to share your experiences during this conversation. Additionally, instead of controlling your child during the last two years of high school, slowly begin to pass the decision-making responsibilities to him, so that he can have experience making decisions in the face of peer pressure before getting to college. It's better for him to make a few minor mistakes while you're there to help him navigate the consequences than make life-altering mistakes while he's away from home.

▮▮ How involved should I be in my teen's life?

Research shows that a young adult's brain isn't fully mature in terms of judgment and impulse control until the midtwenties.[9] Parents and other trusted adults, therefore, are important as supervising mentors, giving advice and direction to young people (consider yourself a consultant). Seek outside help if your teen is involved in activities dangerous to her physical and mental health. Things such as alcohol, drugs, and sexual activity are examples of when involvement is necessary. Actively encourage and support the presence of adult mentors in your child's life. As she grows, wisdom will be sought, and control will be rejected.

▮▮ How should I encourage my child to find an adult mentor?

Set the example. Advisors and mentors are integral to each of our lives. Admit that you don't have all the answers but that experience in life is a valuable teacher. Point your teen to trusted teachers, physicians, coaches, employers, or family friends in your community. Try to identify people with a value system similar to yours—but they don't have to be carbon copies of you. Emphasize to your child the wisdom and strength found in mentors, and then let him cultivate a relationship with his mentor without fear of you feeling incompetent.

Questions Teens Ask

■ I've been dating this boy for four months. He wants to have sex, but I'm not sure. What should I do? Do I owe it to him?

If you haven't worked this through already in your heart and mind, now is the time to decide whether or not you'll become sexually active. First of all, you never owe sex to anyone. It's your choice. Having sex with someone is such an intimate act that it should occur in a long-term, committed relationship where you feel guilt free and safe—that is, marriage.

Remember, the risks of early sexual involvement without the commitment of marriage include sexually transmitted infections, pregnancy, and emotional disappointment, to name just a few. If you tell your boyfriend you won't be sexually active until you're married and he breaks up with you—all he wanted was sex. If he truly loves you, he'll respect you and support your commitment.

Also remember, the intensity of sexual feelings and real love can be two very different things.

■ If I'm careful about using birth control and condoms, what's wrong with having sex?

Having sex is a very important and life-changing decision. It shouldn't be taken lightly. It's not about how careful you are, because birth control and condoms can't protect your heart.

223

You only get one first-time sexual experience. The gift of sex is like having a beautiful birthday present all wrapped with fancy paper and a big bow. If you open it before your birthday, the gift may already be broken and worn out when your big day comes around. The same thing can happen if you start having sex before you're married. This decision can place you at risk for contracting sexually transmitted infections, getting pregnant, and experiencing emotional distress. It can also impact every other area of your life. Waiting to have sex until marriage is one decision you'll never regret. (See chapter 14.)

How do you know if sex is right for you?

Are you married? If you're not married and trying to decide if sex is "right" for you, you need to ask yourself a few other questions. Are you ready to handle the complex situations that accompany the decision to have sex? Are you willing to seek medical treatment if you develop genital warts or contract chlamydia? Are you willing to care for a child who's "accidentally" conceived during the heat of the moment? Are you ready for the pain that comes with a broken heart? These are just a few of the possible outcomes of having sex outside of marriage. Sex is fabulous when it takes place in a healthy marriage. Outside of marriage, sex loses its power because it lacks commitment.

How do you stop going too far if you're really in love?

It's important to realize that love and sex aren't the same thing. For sex to really be the expression of someone's love, it needs to be in a committed relationship. True love seeks what's best for the other person and isn't self-serving. It's considerate and doesn't demand control. These qualities take time to develop in a relationship. Most teenagers think they're "in love," but the relationship hasn't had time to progress through to the deeper levels of commitment. The final level of commitment in a relationship is marriage. Once a couple is married, then sex is the most beautiful expression of one's love for his or her spouse.

Early Sexual Activity
Can Lead to Depression

Depression and suicide is the third leading cause of death in teens in the United States. There is growing evidence to support a connection between early sexual activity in teenagers, depression, and suicide. A Heritage Foundation report found that sexually active teenage girls were three times as likely and sexually active teenage boys twice as likely to experience depression as their counterparts who weren't sexually active. Furthermore, the study reported that sexually active teenage girls are almost three times as likely and sexually active teenage boys almost eight times as likely to attempt suicide as teens who remained abstinent. Additionally, the majority of the teens questioned wished they hadn't become sexually active (72 percent of females, 55 percent of males).[10]

It's difficult to determine if depressed teenagers are more likely to become sexually active or if sexually active teenagers become depressed because of their behavior. The study seems to suggest that both may be true.

Early sexual activity often leads to psychological stress from empty relationships and feelings of self-contempt and worthlessness. While teenagers may become involved in sexual activity to soothe feelings of emptiness and loneliness, sexual activity itself appears to increase the risk of depression and even suicide. Clearly, the evidence suggests that sexual activity in teenagers poses significant mental-health risks.

In order to slow down the physical progression of your relationship, you need to set your boundaries before you find yourself in a situation where it's too difficult to turn back. It's a good idea to group date with other friends who are committed to not "going too far" and avoid being home alone together for long periods of time. Also, volunteer together.

Serving others will not only develop your character, but will develop a new depth in your relationship.

What are healthy ways of showing affection for someone you really care about?

It depends on his or her love language. The book *The Five Love Languages* by Gary Chapman talks about the different ways people feel loved.[11] There are five primary love languages by which each person receives the message that he or she is loved:

1. Quality time—just spending time together.
2. Words of affirmation—telling someone that he or she is valued.
3. Acts of service—helping with a project or doing something for him or her.
4. Gifts—saying, "I'm thinking of you."
5. Physical touch—nonsexual hugs, squeezes, backrubs, or pats on the back.

In your relationship, try to figure out what your friend's love language is, and use it to communicate with him or her. Understanding this key communication tool will go a long way in helping you develop a long-lasting and emotionally fulfilling relationship.

What is love, anyway? Isn't sex love?

After watching the latest Hollywood hits, it's easy to assume that having sex equals love. In real life, sex and love can be two distinctly different things. A lot of sex takes place void of love. Any teen or adult can have sex just for the pure physical enjoyment of it and then get up and move on to another relationship. But the best sex occurs in a committed, caring, long-term relationship—known as marriage! Sex is an important communication tool for people who love each other. Outside of marriage, sex is generally used as an entertainment tool rather than an expression of intimate emotions.

True love is much more than a crush. It's an emotion that causes you to care and give to another person in a sacrificial way. It's seeking his or her best interest over yours. Love grows deeper over time and isn't something that happens overnight. As a young person, the intense feelings you may have for someone may mimic "real" love, but only time will tell.

Can pregnancy occur without having vaginal sex?

Yes. Sperm are capable of swimming long distances. If two people have genital contact but don't have penetrative sex, it's possible to become pregnant, because sperm can leak from the penis and travel to the vaginal cavity.

Can sperm swim through clothing?

Many teens try to express their intense physical desires for one another through simulating sex with their clothes on. In this instance, sperm can't swim through clothing. But if you stimulate one another with your clothes on, it's only a matter of time before the clothes come off. Protect yourself and your heart; don't let your physical relationship progress to this point. Instead, focus on getting to know each other emotionally. Often, engaging in a physical relationship can ruin what might have been a fulfilling emotional relationship.

Can a girl get pregnant if she has sex standing up?

In whatever position you have sex, if sperm are ejaculated into a woman's vagina, pregnancy can occur.

Do boys need sex more than girls?

Most people think boys need more sex than girls. But this isn't always true. There are times, especially when women are older, that they desire more sex than their husbands. The reality is that nobody "needs" to have sex to stay alive, be happy, have a productive life, or be loved and cared for. Even married couples go through periods when they aren't having regular sex, such as during late pregnancy, travel, illness, or emotional distancing. Controlling your sexual urges takes self-control and discipline, the same traits required to be an excellent athlete or student.

How many days a month can you get pregnant?

An egg that's been released from a woman's ovary lives for about twenty-four hours before it breaks up and can't be fertilized. This means that a woman can become pregnant for three to four days in each menstrual cycle, since sperm live between one and three days.

How many sperm does a man release when he ejaculates?

When a man ejaculates, he releases anywhere from 150 to 600 million sperm into a woman's vagina. Only fifty to two hundred sperm may actually make the journey to where the egg has been released.

How much physical contact is okay when I'm dating someone?

When you're first getting to know someone, it's impossible to know if you're actually going to be an item, so keeping your hands to yourself is an excellent policy. Many young people feel obligated to hold hands and kiss on the first date. But when developing the physical aspect of a relationship, starting slow can only be beneficial for your future. If your date wants to become physical right away, you can say you'd like to get to know him first. If your date doesn't respect your boundaries, then the reality is your date doesn't care about you.

People have said that it's best to be friends with someone before you start dating. This is the healthiest way to begin a relationship, because then you aren't thinking about the physical but rather about spending

Character Builders

As teens mature, their capacity to give love to others deepens. Friendships are strong, and romance can mature to an unselfish kind of love, although the majority of high school teens are classically still self-centered. Your goal should be to help your teen transition to "other-centered" relationships before he leaves home. Of utmost importance is to . . .

- **Love your teen unconditionally.** Say "I love you!" daily. If you haven't already, read *The Five Love Languages of Teens* by Gary Chapman.
- **Model caring** for others by volunteering in a service organization.
- **Model loving hard people by sharing** how you're trying to show love to a person who's difficult—a co-worker, an ex-spouse, or a family member.
- **Show your teen a lot of affection**—as much as he'll tolerate—with hugs, backrubs, foot massages, and so on.
- **Look for ways to serve others** as a family and give unselfishly.

time getting to know him as a person. Once you've both decided that you have romantic feelings for each other, discuss your level of comfort for physical affection and how far is far enough. Remember that holding hands leads to kissing, deep kissing leads to petting, and petting can lead straight to sexual intercourse in moments of passion. If you both have decided to wait until marriage to have sex, then you need to keep your physical contact to the activities that won't let you lose self-control. A good rule of thumb is to keep your clothes on and don't touch anything that your bathing suit covers!

How often do married people have sex?

Researchers have posed this question to married couples, and the range could be once a year to every night! The average is around one to three times a week.[12] The more important question is not the frequency of sex, but are husband and wife both enjoying sex? Studies show that married couples enjoy sex more and feel more secure in their relationships than couples having sex who aren't married.[13] Remember, the best sex is in marriage!

When do married couples stop having sex?

Married couples stop having sex when they're physically or emotionally unable to do so. That means that people in their nineties can still enjoy sex.

I have a flat chest; is there any way to make my breasts grow?

Women come in all shapes and sizes. Some women have breasts that are too large for their comfort. Then there are those who have very little fat on their body, which includes breast tissue. If your breasts are small and you've started your period, you may not increase your breast size much. This doesn't mean you can't please your husband once you're married or breastfeed later on. Some women have undergone breast augmentation to enlarge their breasts, but this has several major complications associated with it. Remember, it's not your looks that you want people to like, but the person you are inside.

What causes infertility?

Infertility, or the inability to get pregnant, has become a significant problem in society today. One-third of women who visit infertility clinics and undergo IVF (in vitro fertilization) treatments have a blockage of a fallopian tube caused by a sexually transmitted infection. There are also other medical conditions that can cause a couple to be infertile, such as endometriosis.

What is endometriosis?

Endometriosis is the presence of normal uterine tissue in the wrong place. When endometrial tissue, which lines the uterus, is found anywhere else in the body, it's called endometriosis. Female hormones circulate all through the body, stimulating endometrial tissue growth, no matter where the tissue is, during the month. When the hormone levels drop to produce menstrual bleeding, the endometrial tissue, wherever it is in the body, will bleed too.

Normal endometrial tissue lining the uterus will bleed out into the vagina, but in other parts of the body, the blood can't escape, and pockets of blood will form in the tissue containing it. These pockets are irritating and cause the tissues around them to develop scarring. This endometrial tissue, blood pockets, and scarring is called endometriosis. Endometriosis is often found on the outside surface of a woman's uterus, fallopian tubes, ovaries, bladder, or intestines. Endometriosis can cause a great deal of pain in the pelvis, and the scarring, along with other changes that are a part of endometriosis, can cause infertility.

What is in vitro fertilization (IVF)?

IVF is a method of assisted reproduction in which the man's sperm and the woman's egg (or oocyte) are combined in a laboratory dish, where fertilization occurs. The resulting embryo is then transferred to the uterus to develop naturally. Usually two to four embryos are transferred with each cycle.

Infertility is a disease of the reproductive system that affects the male or female with almost equal frequency. Fewer than 5 percent of infertile couples in treatment actually use IVF. IVF is usually the treatment of choice for a woman with blocked, severely damaged, or absent fallopian tubes. IVF is also used to circumvent infertility caused by endometriosis or a male factor. Many programs also use IVF to treat couples with unexplained infertility of long duration who have failed with other infertility treatments.

According to the latest statistics, the success rate for IVF is 29 percent per egg retrieval. This success rate is similar to the 20 percent chance that a healthy, reproductively normal couple has in any given month of achieving a pregnancy that results in a live baby.[14]

▮ What does "secondary virginity" mean?

Secondary virginity is a term for a person who has been sexually active in the past but makes the decision to not have sex again until marriage. Anyone, at any time, can decide to stop having sex and wait for marriage. This decision will eliminate your chances of getting a new sexually transmitted infection, assuming you don't already have one, becoming pregnant, or experiencing additional emotional pain.

▮ What does abstinence mean?

Abstinence means willingly doing without sexual intercourse. If you want to be technical, sexual intercourse is when a man's penis enters a woman's vagina. But if you broaden the definition beyond the physical and include the emotional, spiritual, and relational, then any time your sexual organs (penis, clitoris, and breasts) are sexually stimulated by the touch of another person, you're involved in a form of sexual activity. Remember, abstinence isn't going without sex forever, but just until you're in a lifelong, committed marriage relationship. Even in marriage, there are periods of abstinence. Regardless of their age or circumstances, people can control their sexual urges and practice abstinence.

▮ What does it mean to be bisexual?

A bisexual is a person who has sex with both men and women.

▮ What is nymphomania?

Nymphomania is an uncontrollable sexual desire in men and women.

The Answers You Need & They Want

Character Builders

Some kids are having sex in high school—but not all of them! Engage in ongoing discussions with your teen about the importance of waiting for sex until marriage. Believe it or not, this will influence her decision on whether to wait to have sex.

- **Model healthy, moral relationships** with appropriate public affection in your own life.
- **Frequently discuss your dream for your teen's sexual happiness in waiting until marriage** for sexual intercourse. If you find out that she's already lost her virginity, encourage her to start over as a secondary virgin. Let her know it's never too late to start over.
- **If your teen is in a serious relationship, spend a lot of time with both of them.** Make sure they aren't alone at either house (where teen sex happens the most). Talk with the other parents for the same commitment on their part to dialogue with their teen.
- **Use the media to fuel discussion** of your own opinions about shallow, sex-filled relationships that misrepresent true love and long-term commitment.
- **Fathers, continue to "date" your daughters, even if you meet resistance. Mothers, "date" your sons.** This lets them know you care about them and want to stay connected.

What is exhibitionism?

Exhibitionism is a perverse act marked by a compulsive need to expose the genitals in public.

What is a pedophile?

A pedophile is an adult who is sexually attracted to children (and acts on the attraction). It's psychologically very damaging to children to be exploited sexually by an adult.

■ What is voyeurism?

Voyeurism is a preoccupation with seeing the sex acts or sex organs of others, especially from a secret vantage point.

■ What is a pelvic exam?

A pelvic exam is an internal examination of a woman's vagina, cervix, uterus, and ovaries. The doctor or nurse uses a speculum, which is an instrument inserted into the vagina that spreads open the walls of the vagina so that the cervix can be inspected for signs of infection. A Pap smear is done to detect any kind of precancer or cancer caused by a sexually transmitted infection called human papillomavirus (HPV). Sexually active women need to check with their physician as the frequency of Pap smears depends on age and other circumstances. Cultures for STIs can also be taken from the cervix or vagina.

A bimanual exam is also done as part of a pelvic exam. The examiner puts two gloved fingers inside the woman's vagina and feels with the other hand on the abdomen for her uterus and ovaries. The examiner is checking for enlargement or tenderness of these organs that could mean pregnancy or pelvic inflammatory disease (infection in your fallopian tubes). Pelvic exams are usually done yearly once a woman has become sexually active or beginning in a virginal girl between ages eighteen and twenty-one. The frequency of Pap smears is currently being debated, so your best bet is to follow your physician's guidance.

■ What is mutual masturbation?

This is when two people stimulate each other's genitals to reach orgasm without having sexual intercourse. During mutual masturbation, sexually transmitted infections can be passed through bodily secretions on the hands of your partner.

What should I do if I've had sex?

If you've already had sex and regret that decision, stop having sex until you thoroughly understand the risks you take on if you remain sexually active. First, ask yourself: Why did I start having sex? Was I pressured into it? Was I hungry for love and thought this would fulfill that need? Was I lonely or depressed, thinking this would fill a vacuum? Was I curious and just wanted to see what "everyone" was talking about? Was I drunk or high on drugs and couldn't say no? Sex isn't worth the risks of contracting a sexually transmitted infection, experiencing a pregnancy, feeling emotional disappointment, and jeopardizing your future marriage. Second, think about your long-term goals and how being sexually active may interfere with them. Third, see your doctor to be sure you aren't pregnant and get tested for STIs. The safest and healthiest choice is to wait until marriage to have sex again.

Why does my doctor want to know if I've been sexually active?

Your doctor needs to know if you've been sexually active in order to rule out possible medical conditions. You need to tell your doctor if you've had any type of sexual contact, whether you've had oral sex, genital contact without penetrative sex, anal sex, or vaginal, penetrative sex. This information is confidential, and it's important to be honest because this information will help you achieve optimal health care. If you've had any form of sexual contact, your physician will need to make sure you don't have a sexually transmitted infection. Since so many STIs don't have any symptoms, it's important to find them before they cause permanent damage.

Why is it so important to be married before I have sex?

Having sex before you're married is risky. Sex with more than one partner increases your chance of getting a sexually transmitted infection, such as chlamydia, human papillomavirus, or genital herpes. You might think, *I'll just use a condom and be safe.* Unfortunately, condoms don't eliminate the risk of contracting an STI. Second, you can become pregnant if you're a girl or responsible financially for a baby if you're a boy. One out of five sexually active girls becomes pregnant by the time she's twenty.

Sex is special. People who have sex before marriage bring a lot of emotional baggage with them, and this may jeopardize the quality of sex in the marriage and increase the chance of divorce. Having sex before marriage may destroy the romance and mystery of the marriage relationship.

▮▮ Am I weird if I'm not dating or never had a boyfriend?

No. Having a boyfriend or dating does have benefits. You feel special, get attention and presents, and have someone to talk to and hang out with. Yet there are so many benefits to being "unattached." You have more time to spend with family and friends. When you're tied down, those relationships get neglected, and you may find that if you suddenly are open for some fun with friends, they've forgotten about you. When you're unattached, you have the ability to focus on your future and the freedom to explore your goals. You won't have the baggage of being emotionally tied up in failed relationships. The majority of boy/girl relationships in high school are shallow and not based on friendship first. It's always best to get to know people for who they are before you let yourself develop romantic feelings for them.

▮▮ How will I know whom I'm supposed to marry?

This is probably the most important question you need to ask yourself and understand if you want to have a happy, healthy marriage. The majority of marriages fail because the partners each married the wrong person. First, avoid some of the pitfalls that jeopardize a marriage from the start:

- Don't decide to get married too quickly. Relationships do the best over several seasons of "weathering," or seeing how you overcome some hurdles together. If you don't give it time, you really don't know the person you're marrying.

- Don't marry too young. Your personality is still evolving through the teen years and early twenties, and you're in for too many surprises if you marry too young.

- Work out any baggage from your family of origin before marriage. Unfortunately, we all have dysfunctional families to some degree that can poison our future marriage. Figure out what your "issues" are, and work on them before you degrade your marriage with them.

Write down on paper what's important to you in a person you want to be with for life. What personality type do you enjoy being with? Do intelligence and looks weigh heavy on your scale? Is spirituality a key factor? How about values and character? What are your family and parenting goals? (If you want five kids and he doesn't want any, that will be a problem and has broken up marriages!) People used to think that opposites attract, but in reality, you'll want to find a person a lot like you with shared interests, values, beliefs, and background. Otherwise your differences will end up causing lots of conflict.

As you spend time together, you'll see how caring or how self-centered the person is. Everyone's on their best behavior when they want to impress someone they care about, but over time and with some hurdles, the real person inside should show his true colors. Be open to close family and friends' opinions about your relationship. They're more objective and may see red flags that you don't see. (Love really is blind at times!)

What should I do if my girlfriend is after me to have sex?

In our society, many girls are the aggressors instead of the boys. This attitude is picked up from TV, movies, and ads where the woman is always enticing the man for sex. It's all about power! Sometimes there are some underlying issues of pain from sexual abuse and the need to feel love, which the woman thinks is connected to sex. Asking some good questions might reveal some other ways for her to be affirmed. But the "No, I'm not interested!" statement should speak for itself. If she doesn't respect that boundary, then she doesn't care about you, and it's time to move on.

Why shouldn't I have sex if I'm in love?

Wanting sex and each other isn't the same as really loving each other. Real love is the kind of love that cares more about the other person than yourself. Real love wants what's best for the other person and is willing to sacrifice for the other person. Is giving her a sexually transmitted infection (because you've had sex with someone who had one) what's best for her? Is getting her pregnant what's best for her right now in her life? If you really loved your partner, you wouldn't want these things to happen to her. The best gift of true love is waiting for marriage where these risks aren't present because you waited. Saying no now makes saying yes in marriage the meaningful "I love you for always" that it's meant to be. If she's the right person, your feelings will grow and last without sex. Just knowing that you're saving sex for marriage can make your relationship even more special. The deliberate decision to abstain from sex before marriage can also help you abstain from sex in marriage during times of illness, pregnancy, or separation from your spouse.

How can my boyfriend and I be close without having sex?

Developing intimacy without sex is a skill that will serve you for life. As married couples can attest, sexual activity doesn't always equate to emotional intimacy. The best things you can do are communicate with your boyfriend about your dreams and desires and keep yourselves out of compromising situations. Talk about your future goals, and create a plan to reach those goals. Additionally, spend time meeting the needs of others. Whether it's volunteering at a retirement center or working to build someone a home, developing common interests through outside activities significantly develops closeness. Additionally, be creative in your dating life. Challenge one another to create times that will build memories; then take time to create photo journals of your time together. After all, if this boyfriend turns out to be your mate, you'll have created a treasure chest of memories for your future.

I want to save sex until marriage. How can I succeed when all my peers are having sex?

First things first: not all your peers are having sex. Many are, but it's not uncommon for teens to exaggerate what they have or haven't done. The best thing you can do to save sex for marriage is to not allow yourself to be caught in a compromising situation (such as home alone without adult supervision late at night). Remember, sex is progressive. Kissing can lead to touching, touching can lead to fondling, and fondling can lead to sex. Holding hands and kissing may seem boring after a while, but if you're committed to remaining abstinent, these are the behaviors that should satisfy you. Make it a policy to group date. If you do date individually, spend time with each other's family. Young couples who spend time with each other's parents generally develop a respect that can protect them from pushing physical boundaries. Also, keep yourself busy. Stay involved in after-school programs, volunteer in your community, and plan your dates. Don't push your curfew. And don't spend time lingering with your girlfriend—it's during these moments of boredom that many young people slip over the sexual line. Always keep in mind that not having sex today will be the greatest gift you can give yourself and your future mate.

How do my boyfriend and I avoid compromising situations?

It's most important to talk about what both of your goals are in your physical relationship. If you're waiting to have sex until marriage, the healthiest choice, then you need a plan ahead of time to avoid moments of passion that can cloud your judgment. Decide beforehand how far you're willing to take your physical relationship. It's important to remember that the further you go, the harder it is to control your physical desires. Make a commitment to one another to keep your relationship pure, and plan activities accordingly. A few tips include dating in groups, not being alone at home together, and avoiding seeing sexually explicit movies.

▮▮ What is the date rape drug? How do I protect myself against being harmed by it?

The date rape drug is called rohypnol. It's a derivative of Valium but is ten times more potent. It's also called "roofies" or "roaches." Rapists use it to take control of their victim and eliminate any memory of the abuse. Under its influence, a person can't move or yell.

The drug can be taken orally and dissolves in liquid. In order to protect yourself from this drug, don't go to parties where alcohol and drugs are being used. If you attend parties where alcohol is served, consider bringing your own beverages, or drink only beverages when you've seen them poured into a glass directly from the bottle. (Avoid punch bowls as well). Also, keep your glass in your hand at all times; never set it down where someone can discreetly slip a drug into your glass without your knowing it.

▮▮ Why shouldn't I drink alcohol?

Alcohol is a depressant and lowers a person's inhibitions. You might be convinced you'd never have sex before marriage, but after a few beers, "Why not?" If you drink alcohol, research shows you're more likely to have sex. Teens who drink are more likely to have more than one partner, which increases the risk of sexually transmitted infections and pregnancy.[15] Many teens also participate in binge drinking (four to five drinks in a row).[16] It's easier for a girl to be raped when she's too drunk to say no or to know what's happened to her.

240

■ What's the problem with binge drinking?

Binge drinking is dangerous and can kill you. Binge drinking is considered drinking four or more drinks rapidly in a row. Consuming alcohol this quickly causes your blood alcohol level to rise and become toxic to your brain. Research appears to indicate that the teen brain is more susceptible to the toxic affects of alcohol. In addition, this type of drinking lowers an individual's inhibitions, which means you're more open to risk behaviors. In fact, a majority of first-time sexual encounters between teenagers involve alcohol.[17]

Moving Out

College and Beyond

"I can't wait until I move out!" were the words you heard last week from your teenager. And if you're honest, you probably muttered under your breath, "I can't wait either." Face it, an adolescent's quest for independence is perhaps more exhausting than keeping your ten-month-old away from the electrical outlets. If you're like most parents, you've been working your way to this stage of life for eighteen years. Some days you may feel exhilaration at the thought of having your teenager move out. Other days you may worry about whether or not she's ready for the world. Rest assured, you've done all you can do! Now it's time to switch roles from hands-on parenting to a key advisor.

Basically, the relationship you've developed with your child will determine how broad of a role you'll play in her life from this point forward. At this stage, many teens tend to flee from home to the reckless abandon of most college campuses in order to find themselves. Hopefully, during the last few years, you've given your child just enough rope to find herself before heading off to college.

As your child journeys down the road to independence, the questions or concerns you may have, or the questions your young adult may be asking, might be too difficult to articulate in person. Consider handling these delicate interactions with letters, especially since many young adults aren't living at home. If you happen to be one of those rare parents who are articulate and still have the attention of your teen, you're more than welcome to handle these questions face-to-face. But for the rest of you, hopefully the contents of these letters will help you develop the message you want to communicate to your young adult as you deal with some of these tough issues, whether you're married, divorced, or never married.*

Parents' Questions

■■ **What do I tell my young adult who wants to come home for the holidays with her nonmarried, cohabiting partner?**

The answer to this question will depend on whether you've discussed cohabitation with your grown child and indeed whether you approve or disapprove of cohabitation. This letter is written from the perspective of a parent who has discussed cohabitation or sexual activity prior to marriage and believes this is an unhealthy decision. Regardless of how this letter or discussion is handled, love must prevail, and the freedom to come home for unconditional love is always an option.

---

* You'll notice that some letters from parents are written from a faith perspective. While the Medical Institute isn't faith based but a medical scientific organization, it recognizes the importance of faith in sexual decision making. Parents of faith are encouraged to express their faith in letters to their grown children. A word of caution, however: if a grown child has rejected your faith, don't attempt to force it on him. At this age, he's more likely to be influenced by how you live out your faith daily than by words on paper. Obviously, parents with no faith could modify these letters accordingly.

The Answers You Need & They Want

My dearest daughter,

Thank you for wanting to come home for the holidays and for being sensitive to our beliefs and values. Your father and I look forward to your visit and meeting your new boyfriend. As parents of a grown adult, we of course have long ago released you to follow your own path. We would make one condition of your visit, and that is that you and your boyfriend sleep in separate bedrooms while you're staying in our home. For our part, we resolve to resist the temptation to offer you parental advice or express our concern in regards to your current lifestyle. While your father and I are concerned for your future, we love you very much, and we look forward to having you home for the holidays.

Love,
Mom

What do I tell my daughter who's getting married about sex in marriage?

This is an easy question to avoid, because it may be difficult due to your own personal baggage. There's no one answer to this question, since so many factors are involved. Is the father or mother answering the question? Is the daughter entering marriage as a virgin or as sexually experienced, especially with her fiancé? Is the daughter's fiancé a virgin or sexually experienced, even from a previous marriage? Is the parent who's speaking married or divorced? Does the family have a spiritual heritage? This question is probably one of the most ignored discussions in this entire book, but in many ways, it's perhaps one of the most important. This letter is written by a father with a spiritual faith talking to his daughter who is a virgin. You should modify it for your circumstances.

My dearest daughter,

Your mother and I are looking forward to your marriage. You were wise to get premarital counseling, and I know you'll be committed to your vows of "till death do us part." Your counseling may have discussed a few basic male/female differences, but I doubt it addressed some of the tougher issues.

I've written my thoughts down because, quite frankly, I might forget or stumble over some points. Besides, in your excitement of getting married, you probably wouldn't hear half of what I say, so maybe in the months to come you can reread this letter and hopefully share it with your husband.

I hope I have conveyed to you in our previous talks how beautiful and wonderful sex can be in a committed marriage. I commend you for waiting for sex until your wedding night. For some, especially for a woman, it can be difficult to say yes to sex after saying no for so many years. Perhaps the best advice I can give you is just to be patient. I can also guarantee you that sex will be better ten years into your marriage than even on your wedding night.

I hope your wedding night and honeymoon are all bells and whistles with fireworks like a Fourth of July in Washington DC, but if they aren't, don't despair.

One thing that might cause some problems would be getting honeymoon cystitis (a bladder infection that occurs during the first few days of marriage due to frequent intercourse). If you develop painful urination, call your doctor for medication. You might want your physician to give you a written prescription, which you can fill if it's needed, for a urinary tract antibiotic and for Pyridium to control the pain. (Pyridium will change the color of your urine.) Hopefully, you won't get an infection, but if you do, take your medication and realize that it won't be a recurring problem.

Even if your sex life is incredibly fulfilling on your honeymoon, I must tell you that it won't always be like that. Both men and women go through seasons of sex. Poor health may put a damper on sex for a while for either spouse. A business failure or problems at work may seriously affect your husband. Two children in diapers and the "baby blues" may make sex difficult for a while for you. I guess what I'm trying to say is that sex within a marriage will vary from time to time; don't be discouraged. You have before you a whole lifetime and different seasons of life to find out how to please each other. Simply put—be patient, but at the same time be a student of what turns your husband on and how to please him.

No two couples are exactly alike, but most likely there will be differences in how the two of you view sex. In general, men want more sex more often than women, but this will vary with seasons of life, and as you get older, this could reverse. There's no right or wrong answer about the frequency of sex, and it will change with age, children, and external circumstances. The main thing is to learn to communicate with each other your desires, needs, frustrations, and expectations.

Men in general feel rejected if their wife doesn't want to have sex. Wives, on the other hand, generally feel no rejection if their husband is too tired for sex.

My advice is to make sure your husband knows that you aren't rejecting him, you love him, and you're willing to give him a rain check to look forward to.

At other times, you might sense your husband really needs sexual release, and basically you give him the freedom to satisfy himself without attempting to satisfy you or bring you to a climax. To your husband, this unselfishness on your part is going the extra mile.

In regard to simultaneous climaxes, it's wonderful when it happens, but it's also okay when it doesn't. Allow each other the freedom from having to perform perfectly every time you have sex.

Sex is such an intricate part of marriage that if you're having problems, you should get professional help. Be careful talking about sex, the most intimate part of your marriage, especially to anyone of the opposite sex. I'd suggest you get help from a counselor who's not only qualified, but who also shares your faith and values.

I believe your entire bodies belong to each other, but with this one caveat— every aspect of your sex life must be mutually satisfying. Trouble abounds if one of you forces some touch or sex act and it isn't mutually satisfying. Oral sex tends to be a guy thing, but it's something the two of you will have to decide for yourselves. From a medical standpoint, however, you must know that if you or your husband has "fever blisters," genital herpes can result from oral sex.

Sex during a menstrual period is another controversial area. Sex during this time in a woman's cycle is usually not as pleasurable, especially for the female. It's in these areas and other areas of your marriage that communication between husband and wife is so critical. Again, if you're reaching an impasse—seek counseling.

There may be times in your marriage when for medical reasons the two of you can't have sexual intercourse for a period of time. Pregnancy is just one example. I'd encourage you to consider your husband's needs at this time. If it's agreeable to your husband, you could manually stimulate him to release his sexual tensions. You may prefer for it to be mutual stimulation in times when sexual intercourse isn't possible for periods of time due to illness, during late pregnancy, or after delivery, if it's mutually satisfying. Again, you must communicate at a very deep level. With time, it will become easier to talk about this and any other issue in your marriage.

In closing, I just know you're going to have a good marriage, which includes a great sex life. The great thing about sex within a committed marriage determined to go the distance is that you're not on stage and you don't have to perform perfectly every time. Allow each other the freedom to fall flat on occasion. Learn to laugh at yourself and to laugh together as a couple.

Have a great marriage.

We love you,
Dad

▮▮ What do I tell my son who's getting married in regards to sex in marriage?

This might be a hard question for you to answer, and it will depend on your son's situation, but here is a letter written to a son who hasn't been sexually active.

Dear Son,

Your mother and I are so looking forward to your marriage. You were wise to get premarital counseling, and I know you'll be committed to your vows of "till death do us part." Your counseling probably discussed a few basic male-female differences, but in this letter I'll address some of the tough issues.

I hope I've conveyed to you in our previous talks how beautiful and wonderful sex can be in a committed marriage. I commend you for waiting for sex till your wedding night. You can go into marriage with no fear of giving a sexually transmitted infection to your wife and no memories from the past. Media unfortunately has given many people the wrong impression of what sex is like in a good, vibrant marriage. It's special and wonderful, but TV and movies only show the peaks and the highs, not the lows that every good, married sex life transitions through. So let's begin.

I'm sure that your counselor discussed the differences in sexual arousal between males and females, but let me give you my take on the issue. Males are visual, and women are relational and emotional. A man can have a fight with his wife, but when he sees her in a sexy nightgown, he's ready to have sex immediately. Women, however, don't easily forget the fight from two hours ago or perhaps two days ago. Women are turned on by romance and kind words.

I trust your bride-to-be has been seen by her physician and you two have discussed what form of birth control, if any, you want to use. Her physician can usually spot any potential major problem, but sex for a woman the first few times can be a little bit painful, so please be patient with your wife. Patience and understanding your wife in the beginning of your sex life together will pay huge dividends for you in the future.

Taking time and getting to know each other's bodies is especially important for your wife, as this will provide the lubrication she needs to make sex really enjoyable for both of you but especially for her. In the beginning, she might need some extra lubrication, so I'd suggest you take along a tube of water-soluble lubricant that any pharmacist can provide for you. Also, something that men don't often hear about is premature ejaculation. Don't be embarrassed if this happens; it can be normal given the stress of the day and also the anticipation of something you've undoubtedly longed for.

If your honeymoon is fabulous and your sex life is great, I must tell you that it won't always be like that. Both males and females go through seasons of sex within marriage. Poor health may put a damper on sex for a while for either spouse. A business failure or problems at work may seriously affect your sexual drive. Two children in diapers and the "baby blues" may make sex difficult for a while for your wife. You have before you a whole lifetime and different seasons of life to find out how to please each other. Simply put—be patient, but at the same time be a student of what turns your wife on and how to please her.

No two couples are exactly alike, but most likely there will be differences in how the two of you view sex. Males in general want more sex more often than females, but this will vary with seasons of life, and as you get older, this could reverse. There's no right or wrong answer about the frequency of sex, and it will change with age, children, and external circumstances. The main thing is to learn to communicate with each other your desires, needs, frustrations, and expectations. If both of you are satisfied, it really doesn't matter how often you're having sex.

Men in general feel rejected if their wife doesn't want to have sex. Wives, on the other hand, generally feel no rejection if their husband is too tired for sex. If you feel you're getting shorted on sex, then take the time to prime the pump. Bring home some flowers, go out for a romantic dinner or a weekend getaway, and at the right time, convey your frustrations to your wife. Timing is everything in life and in marriage.

In regard to simultaneous climaxes, it's wonderful when it happens, but it's also okay when it doesn't. Allow each other freedom from having to perform perfectly every time you have sex.

Sex is such an intricate part of marriage that if you're having problems, get professional help. Be careful talking about sex, the most intimate part of your marriage, especially to anyone of the opposite sex. I'd suggest that you get help from a counselor who's not only qualified, but who shares your faith and values.

I believe your entire bodies belong to each other, but with this one caveat— every aspect of your sex life must be mutually satisfying. Trouble abounds if one of you forces some touch or sex act and it's not mutually satisfying. Oral sex tends to be a guy thing, but it's something the two of you will have to decide for yourselves. I believe, however, that it must be a mutual decision and no one spouse should force it upon the other spouse. From a medical standpoint, however, you must know that if you or your wife has "fever blisters," genital herpes can result from oral sex. On the other hand, I'd caution you in regard to rectal intercourse, but for health and physical reasons. The rectum simply wasn't designed for penile intercourse.

Sex during a menstrual period is another controversial area. First of all, sex during this time in a woman's cycle is usually not as pleasurable, especially for the female. It's in this area and other areas of your marriage that communication between husband and wife is so critical. In this area of sex during a menstrual period, it's always wise for a husband to yield to his wife. Again, if you're reaching an impasse, seek counseling.

There may be times in your marriage when for medical reasons the two of you can't have intercourse for a while. A period of time during pregnancy is just one example. I'd encourage you to express your needs to your wife. Perhaps she's willing to manually relieve your hormones and your sexual tension. In my opinion, this is preferable to masturbation by yourself. Your wife may prefer mutual stimulation in times when sexual intercourse isn't possible due to illness, for periods of time during late pregnancy, or after delivery, if it's mutually satisfying to both partners. Again, you must communicate at a very deep level that at first may be very difficult for one or both of you. With time it will become easier to talk about this and any other issue in your marriage and to seek to truly satisfy and please each other. This is the meaning of true intimacy, where you can take your mask off and be yourself with no fear of rejection.

In closing, I just know you're going to have a good marriage, which includes a great sex life. The great thing about sex within a committed marriage determined to go the distance is that you're not on stage and you don't have to perform perfectly every time. Allow each other the freedom to fall flat on occasion; that's okay. Learn to laugh at yourself and to laugh together as a couple.

Love,
Dad

My daughter has found the love of her life and wants to get married, but she hasn't finished college. What should I do?

There's no easy answer to this question, and ultimately it's your daughter's decision, but as a parent you can provide guidance and direction. The first questions to ask are: Do you think your daughter has made a wise choice? What do her friends think of this match? If you have older sons or daughters, what do they think of their sister's choice?

If you believe that your daughter is mature enough for marriage and she and her boyfriend are a good match, then consider giving your blessing on the marriage and being willing to help them out financially until she finishes college. In most instances you'd be helping with college anyway, so you're using funds that were already committed, although additional funding might be required. Perhaps the offer to help them financially is conditioned on their having premarital counseling, and indeed many churches are even making counseling mandatory before the wedding can take place.

If you aren't sure about the person your daughter has chosen, then counseling is even more important. It would be best for your daughter and her boyfriend to discover with the aid of a counselor that perhaps they'd be wise to call off the marriage or at least delay it.

What are the possible repercussions for not giving your blessing and financial help? Your daughter and her boyfriend could just decide to cohabit, and due to lack of funds and commitment, the relationship could blow up before marriage. Your daughter could be left pregnant or a single parent with a child in tow. Or they could get married without your blessing, and in part due to financial struggles and lack of counseling and preparation for marriage, their marriage could self-destruct and end in divorce.

Even if you think your daughter's choice is wrong, the marriage could work if she and her boyfriend get premarital counseling. They need to clearly see their differences but accept those differences, with the resolve that their marriage will take a lot of work on both parts. They must be committed to making it work, no matter what.

The key to this discussion and many others is the resolve to stay cool, calm, and objective without raising your voice or saying words you'll later regret. Remember, at this age you can't control your children or tell them what to do—you need to provide options that in time they may accept as their own.

What do you tell your young adult who has told you she intends to become sexually active?

This question, as well as all of these questions, can be difficult to answer, and there are many possible answers that depend upon your view of sexuality and what is right and wrong. The answer will probably be different if you're married than if you're divorced and living with someone. You'll have to modify the letter or answer depending on your personal faith, worldview, and moral convictions. This letter is the response of a mother who feels that her grown child is making a mistake and that in all probability it will result in pain in the future. One constant that should be a part of any version of this letter, however, is unconditional love for your child even if you disapprove of the decision she's making.

Dear Daughter,

Thank you for your willingness to share with me your decision about being sexually active. I know that it was probably a very difficult decision.

Let me first say that even though you must know I was disappointed by your decision, I hope it was clear that my love for you remains no matter what choices you will make now or in the future. If you hear nothing else, please know that I love you. There's nothing you could do or say that could ever cause me to stop loving you. Your father and I will always open the door for you to come home, even though we may have to put restrictions on what takes place under our roof. I hope you understand that.

I couldn't tell for certain whether your decision is totally made or whether you were asking me to give you permission to become sexually active. It should have been no surprise, based on our previous discussions about sex, that I couldn't give you my personal approval.

My response, in part, was based on my faith, but equally important is that no mother wants to see her child, regardless of her age, get hurt or even enter into situations where she might get hurt. I believe your having sex outside of marriage will result in some pain at some point in your life, sooner or later.

If your decision is final, then you must make some hard and fast decisions. If he's had sex before, he needs to be checked for STIs, because most STIs show no symptoms, and there's no way to know if you have them except by being tested. Some can be treated, but if he has a viral STI, then you must understand that the odds are good that eventually you will become infected. Can you accept that? While consistent and correct use of condoms may reduce the risk of transmission for most but not all STIs, your risk of acquiring an STI, especially a viral STI, from your partner is greater over time with multiple acts of sex even with the correct use of a condom. It also needs to be said that less than 100 percent correct use may not even help in reducing the risk.

Assuming that you don't want children now, you'll need to talk to your physician about the best choice of birth control for you. While the pill is close to 100 percent effective if taken perfectly, you must know that the overall first-year failure rate even for the pill is about 8 percent. Why? Because we're humans, and sometimes we just forget to take our medications. Also, the pill offers no protection against STIs.

Marriage is a great stabilizer for men, and most men in marriage will be faithful to their wives. A man is much more likely to be unfaithful to a nonmarried partner. If your partner has sex with somebody else and contracts an STI, it's likely he'll pass it on to you, especially if you aren't using condoms correctly 100 percent of the time.

Have you thought about what will happen if you become pregnant? You know, of course, my feeling about abortion, but have you thought about what you would do? Would your partner marry you, and is this someone you want to spend the rest of your life with? If he wouldn't marry you, would you try to rear the baby by yourself? Would you release your baby for adoption? Would you have an abortion? There are no easy answers to having a child outside of marriage.

There's a good chance you won't marry the first person you have sex with. Even if you don't get an STI or get pregnant, how will the time you spend cohabiting affect your future marriage relationship? Will the excitement of sex with multiple partners put a damper on sex in a future marriage relationship because of past memories, scars, or expectations? I can't tell you this will happen, but there's a likelihood of it, and no parent wants to see their child get hurt or have a marriage that's less than it could be. I'm also not saying that hurts and scars can't be healed through time and counseling, but that in itself can be costly in terms of finances and personal pain.

Know that I love you and I'm ready to give you a hug or talk to you at any time in the future, even though I may disapprove of the path you've chosen. It will be difficult, but for my part I have spoken what's on my heart, and I promise not to bring up the subject with you in the future unless it's a discussion you initiate.

I love you.
Mom

What do I tell my grown son who has just told me he's a homosexual?

Your answer will depend in part on previous discussions you've had with your son in regard to homosexuality, as well as your belief system. This answer is from a mother who disapproves of the gay lifestyle but loves her son very much.

Dear Son:

I know you're aware of the feelings your father and I have about the homosexual lifestyle. It's been a long time since we've talked about this subject, and I hope we've conveyed that our disapproval is not against the homosexual person but rather against the chosen lifestyle. I would be lying if I said I'm not crushed by your decision, but also know that you're still my son whom I very much still love and care for in a way probably beyond your capacity to understand. I express these feelings not to place any guilt on you, but merely to explain the pain I now feel.

The practice of homosexuality is against your father's and my value system, but equally important is that we fear the risk of HIV and premature death, as well as the other potential emotional and physical complications from this lifestyle. I also think that most parents hope and pray that one day their child will grow up and find a spouse to marry and that grandchildren will soon follow. Having children is the hope and dream of most married couples. Perhaps it's also the wish of us as human beings who know that one day we will die but our children and grandchildren may be our legacy.

Part of the pain I feel is the guilt I now have. Did I as a mother raise you in a manner that predisposed you to this lifestyle? Was there any sexual abuse in your early childhood or adolescence? I know we don't have all the answers, but I do know that, regardless of the factors, a choice is involved. With professional help, an individual can leave the homosexual lifestyle if the desire to change is present. Just like with an alcoholic, recovery is possible if the individual is willing. This area I know is controversial, but I have personally met and visited with individuals who have successfully left the homosexual lifestyle as well as later entered into a married heterosexual relationship. I'm not saying that change is easy but that it's possible. I won't dwell on this possibility, but I merely lay it out on the table along with the offer of financial help for counseling if that's a path you choose to follow in the future.

I know that there are many medical consequences to consider besides HIV infection. I plead with you to talk with your physician about the lifestyle you've chosen to lead and seek the best medical advice possible. Perhaps in time you can talk to your father about your lifestyle.

In closing, let me say that I love you so very much. You're always welcome home, but we would need to talk about how to handle the situation if you wanted to bring a male friend with you. This, of course, would have to involve your father, but I personally would have to ask you to stay in separate bedrooms. I hope you understand.

I love you.
Mom

How do I respond to my grown child when he asks why it's wrong to have sexual intercourse prior to marriage if a couple is mature and cares for each other?

The answer to this question will depend in part on the faith of the parent and of the grown child. At this age, resist the temptation to lecture or blow up in anger. As a parent, no matter the extent of your worries and concerns, you can't control the actions of your grown child. It's best to acknowledge that this is his decision and your love for him will continue no matter what he decides, but tell him that here are your thoughts and the reasons you hope he'll consider before making his final decision. This letter is written by a father of faith to his grown child who has at least been exposed to his parent's faith and beliefs.

Dear Son:

You know that our faith is clear that sex is meant to occur only between a husband and wife in the context of a lifelong, mutually faithful relationship called marriage. You know that I believe sex within the context of marriage is wonderful and beautiful. Sure, sex can be wonderful and pleasurable outside of marriage, but it's the best (safest and healthiest) within marriage.

In marriage, where the couple has committed to stay together for a lifetime, they have the freedom to be intimate not only in the sexual act, but with every aspect of their life and marriage. With the true intimacy that's found in a committed marriage, the wife and the husband have the ability to take off their masks and share their innermost dreams and feelings without the fear of failure, ridicule, rejection, or even abandonment.

Sexual intercourse between two people who care for each other is powerful and wonderful. What happens when the relationship breaks up for whatever reason? There's usually pain and rejection for at least one party, perhaps both. It can be like taking off a bandage when the bandage is stuck to the skin and flesh is literally ripped apart. It hurts and often leaves a scar—and the individual remembers that hurt and pain. The human body is resilient to pain and usually recovers, but scars remain that can interfere with a future relationship—especially in marriage.

Deep intimacy in future relationships can be hindered because of the memory of being hurt last time. There can be hurt and pain even in relationships that haven't experienced sexual intercourse, but sex is so powerful that the scars and hurts are likely to be more severe and more prone to interfere with deep intimacy in a later marriage.

A child can also result when sexual intercourse occurs, and then you're faced with difficult decisions. While some choices are better than others, none are easy and without pain. Also, the more partners you have before marriage, the greater the likelihood of acquiring a sexually transmitted infection and potential lifelong complications. Since most STIs are asymptomatic, if either you or your partner has had sex in the past, it's possible to acquire or transmit an STI to each other without knowing it unless you've been screened and treated as necessary. While bacterial STIs can be treated, viral STIs can't be cured, although some burn themselves out over time. Some persist for a lifetime.

Another possible problem with having sex before marriage is that you may end up marrying the wrong person. Sex may mask your differences and blind you to a person's true personality, thereby making a future marriage difficult or possibly causing it to end in divorce. It's good to marry someone you're attracted to, but over time, passion may fade a bit as a more stable and deeper love develops. A marriage built only on passion will likely not last for a lifetime.

As a parent, I don't want to see you get hurt. I know that sex outside of marriage is likely to cause pain and suffering sooner or later. I hope you'll reconsider your decision. If you think you've found the person you want to spend the rest of your life with, then get to know each other without sex possibly blinding your eyes to each other's faults and blemishes. Get counseling, and if both of you decide you truly want to stay together for a lifetime, get married. Then enjoy sex in the context of marriage, where it's not only the best sex, but also the healthiest sex.

Regardless of your decision, I will always love you.
Dad

The Answers You Need & They Want

Questions Young Adults Ask

◾ What's wrong with casual sex?

Casual sex can ruin your opportunity to enjoy a fantastic sex life in the future. The problems associated with casual sex include sexually transmitted infections, emotional distress, the possibility of pregnancy, and an inability to develop close relationships in the future.

When you have sex with a person, you are not only having sex with that individual, but with all of his previous partners and his partners' partners. Also, if a person is willing to have casual sex with you, chances are very good that he has had many sexual partners before you and could very easily have one or more STIs. Since most STIs have no symptoms, it's almost impossible to know if your potential partner has an STI. There's also the risk of a nonmarital pregnancy. If a pregnancy occurs without a committed marital relationship, most people make decisions they'll someday regret. The bottom line is that sex was created to be a special bond in a permanent marital relationship.

◾ Do men need sex more often than women?

What does "need" actually mean? Food, water, and oxygen are what we need to live. While sex is certainly a fantastic part of life, a person can live a long, happy, and fulfilled life without sex. Most men do desire sex more than women do. But the funny thing is that men and women desire sex in different amounts during various phases of life.

◾ If I have been infected with a sexually transmitted infection, will it affect my ability to have sex in marriage or my chances of having children?

As with other areas of sex, the answer to this question depends on whether a male or female is asking the question. The question is introduced by the words "have been," which implies that the STI is no longer present. Bacterial and parasitic STIs (gonorrhea, chlamydia, syphilis, bacterial vaginosis, and trichomonas infections) can be treated, and most go away over the course of months and in some cases years, even if not treated. (The scars or damage that may result are likely to remain for a lifetime.)

Viral STIs (HIV, herpes simplex virus [HSV], and human papillomavirus [HPV]), however, can't be treated completely and may last a lifetime. HIV and HSV are lifelong. With HPV, the body usually clears most infections after a number of months; some infections persist and may lead to cancer. Both males and females with a past history of an STI (and even those who are sexually experienced but have no history of an STI) who are getting married should be seen and tested as needed by a physician to make sure that they aren't still carrying an STI from the past. An STI may have no symptoms and could be passed on to their marriage partner.

STIs are sexist. Men generally don't experience the problems females have in regards to both initial pain as well as complications such as infertility and inability to experience pleasurable sex in marriage. Men may have temporary infertility due to chlamydia or gonorrhea infection, but this is usually reversed by treatment or passage of time. With some STIs, like genital herpes, the male may think he's cured since he hasn't had any blisters or symptoms for years. The virus, however, may still be present and could be passed on to his spouse in the future. If that happens, the male's frequency of sex within the marriage may be altered by the wife's recurrent outbreaks of herpes that can last for years. A man may face possible resentment by his wife because he transmitted this very painful infection to her.

Up to one-third of couples undergoing in vitro fertilization are infertile because of scarring from previous STIs (chlamydia and gonorrhea). Most women with chlamydia and gonorrhea have no symptoms, and even though the infection is eventually treated, irreversible damage that may cause infertility may have already happened.

A past history of an STI may or may not cause problems in a future marriage. Anyone getting married who has had sex with a previous partner should be evaluated and treated, if necessary, for any STIs. If

The Answers You Need & They Want

an STI is found that can't be treated and cured, then the couple needs to be counseled, and the uninfected partner needs to understand and accept the potential risk of being sexually active. The best way to avoid the potential pitfalls of this situation is for both partners to be abstinent before marriage and then faithful within marriage.

I used to be sexually active, but now I want to be abstinent. Is it okay? How do I do it?

Returning to an abstinent lifestyle is not only okay, it's the best choice you can make for your future health, hope, and happiness. You can't change the past, but you can make changes that will affect your future.

How do you do it? Simply make it known at the beginning of any new relationship that you've made the decision not to have sex again until you're married. This decision could end some relationships before they get started, but it's the best way to keep from being sexually involved outside of marriage.

Once you've made the decision to remain abstinent, talk with your physician about your decision. Your physician will likely test for any asymptomatic sexually transmitted infections that you may have. Women should have yearly Pap smears. Bacterial STIs can be treated, but unfortunately, viral STIs can't be cured and can last for a lifetime.

Is there any danger in having sex while I'm engaged?

The engagement is a time for a couple to get professional counseling to uncover any basic problems that are likely to lead to divorce. They either deal with these issues or cancel the engagement. Sexual intercourse during this time may mask some basic personality differences that might lead to divorce.

Even if contraception is used, there's always a chance of pregnancy that will leave you and your partner with tough decisions to make. A pregnancy may cause you to marry even though counseling indicates that your future marriage is heading for trouble. Even if counseling indicates a perfect match, you may be faced with the problem of walking down the aisle visibly pregnant or having your teenager do the math and find out that she was born seven months after the wedding date. An abortion before marriage might terminate the life of the only child you as a couple ever conceive. If the engagement is called off, you'll face tough decisions, some better than others but none without pain. To keep the baby as a single mom, to release the baby for adoption, or to terminate the pregnancy all have severe consequences.

If either or both of you have had previous sexual experiences, there's a possibility of acquiring or transmitting a sexually transmitted infection that was asymptomatic. For this reason, regardless of whether sex takes place before the wedding or after the wedding, screening for the possibility of asymptomatic STIs should be done prior to sexual intercourse. Some STIs can be cured, some cannot, and the uninfected partner must understand and accept those risks prior to initiating sex.

If the uninfected partner accepts those risks and becomes infected before the wedding and the wedding is later called off, he or she will then face the problem of possibly transmitting that nontreatable STI to any future partner, including a future spouse.

When should I get married?

The simple answer is when you're ready financially and emotionally to support yourself and another person. Several generations ago, individuals married in their teens, but it's a rare teenager today who is emotionally and financially ready to support a marriage and any children that may follow. Teenage marriages today, unlike those several generations ago, are rarely successful.

Starting in your early twenties, you should have the freedom to acknowledge and desire marriage and be open to the possibility of marriage if you find someone who fits your criteria for a spouse. In preparation for marriage, it's a good idea to start thinking of the characteristics, goals, and qualities you desire in a future spouse. While you're unlikely to find a spouse who completely fulfills your wish or dream list, it is a beginning. There are likely to be some characteristics, such as sharing your faith, that you won't compromise.

There's been a gradual increase in the average age of marriage in recent years, but many are questioning the wisdom of this trend. In part, this increase is due to the growing need for college and postgraduate education and the perceived need to further careers for both males and females prior to marriage.

A female's fertility and ease of childbearing is the greatest in the early- to mid-twenties. This doesn't mean a woman can't conceive and bear children in her thirties and forties, but fertility does progressively decrease yearly in the late twenties and into the thirties. Starting a family at a younger age is more critical for those desiring a large family, especially if one desires a little spacing between children. There's also an increased risk of certain genetic disorders, such as Down syndrome, with increasing maternal age, especially in the late thirties and early forties. While couples in their twenties may be more immature and less financially established than couples in their thirties, they tend to be more adaptable to change and may have more energy and stamina to easily cope with an active toddler.

This doesn't mean that individuals should get married at an early age just for the sake of being married. It just means to be open to marriage starting in your twenties if you find somebody who fits your criteria for a spouse. Regardless of your age, it's always wise to receive premarital counseling and even better to get some counseling prior to a formal wedding announcement. If a counselor, friends, and family have reservations about the person you're planning to marry, consider this to be a very large red flag. If this happens, you should proceed very slowly or even put the marriage on hold for a period of time.

What's wrong with living together?

The trouble with cohabiting as a sort of trial for marriage compatibility is that it seldom works. While some couples cohabit for sex, convenience, or to save money, many cohabit in hopes of avoiding a divorce. Most children of divorce desperately want to avoid the mistakes of their parents.

21 Reasons for Marriage

LIVE LONGER! GET MARRIED! This isn't a bumper sticker you're likely to see driving down the highway. To say that Americans today view marriage differently than three decades ago is quite an understatement. Since 1970, the average age at first marriage has increased substantially, along with rates of divorce and nonmarital births. At the same time, rates of cohabitation (people living together outside of marriage) have increased as well.[1]

The trend is obvious—fewer Americans are married, and a greater proportion of children are being raised in single-parent homes. The response of many in our society to this data is a resounding, "So what?" The Institute for American Values compiled this list of twenty-one reasons why marriage matters. For more insight, visit their website at www.americanvalues.org.

1. Marriage increases the likelihood that fathers have good relationships with their children.
2. Cohabitation is not the functional equivalent of marriage.
3. Growing up outside an intact marriage increases the likelihood that children will themselves divorce or become unwed parents.
4. Marriage is a virtually universal human institution.
5. Divorce and unmarried childbearing increase poverty for both children and mothers.
6. Married couples seem to build more wealth on average than singles or cohabiting couples.
7. Married men earn more money than do single men with similar education and job histories.
8. Parental divorce (or failure to marry) appears to increase children's risk of school failure.

Since only about 30 to 40 percent of marriages today last for a lifetime, it's natural for single young adults to want to avoid divorce. But look at the facts. The problem with cohabiting as a form of trial marriage is that most trials don't work. About 60 percent of cohabit-

9. Parental divorce reduces the likelihood that children will graduate from college and achieve high-status jobs.
10. Children who live with their own two married parents enjoy better physical health, on average, than do children in other family forms.
11. Parental marriage is associated with a sharply lower risk of infant mortality.
12. Marriage is associated with reduced rates of alcohol and substance abuse for both adults and teens.
13. Married people, especially married men, have longer life expectancies than do otherwise similar singles.
14. Marriage is associated with better health and lower rates of injury, illness, and disability for both men and women.
15. Children whose parents divorce have higher rates of psychological distress and mental illness.
16. Divorce appears to significantly increase the risk of suicide in both parents and adolescents.
17. Married mothers have lower rates of depression than do single or cohabiting mothers.
18. Boys raised in single-parent families are more likely to engage in delinquent and criminal behavior.
19. Marriage appears to reduce the risk that adults will be either perpetrators or victims of crime.
20. Married women appear to have a lower risk of experiencing domestic violence than do cohabiting or dating women.
21. A child who is not living with his or her own two married parents is at greater risk of child abuse.

ing couples don't marry. Of the remaining 40 percent who marry, the divorce rate is close to 75 percent. This means that approximately 10 percent of cohabiting couples will marry and stay married for a lifetime.[2]

The Effects of Cohabitation

Many young adults feel that living together is a great alternative to marriage. Most have experienced the pain of never seeing a marriage work. These young adults don't realize that by cohabiting, they could actually be sabotaging their chances at experiencing a fabulous marriage in the future. Here are some facts about cohabiting:

- Cohabiters experienced significantly more difficulty in their marriages with adultery, alcohol, drugs, and independence than couples who hadn't cohabited. Apparently marriages preceded by cohabitation are more prone to problems often associated with other deviant lifestyles—drug and alcohol use, more permissive sexual relationships, and an abhorrence of dependence—than marriages not preceded by cohabitation.[3]
- Compared to married couples, cohabiting couples have less healthy relationships. They have lower relationship quality, lower stability, and a higher level of disagreements.[4]
- Cohabiters are much more violent than marrieds. The overall rate of violence for cohabiting couples is twice as high as for married

What's missing in a trial marriage? Commitment! Commitment is the result of a piece of paper called a marriage certificate and vows made to each other to stay together "till death us do part" in front of witnesses. In a trial marriage, either party can leave anytime for any or no reason at all. Rather than cohabiting, it would be more beneficial to get counseling and uncover potential differences, which will allow you to decide whether to proceed with marriage or not.

Every couple living together, married or not, will have differences and conflict, and yes, even fights. The big question is whether or not there's resolve to work out differences, work through conflicts, and even learn how to fight fairly. Commitment means that as a couple you will take couples, and the overall rate for "severe" violence is nearly five times as high.[5]

- One of the most respected studies in the field of psychiatry, conducted by the National Institutes of Mental Health, found that women in cohabiting relationships had rates of depression nearly five times higher than those of married women, second only to those of women who were divorced.[6]

- The National Sex Survey reports that cohabiting men are nearly four times more likely than husbands to have cheated on their partner in the past year. While women are generally more faithful than men, cohabiting women are eight times more likely than wives to cheat.[7]

- Research strongly and consistently indicates that marriage is a wealth-building institution. Married people typically earn and save more than their unmarried counterparts.[8]

The very thing that young couples think can enhance their future relationships in fact can serve to undermine them.

the time and effort to make a marriage work no matter what. Commitment is needed for any relationship to endure. Marriage provides commitment; trial marriage rarely does.

▮▮ Can a person never marry and be happy?

Yes! You can read the stories of those who have lived in singleness for a lifetime and have had both happy and productive lives. Some individuals are called to singleness because of faith (Catholic priests, monks, nuns), and some are single because their chosen profession was their love and they chose not to marry. Some individuals desired marriage but just never found the right person or the right person at the time in life when marriage was considered an option.

A single person needs to find, through alternative sources, the companionship and emotional strength that a husband and wife provide for each other. A single person needs a healthy base of friends who can help share his or her burdens, hopes, and dreams. A singles ministry at a church or synagogue might supply a base of support as well as a social outlet. It might even lead to marriage at an older age.

Many of these principles apply to the never married as well as the person who's single due to death or divorce. Regardless of whether we're single lifelong or single due to death or divorce, we all need companionship and love. While sex between a husband and wife who are committed to each other is wonderful and beautiful, we can live without sexual intercourse if we have family and friends, have a purpose in life, and know we are loved.

Part 3

The State of Sex Today

Truth or Consequences

Sexually Transmitted Infections

"Sex, drugs, and rock 'n' roll!" may have been the liberating mantra of your youth. Unfortunately, kids today don't understand why the sixties were such a big deal. After all, they've grown up in a society bombarded by sexuality. Sex is no longer a secret. Music lyrics, television shows, and Hollywood celebrate sex seemingly all day, every day. Because of this, the social scene surrounding sexually transmitted infections has vastly changed from the days of Woodstock. Casual sex is as common for youth today as going to the movies. In fact, to some adolescents, sex is just a game—something to do when they're bored.

The difference between now and then is that forty years ago there were only two significant STIs (then known as venereal diseases): syphilis and gonorrhea. Both were easily treated with antibiotics. Today there are nearly thirty STIs that paint the sexual landscape, and some, like HIV, often have deadly consequences. In addition, teens today are having sex with more partners—thus putting themselves and others at significant risk of contracting viral infections that can't be cured.

Hopefully, this section will help you communicate more effectively to your children and those around you about the significant impact of STIs and why condoms often fail to prevent the spread of these infections.

▮▮ What is a sexually transmitted disease (STD) or a sexually transmitted infection (STI)?

Sexually transmitted disease (STD) and sexually transmitted infection (STI) are terms now used for what used to be called venereal disease (VD). STDs are the result of an infection with various types of "germs" (bacteria and viruses) and "parasites." Examples of bacteria are chlamydia, gonorrhea, and syphilis. Examples of viruses are HIV, genital herpes, hepatitis B, and human papillomavirus. Trichomoniasis is caused by a protozoan parasite called trichomonas vaginalis.

When an individual is first infected, it's called an STI. If part of the body malfunctions because of the STI, the infection is then considered a disease (STD). For example, when an individual is infected with HIV, the person would be considered as having an STI. However, when the person develops full-blown AIDS, which can be years later, it would be called an STD.

One way in which STIs differ from each other is how they're spread. Some STIs (gonorrhea, chlamydia, trichomoniasis, and HIV) are spread through body fluids such as semen, vaginal secretions, and blood. Others (genital herpes, syphilis, and HPV) are spread by direct skin-to-skin contact.

Most STIs are spread almost exclusively by intimate sexual contact and usually infect the genital area, mouth, or rectum. The delicate lining of these areas and their warmth and moisture allow the growth of the STIs. Some STIs, such as HIV or hepatitis B, can also be transmitted by exposure to another person's blood (contaminated blood or needles). STIs aren't spread from toilet seats, shaking hands, and other nonsexual contact. Due to better screening of blood and blood products, it's now exceedingly rare to acquire HIV or hepatitis B or C through a blood transfusion.

The State of Sex Today

Why are sexually transmitted infections and diseases important?

Sexually transmitted infections and diseases can produce lifelong consequences for anyone who becomes infected. These problems can destroy future hopes and opportunities and can make life difficult. STIs can permanently damage and infect a person's body and even cause death. These infections and the diseases they cause are much more common than most people realize. It is now estimated that there are approximately 18.9 million new cases of STIs yearly in the United States.[1]

Since some of these infections are viruses, they have no cure and can infect a person for his or her entire life. Some infections, such as chlamydia and gonorrhea, can damage a woman's fallopian tubes so severely that pregnancy may not be possible without undergoing in vitro fertilization. HIV/AIDS is life threatening, HPV may be, and hepatitis B and C may result in chronic illness. Human papillomavirus (HPV) can cause a woman to develop precancerous and cancerous growths on her cervix—more than 99 percent of all cases of cervical cancer are linked to HPV.[2]

One of the biggest risk factors for becoming infected with an STI is having multiple sexual partners. Having sex with only one faithful, uninfected partner for a lifetime is the best way to avoid STIs. This scenario is seldom found outside of marriage.

What is chlamydia?

Chlamydia is a very common sexually transmitted infection. It's an STI that men carry and can pass on but rarely experience any long-term consequences from. Women, however, often suffer many long-term consequences from contracting it. Chlamydia can cause infertility when the infection moves through a woman's cervix and uterus into her fallopian tubes. If a woman who has had pelvic inflammatory disease or PID (an infection of the fallopian tubes) becomes pregnant, she has an increased risk of experiencing a tubal or ectopic pregnancy. An ectopic pregnancy places the mother's life at risk and requires a woman to either have surgery or take medication for treatment. Babies rarely survive an ectopic pregnancy.

The disturbing thing is that up to three out of four women who are infected with chlamydia experience no symptoms and don't know they're infected—and all the while, the infection can be permanently damaging their fallopian tubes. Even when chlamydia is diagnosed and treated with appropriate antibiotics, the tubes may be irreparably damaged, resulting in infertility. Approximately 5 to 10 percent of all sexually active teenagers are infected with chlamydia and are at risk of becoming infertile.

▮▮ What are the signs and symptoms of chlamydia?

Generally men experience no symptoms at all. Occasionally they may have some discharge from their penis or pain with urination. Even though they may not experience any symptoms, if they're infected, they can pass on this infection to a woman during sexual intercourse (vaginal, anal, or oral) or genital contact without penile insertion.

If a woman becomes infected, she usually won't experience any symptoms but could develop pelvic inflammatory disease (PID). PID can be silent or present with high temperature and severe pelvic and abdominal pain. Infertility may result from PID regardless of symptoms being present. She may also have vaginal discharge that's different from her normal vaginal secretions. The discharge can smell foul and look discolored. If a woman has had sexual intercourse with a new partner (or her partner has had a new sexual partner) and she starts having a fever and pelvic pain, she should see a physician immediately. If the physician finds she has PID, antibiotics will be started to minimize the scarring of her reproductive organs. Since the majority of women with chlamydia have no symptoms, it's recommended that all single, sexually active adolescent women be screened for this STI at least annually.[3]

How can I avoid getting chlamydia?

The only way to totally avoid becoming infected with chlamydia is to not have sexual intercourse (vaginal, oral, or anal) or to have intercourse only within the context of a lifelong, mutually faithful, monogamous relationship with an uninfected partner. This scenario seldom occurs outside of marriage. If you've had sexual intercourse in the past and are under twenty-five and single, you should be evaluated and screened (if necessary). If you're a carrier of chlamydia, you should be treated with antibiotics even if you have no symptoms. Condoms, if used 100 percent of the time, may reduce the risk of infection by approximately 50 percent or less.[4] However, they'll never totally eliminate the risk of transmission.

What is gonorrhea?

Gonorrhea is an infection of the genital organs of a man or woman caused by a germ called *Neisseria gonorrhea*. This germ is easily passed from man to woman or woman to man during sexual intercourse. It's also easily passed during oral and anal sex. In men, the infection can cause scarring of the urethra (the tube for urinating). If a woman is infected, she'll often develop scarring in her fallopian tubes or around her ovaries. This scarring may render her infertile and can cause her to experience severe pelvic pain for many years. This pain may be so severe that a hysterectomy may be needed to eliminate the pain. Though gonorrhea isn't as common as chlamydia in the United States, it's still a very dangerous infection.

What are the signs and symptoms of gonorrhea?

If a man is infected with gonorrhea, he'll often have a discharge from his penis and burning with urination when he first becomes infected. Then, after a period of time without symptoms, the germs could cause scarring of his genital organs, or he could pass the infection on to a sexual partner.

Many women don't experience symptoms from gonorrhea infection. If they do have symptoms, the most common are fever and pelvic pain resulting from pelvic inflammatory disease (PID). If a woman has had sexual intercourse and has never been tested for gonorrhea, she needs to see a physician, especially if she starts developing a fever and pelvic pain. Antibiotics can kill the bacteria, but it's possible the fallopian tubes may already be damaged. Individuals who suspect they are infected with gonorrhea should be tested and treated immediately if gonorrhea is present. Anyone who has sexual intercourse with a new partner or whose partner has had sex with someone else should be evaluated for gonorrhea as well as for other sexually transmitted infections.

How can I keep from being infected with gonorrhea?

The only way to totally avoid becoming infected with gonorrhea is to not have sexual intercourse (vaginal, oral, or anal) or to have intercourse only within the context of a lifelong, mutually faithful, monogamous relationship with an uninfected partner. This scenario seldom occurs outside of marriage. Condoms, if used 100 percent of the time, may reduce the risk of infection by approximately 50 percent or less.[5] Condoms will never totally eliminate the risk of transmission.

What is syphilis?

Syphilis is a sexually transmitted infection caused by an organism called *Treponema pallidum*. This germ is easily transmitted from one person to another during sexual intercourse (vaginal, anal, or oral). It can be a dangerous infection. When a person is first infected, he or she will usually have a painless sore at the place where the syphilis germ penetrated the body. For a man, this can be on the penis. For a woman, it can be on the labia or farther up in her vagina where she would have no symptoms and therefore not know she was infected. If a person doesn't see a physician for diagnosis and treatment, the sore will heal, and the infected individual will believe he or she is well. However, the infection has only gone underground in a person's body, and a few weeks later, "secondary syphilis" develops. Symptoms of secondary syphilis are many and varied, including fatigue, fever, hair loss, skin rash, and other problems. If an individual doesn't get diagnosed and treated at that point, the process then can go underground again and is now called "tertiary syphilis" (third-stage syphilis). This late stage of syphilis can cause several serious health problems later in life.

What are the signs and symptoms of syphilis?

The first sign of syphilis is a painless sore that's usually a quarter inch to one inch in size. This sore is called a chancre (pronounced "shanker"). When the sore heals after about two weeks, a person may think that he or she is well. Within a few weeks, however, signs of secondary syphilis develop, which include fatigue, fever, hair loss, skin rash, warty-looking growths (condyloma latum) around the vulva and anus, and enlarged lymph nodes in various parts of the body. Secondary syphilis can also cause inflammation of the liver and kidney, changes in the bones, and eye infections. Tertiary syphilis (third-stage syphilis) develops in about 25 percent of people infected with syphilis and can result in damage to the large arteries of the body, the heart valves, and the brain.[6] At the end stage, syphilis can cause dementia.

How can I keep from getting syphilis?

The only way to totally avoid becoming infected with syphilis is to not have sexual intercourse (vaginal, oral, or anal) or to have intercourse only within the context of a lifelong, mutually faithful, monogamous relationship with an uninfected partner. This scenario seldom occurs outside of marriage.

Condoms, if used 100 percent of the time, may reduce the risk of infection by approximately 50 percent or less.[7] Condoms will never eliminate the risk of transmission. If you think you might have had sex with someone who could be infected with syphilis or any other sexually transmitted infections, or if you have any rash or sore in the genital area, you need to see a health-care provider and be evaluated and tested as needed.

Since syphilis and other STIs don't always have obvious symptoms, it's important to tell your physician if you or your partner have had sex with other individuals so that screening for syphilis and other STIs can be considered. This is especially true for pregnant women because untreated syphilis can be passed from mother to child with devastating results.

What is HIV/AIDS?

HIV (human immunodeficiency virus) is a virus that invades the immune system of the body and destroys it over time. A person is infected with HIV by exposure to infected blood, semen, or vaginal secretions during any type of sexual encounter. Once people are HIV infected, they're infected for life, as we have no cure for any virus, including HIV. With modern drugs and early diagnosis of HIV infection, however, we can keep many individuals from ever progressing to full-blown AIDS. The destruction of the immune system over time reduces a person's ability to fight off infections and some cancers, at which time the HIV-infected individual is said to have AIDS (acquired immunodeficiency syndrome), which is treatable but not curable. Advances in the treatment of AIDS have turned this disease into a chronic illness that can be controlled for years. Some individuals have no evidence of infection while being treated. Most people with AIDS, however, eventually die from infections that can't be controlled, unless they die from another cause first.

What are the signs and symptoms of HIV?

Infected individuals may initially experience flulike symptoms (fatigue, fever, aches, and sometimes a rash) for a limited period of time. After the initial infection, most individuals have no recognizable symptoms for years, even though they're capable of infecting their sexual partner during this period of time. Typically after about ten years, the body's immune system is weakened enough to cause symptoms, and the individual is said to have AIDS (acquired immunodeficiency syndrome).[8] Early diagnosis of HIV infection and new therapies may further delay the onset of full-blown AIDS as well as allow the infected person to alert any potential sexual partners of the risk of acquiring HIV.

How can I prevent becoming infected with HIV?

Avoiding drug use and tattoos or body piercings from a place that doesn't have a current inspection certificate from your local health department is one sure way to avoid infection. If you're single, abstain from sexual activity. If you get married, be faithful. If you haven't had sex (vaginal, oral, or anal) and don't shoot drugs, your chances of getting HIV/AIDS are extremely low.

While consistent and correct use of a condom can reduce your risk of getting HIV, it doesn't totally prevent you from contracting HIV. If a condom is used 100 percent of the time, your chance of infection is reduced by about 85 percent, but that still leaves a 15 percent risk of becoming infected with a potentially fatal disease.[9] Inconsistent condom use, which is more common, offers significantly less risk reduction, if any. If you've already had sex, get checked out, and make a decision in the future not to put yourself at risk for acquiring HIV.

What is genital herpes?

Genital herpes is a sexually transmitted infection caused by the herpes simplex virus (HSV). Genital herpes most commonly infects a man's penis and, less commonly, the skin around the genital area. It commonly infects a woman's vulva, vagina, or cervix and the skin adjacent to her genitalia. If individuals have oral or anal sex, herpes can spread to those areas as well.

A negative consequence of contracting genital herpes is that once people become infected, they may be infected for life. Approximately 70 percent of individuals infected with genital herpes will have recurrences.[10] The frequency of these recurrences usually decreases over time, but it's possible for some individuals to have outbreaks throughout their life. These outbreaks can range from every few weeks to every few years. It's also possible to pass this infection on even when there's no obvious outbreak. Genital herpes is generally not dangerous in adults, but occasionally it may spread to the central nervous system and cause meningitis or encephalitis. Genital herpes can, however, cause severe discomfort to an infected individual.

What are the signs and symptoms of herpes?

Burning sores in the genital area are usually the first sign of a herpes infection. For a woman, this burning may be so severe that she can't urinate because it makes the burning worse. This initial infection usually heals within a couple of weeks.

After the initial infection, there may be outbreaks of new sores in the same area as the original infection every few weeks or months. Subsequent infections tend to only last a few days and generally aren't as painful. The sensation a person gets just before a recurrence is called a prodrome and may include fever, chills, tingling, burning, or pain. While there's no cure for genital herpes, antiviral medications can reduce the severity of symptoms and shorten the duration of the lesions.

A devastating aspect of herpes infection for a woman is that if she breaks out with herpes at the time she's delivering a baby, her baby could become infected. The presence of herpes lesions at the time of delivery will almost always necessitate a C-section in an attempt to minimize the risk of a mother transmitting herpes to her child. For the initial episode of genital herpes, the risk of transmission when a baby is delivered vaginally is about 50 percent. If it's a recurrent episode, the risk decreases to under 3 percent.[11]

How can I keep from becoming infected with herpes?

The only way to totally avoid becoming infected with genital herpes is to not have sexual intercourse (vaginal, oral, or anal) or have intercourse only within the context of a lifelong, mutually faithful, monogamous relationship with an uninfected partner. This scenario seldom occurs outside of marriage. Condoms may reduce the chance of becoming infected with genital herpes, but they never eliminate risk. Part of the reason is that herpes can be anywhere on the genitals and surrounding areas of skin, and condoms don't cover the entire genital area.

Genital herpes is extremely common. About one in five Americans over the age of eleven test positive for the herpes simplex virus. While approximately 1 million Americans get infected with HSV yearly (called incidence), a total of about 45 million Americans have antibodies for the genital herpes virus (called prevalence) because once infected, the antibodies persist for a lifetime.[12] If you have sexual intercourse with more than one person and your sexual partners have had intercourse with other people, it's possible that you will become infected with this virus.

What is human papillomavirus?

Of the nearly 19 million new sexually transmitted infections that Americans acquire yearly, HPV is the most common, with an estimated 5.5 million new cases yearly in the United States.[13] Of all Americans living, however, more are infected with genital herpes than HPV, since in most individuals the body clears itself of the HPV virus over the course of a year or two. Unfortunately, some individuals don't spontaneously clear HPV from their body, and certain strains of HPV in women can lead to precancer (cervical dysplasia) or cancer if not diagnosed and treated.

Since HPV is so common and infectious, if you have sexual intercourse with more than one person who has had sex with other people, you may become (or have been) infected with this virus. Approximately 45 to 60 percent of sexually active adolescents do become infected, regardless of whether they use condoms. About one in five women infected with HPV will experience an abnormal Pap smear, genital warts, precancer, or cancer of the cervix.[14]

One of the more dangerous aspects of HPV infection is that 99 percent of women infected with the virus don't know it because there are no symptoms. Thus a woman can develop precancer or cancer of her cervix and never know she has a problem until she has an abnormal Pap smear. For this reason, it's recommended that all adolescent women who have had sexual intercourse—even one time—have regular Pap smears. The timing and frequency of Pap smears is currently under debate, so individuals at risk should check with their physician.

▌▌ What are the signs and symptoms of HPV infection?

Most people who are infected with HPV don't know it, except for about 1 percent who have genital warts. The warts can vary from a small bump, which is hardly noticed, on the man's penis or the woman's vulva to large warts that are easily seen.

Most genital warts are caused by strains of HPV that don't turn into cancer. However, a physician should still evaluate them, and in women, a Pap smear is needed to identify cancer-causing strains of HPV. In addition, physicians will probably screen for the presence of other sexually transmitted infections.

The most common problem linked to HPV is that specific strains of the virus may cause a woman to experience precancer or cancer of her cervix. Over 99 percent of all precancer and cancer of the cervix is caused by HPV.[15] There are approximately 3.5 million cases of atypical cells (dysplasia) in the United States each year and thirteen thousand cases of cervical cancer, which result in approximately four thousand deaths.[16]

▌▌ What can I do to prevent becoming infected with HPV?

The only way to totally avoid becoming infected with HPV is to not have sexual intercourse (vaginal, oral, or anal) or to have intercourse only within the context of a lifelong, mutually faithful, monogamous relationship with an uninfected partner. This scenario seldom occurs outside of marriage.

Condoms don't appear to reduce the risk of becoming infected with HPV even if they're used 100 percent of the time. Some studies suggest that condoms may reduce the risk of HPV-associated diseases such as genital warts, cervical dysplasia, and cancer in women.[17] There is no

The State of Sex Today

cure for HPV. The warts caused by HPV can be treated, but this treatment is uncomfortable, and the warts can recur and require treatment again. Although cervical dysplasia and cancer of the cervix can usually be successfully treated, treatment can damage the cervix and interfere with future fertility and pregnancy.

ⅠⅢ What is viral hepatitis?

Viral hepatitis is the inflammation of the liver as a result of infection by a virus that selectively chooses the liver to infect and inflame. One group of viruses causing hepatitis is classified as hepatitis viruses. Hepatitis B virus is commonly spread through sexual contact. Hepatitis C is another virus that can sometimes be sexually transmitted. While the primary method for the spread of hepatitis B and C is nonsexual contact with another person's blood (blood transfusion, contaminated needle, razor, knife), these viruses (especially hepatitis B) can be transmitted through sexual intercourse.

The problem with hepatitis is not only that a person can become a carrier of the virus and infect others, but that occasionally the infection will damage the liver and even lead to liver cancer over a period of months or years. With improved methods for screening the blood supply in the United States, it's now extremely rare for a person to contract hepatitis B or C through a blood transfusion or use of other blood products. Hepatitis A isn't transmitted by vaginal intercourse but can be transmitted by oral sex and men having sex with men.

ⅠⅢ What are the signs and symptoms of hepatitis?

When people first become infected with viral hepatitis, they may develop flulike symptoms. These can include fatigue, mild fever, nausea, vomiting, and a general feeling of discomfort in the abdomen. A loss of appetite and weight may also result. Because of the infection to the liver, infected individuals may develop dark-colored urine, and their skin may become yellow (jaundiced) in color. If they develop chronic hepatitis and then develop cirrhosis or liver cancer, they can have symptoms related to these diseases. Both of these diseases can lead to death.

▮▮ How can I keep from being infected with hepatitis?

In the United States, the most common types of hepatitis are A, B, and C. Hepatitis A is usually acquired by consuming food and beverages contaminated with fecal matter, although it can occasionally be in a person's blood for a short period of time. Hepatitis B and C are often found in an infected person's blood. Any exposure of nonintact skin to infected blood can result in infection. The only way to avoid being infected with hepatitis B and C (and occasionally A) is to avoid exposure to blood contaminated with any of these viruses. Vaccines for hepatitis A and B, which are about 90 to 95 percent protective, greatly reduce the risk of infection.[18] No vaccine exists for hepatitis C. Because blood is now carefully screened for hepatitis, transfusions rarely contribute to transmission in this day and age.

Avoiding exposure to contaminated blood is the first step you can take to protect yourself; this includes not using IV drugs, not sharing household items such as razors or toothbrushes with infected persons, and staying away from tattooing and body piercing establishments that aren't routinely inspected for sanitary practices by a health department. Hepatitis B and C can also be spread through a variety of sexual practices, and hepatitis A can be spread through oral sex. Therefore, the second thing you can do to protect yourself from the hepatitis viruses is to abstain from intercourse or to have intercourse only within the context of a lifelong, mutually faithful, monogamous relationship (marriage) with an uninfected partner.

▮▮ What is trichomoniasis?

Trichomoniasis is a sexually transmitted infection caused by a parasite called *Trichomonas vaginalis*. New studies suggest that trichomoniasis is almost always transmitted by sexual contact. Most men who are infected have no symptoms, and trichomoniasis doesn't damage a man's body. An infected woman will often experience irritating discharge that's profuse and greenish in color. Trichomoniasis has recently been found to be occasionally associated with pelvic inflammatory disease in women. If a woman thinks she might be infected with trichomoniasis, it's important that she be tested and treated as soon as possible. In addition, having trichomoniasis can increase a person's risk of contracting HIV if exposed to the virus.[19]

What are the symptoms of trichomoniasis?

Most people who are infected, particularly men, have no symptoms. Women will often have a very heavy, frothy, greenish, vaginal discharge that's very irritating. If a woman has abnormal discharge or begins having a fever and pelvic pain, she needs to be seen by a physician as soon as possible.

How can I keep from becoming infected with trichomoniasis?

The only way to totally avoid becoming infected with trichomoniasis is to not have sexual intercourse (vaginal, oral, or anal) or to have intercourse only within the context of a lifelong, mutually faithful, monogamous relationship with an uninfected partner. This scenario seldom occurs outside of marriage. If you think you might have been exposed to someone who has a trichomoniasis infection or any sexually transmitted infection, you should see a physician to be evaluated and treated if necessary.

How can I tell if a person has a sexually transmitted infection?

Unless a person has sores, blisters, or warts on his or her genitals, you can't tell by looking at a person whether he or she is infected with an STI or not. More than half of the people who are infected with STIs have no symptoms and don't know they're carrying such an infection. STIs can be transmitted to another person through sexual intercourse in the absence of symptoms. We now know that most people who become infected with an STI are infected by a sexual partner who doesn't have sores, discharge, or obvious symptoms at the time the STI is passed from the infected person to the uninfected partner.

In addition, many people don't tell the truth even if they know they're infected with an STI. They may fail to do this because many fear that if they reveal their infection to a potential sexual partner, the partner will refuse to have sex with them. Surprising as it may seem, a significant number of people infected with HIV/AIDS don't share this information with potential partners, even though they may be passing on a deadly disease.

Will having a sexually transmitted infection hurt my sex life?

People who become infected with STIs often feel dirty, sexually unattractive, and depressed. This is particularly true with infections such as genital herpes. Herpes can cause pain during intercourse and is a constant reminder to individuals that they have an STI. In addition to the emotional turmoil caused by an STI, most people who know that they have a chronic infection worry about passing the infection on to someone they care about during intercourse.

Can a pregnant mother pass her sexually transmitted infection to her baby?

Many STIs can be transmitted during pregnancy, at the time of childbirth, or even later when the mother is nursing her baby. Because of this, it's terribly important that a woman who might be at risk for or has become infected with an STI see a physician early in pregnancy to be tested and then treated if possible. Some diseases that can be transmitted from mother to child include the following:

The State of Sex Today

- Hepatitis B can be transmitted to the baby during pregnancy and can cause the infant to have hepatitis B and become a chronic carrier and transmitter of that disease. In addition, infants who acquire hepatitis B are at high risk for chronic disease and cancer of the liver.[20]
- Human papillomavirus (HPV) can be transmitted to a baby at delivery, and the infant potentially could develop polyps on its vocal cords that could require surgery.[21]
- Chlamydia can be transmitted to the baby and cause an eye infection; one type of eye infection can even lead to blindness if left untreated. Chlamydia can also cause viral pneumonias in the infant during the first few months of life.[22]
- HIV can be transmitted to a baby during delivery or when the mother nurses her newborn baby.

Can you get sexually transmitted infections from oral sex?

Yes! Most STIs can be transmitted during oral sex. It isn't possible to become pregnant through oral sex, but STIs are still a real danger. Some STIs, including syphilis, gonorrhea, genital herpes, and chlamydia, are easily transmitted during oral sex. Even HIV can be transmitted by oral sex.[23]

Can I get a sexually transmitted infection if I use a condom?

Yes! While consistent and correct condom use can reduce the risk of most STIs, condoms never totally eliminate risk. Even if you use condoms perfectly 100 percent of the time, you still can become infected with any number of STIs.

If condoms are used 100 percent of the time, they appear to reduce the risk of HIV transmission by approximately 85 percent. For other STIs such as chlamydia, gonorrhea, genital herpes, and syphilis, transmission is reduced by 50 percent or less.[24] With the possible exception of genital herpes and HIV/AIDS, we have no reliable scientific studies that show any risk reduction from inconsistent condom use. Even if condoms are used perfectly every time, there are still risks due to slippage or breakage. For some STIs, there are risks because the condom doesn't always cover all of the infected areas of the genitalia and surrounding skin. Unfortunately, the vast majority of individuals are unable to use condoms both consistently and correctly.

It's also important to understand that risk is cumulative. For example, in the situation of a woman having sex with a male partner with gonorrhea, the estimated risk per one act of sex without a condom is believed to be approximately 50 percent.[25] If a condom is used perfectly 100 percent of the time and the slippage and breakage is 3 percent, then the estimated risk for the female to acquire gonorrhea from her infected male partner is 1.5 percent. The calculated cumulative risk of condom failure in the scenario above is 14 percent for ten acts of sex with an infected individual, 26 percent for twenty acts of sex, and 37 percent for thirty acts.[26] Incorrect and inconsistent condom use dramatically accelerates the cumulative risk.[27]

Can I get a sexually transmitted infection with my first act of sex?

Yes. If your sexual partner has had sex with previous partners, you can contract an STI if your partner is currently infected. If your partner has ever been infected with herpes, hepatitis B, hepatitis C, or HIV, he or she may well still be infected—since these infections generally last for a lifetime.

Can I get a sexually transmitted infection if I only have sex with one person and we were both virgins when we married and started having sexual intercourse?

No. STIs are transmitted from one infected person to another person through sexual activity—oral, vaginal, or anal intercourse (or through genital contact without penile insertion). If neither you nor your spouse has ever had sexual intercourse with anyone else and you both are faithful to each other, then you'll almost never get a sexually transmitted infection or disease. Possible exceptions would be those STIs transmitted through blood that could be passed through lab accidents, accidental needle sticks, and, rarely, through contaminated blood or blood products.

■■ How are sexually transmitted infections treated?

Some STIs can be treated and cured with antibiotics. These include syphilis, gonorrhea, chlamydia, and trichomoniasis. This statement, though, can be too reassuring. For example, if chlamydia and gonorrhea are present and not detected, they can cause damage to a woman's fallopian tubes and cause her to become sterile even though she doesn't know she's become infected. Yes, once her infection is found, she can be treated, but by then it may be too late for her fertility. Syphilis can be treated with antibiotics, but that must be done early in the course of the disease to minimize its potential irreversible impact.

Viral infections such as genital herpes and HIV have no cure. Although drugs may control HIV/AIDS, once someone becomes infected, it's usually for a lifetime. Suppressive antibiotics and antifungal medication may also be necessary when treating a patient with HIV/AIDS. In addition, even if a person is taking drugs to control these infections, he or she can still transmit the infection to a sexual partner. Genital warts caused by HPV can be treated, but often this is a prolonged and uncomfortable process. In addition, HPV can cause precancerous or cancerous changes to the cervix that must be treated with either minor or major surgery or even radiation.

■■ Should I be tested for sexually transmitted infections?

If you've had sexual intercourse with a person who has had intercourse with other partners, you should mention this to your physician, and he will decide if you need to be screened for STIs. It's currently recommended that all single, sexually active females under the age of twenty-five be screened for gonorrhea and chlamydia at least annually. Single, sexually active males should be evaluated and be tested as necessary. High-risk individuals, including those with a past history of an STI, are usually tested more often.

Any ulcerative lesion should be screened for genital herpes (HSV) and syphilis. Most individuals should probably also get tested for HIV.

It's important to tell your physician your sexual history, as certain individuals may need to be screened for other STIs as well. Each time you change sex partners or your partner gets a new partner, your risk for catching an STI increases, and you should check with your doctor about whether you should get tested again. Remember, most STIs don't cause any symptoms—at first.

Choosing to remain sexually abstinent until marriage, marrying an uninfected individual, and then remaining faithful in the marital relationship will ensure a much healthier and happier sexual experience.

▮▮ What should I do if I think I have a sexually transmitted infection?

Any individuals who think they might have an STI or are notified that their partner is infected need to be evaluated by a physician or nurse-practitioner as soon as possible. It's imperative to be totally honest with your doctor so he can perform the necessary screening tests. That might be a blood test, a urine test, or a swab of the cervix or urethra. Since most individuals don't know that they're infected, it's important to let your physician know at any visit, especially the yearly checkup, of any sexual exposure (vaginal, rectal, or oral).

The State of Sex Today

15

How Safe Is Safe?

What You Need to Know about Contraceptives

■ Do oral contraceptives protect against sexually transmitted infections?

No, oral contraceptives are only effective in reducing the risk of becoming pregnant. They provide absolutely no protection against STIs.

■ What are oral contraceptives, and how do they work?

Oral contraceptives (OCPs), or birth control pills, are pills that contain synthetic estrogen and progesterone (two natural hormones for the human female body). These synthetic hormones work by "putting the ovaries to sleep." In this condition, the ovaries don't release an egg monthly. If the ovaries don't release an egg, a woman can't become pregnant. OCPs also alter cervical mucus to interfere with sperm penetration, and they alter the endometrial lining.

While a woman is using the pill, her ovaries don't produce as much estrogen and progesterone. The estrogen and progesterone for her body come from the pills she's taking by mouth.

If birth control pills are taken perfectly, they're very effective. Less than 1 percent of women who take the pills properly will become pregnant each year. The primary problem with OCPs is that many women forget to take their pills or take them incorrectly. Using the pill incorrectly may result in a pregnancy. Surprisingly, the failure rate for the pill during the first year of use is 8 percent, due to inconsistent use or improper dosing. (OCPs, in addition to preventing pregnancy, may decrease abnormal and painful bleeding and decrease the risk of ovarian cyst formation.)

What is the contraceptive patch?

A contraceptive patch is a way of delivering continuous levels of hormones through the skin. The contraceptive patch contains hormones similar to those in birth control pills. Hormonal contraceptives aren't for everybody, because side effects may make you sick, moody, tired, bloated, irritable, and easily annoyed. Most side effects of the contraceptive patch aren't serious, and those that are occur infrequently.

What is a dental dam?

A dental dam is a square piece of latex that's used for hygienic reasons during dental procedures. Scientists have never checked to see whether using a dental dam during oral sex reduces a person's chance of catching a sexually transmitted infection. Recommendations to use dental dams during oral sex are based on urban legends.

How do emergency contraceptive/morning-after pills work?

The emergency contraceptive/morning-after pill has three possible ways it can work:

- Ovulation is inhibited, meaning the egg won't be released.
- The normal menstrual cycle is altered, delaying ovulation.
- The pill can alter the lining of the uterus so that if the first and second actions fail, the tiny baby will die because it cannot attach to the lining of the uterus.

What are condoms, and how do they work?

Condoms are devices usually made of latex rubber. They are made large enough to fit over a man's erect penis. In order to be effective, however, the condom must be tight enough to stay in place during sexual intercourse.

Condoms can be used for two purposes. First, they catch a man's semen when he ejaculates so the sperm in the semen don't get into a woman's reproductive tract. Second, the condom can prevent part of the genitalia of one person from touching part of the genitals of another during sexual intercourse.

A major problem with condoms is that people often don't use them correctly or don't use them every single time. Both correct and consistent condom use are necessary to reduce transmission of sexually transmitted infections. It's important to understand that some STIs are highly infectious. For example, a woman has an estimated 50 percent chance of getting gonorrhea from an infected male partner each time she has sex with him if no condom is used. It's obvious why inconsistent or incorrect use (such as genital contact prior to putting on a condom) can easily lead to infection. Another problem is that condoms don't cover or protect the entire genitalia of either the man or the woman, and an STI that's transmitted skin to skin (such as HPV or HSV) can still be transmitted if there's any genital contact.

In addition to these problems, semen can leak out when the condom is removed, and condoms can either break or slip off, allowing leakage of fluid that can have both sperm and germs present. Typically, about fifteen out of one hundred women who rely on condoms to prevent pregnancy become pregnant during the first year of use.[1] If a condom is used correctly 100 percent of the time, the risk of acquiring HIV is reduced by approximately 85 percent. For more contagious STIs such as gonorrhea, chlamydia, genital herpes, and syphilis, a person's chance of infection is reduced by approximately 50 percent or less if the condom is used for every act of sex.[2] While studies are limited, there appears to be minimal to no risk reduction for bacterial vaginosis, trichomonas infection, and HPV infection. With the possible exception of HIV and genital herpes, there appears to be no risk reduction from inconsistent condom use. Unfortunately, very few individuals are able to use a condom consistently and correctly over many months of use.

For those allergic to latex, there are polyurethane male condoms. They appear to have higher slippage and breakage rates than latex condoms.

▮ What is a female condom?

A female condom is a contraceptive method used by women to prevent pregnancy and sexually transmitted infections. It's a soft, plastic (polyurethane), tubelike device that a woman can insert into her vagina to collect sperm and secretions. The typical-use, first-year failure rate for the female condom is estimated to be 21 percent.[3]

▮ What is an IUD, and how does it work?

An intrauterine contraceptive device (IUD) is a small, plastic device that can be inserted by a physician through a woman's cervix and into her uterus to prevent pregnancy. This procedure is done in a physician's office, usually during or immediately after a menstrual period so that a woman can be sure she isn't pregnant. No one knows exactly how an IUD works, but it seems fairly certain that the contraceptive effect

The State of Sex Today

is produced in several ways. For the most part, IUDs appear to either kill sperm or keep them from swimming through the uterus into the fallopian tubes, so IUDs generally prevent conception. IUDs also appear to sometimes interfere with implantation after conception has already occurred. Some people consider this to be a very early abortion. The estimated typical-use, first-year failure rate for an IUD is less than 1 percent.[4]

▮ What is a diaphragm?

A diaphragm is a dome-shaped rubber cap with a flexible spring rim. Actually, a diaphragm should be called the diaphragm-plus-jelly contraceptive, because the diaphragm itself doesn't produce any significant contraceptive effect. The diaphragm merely holds the contraceptive jelly against the cervix; it's the jelly that kills the sperm. If the contraceptive jelly is put into the vagina without a diaphragm, the jelly will "glob up" into one corner of the vagina, making it relatively ineffective as a contraceptive.

Since the diaphragm doesn't completely seal off the upper vagina, sperm can swim around the edges of it. When they do this, they're killed by the contraceptive jelly. Even if you have a small hole in your diaphragm, any sperm that swim through the hole are usually killed by the jelly held in position by the diaphragm. This form of birth control isn't usually used by teenagers. The estimated typical-use, first-year failure rate for a diaphragm is 16 percent.[5]

▮ What is Depo-Provera, and how does it work?

Depo-Provera is a synthetic hormone (progesterone) that's injected by a health-care professional into a woman's buttocks or arm muscle every three months. Depo-Provera is very effective in preventing pregnancy. It does so by inhibiting ovulation (the monthly release of a mature egg from the ovary), by changing the cervical mucus to help prevent sperm from going into the uterus, and by changing the uterine lining to prevent the implantation of a fertilized egg if a woman were to ovulate and the sperm did reach and fertilize the egg. It's rare for this third event to happen because it's very uncommon for a woman to ovulate if she receives her Depo-Provera regularly.

Though Depo-Provera is effective in preventing pregnancy (typical-use, first-year failure rate is 3 percent[6]), it can be dangerous for an unmarried adolescent to use. The danger is that she can feel that she's safe to have intercourse. She's not safe from any sexually transmitted infection, however, and is potentially exposing herself to great risk. In addition, Depo-Provera can cause loss of hair, acne, weight gain, feelings of constant premenstrual tension, and irritability. An individual who's contemplating the use of Depo-Provera needs to consider all of these issues.

What is natural family planning (NFP), and how does it work?

Natural family planning is a technique that trains a woman and her husband to predict when she's going to ovulate and to avoid sexual intercourse from a few days before to a few days after ovulation. With proper training, most couples are able to predict when ovulation will occur, and with self-control, the couple can avoid sexual intercourse at that time of the month and prevent pregnancy from occurring. If a woman has extremely irregular menstrual cycles, it's difficult to predict when ovulation might occur, and it's unlikely that natural family planning will be successful in this situation. Obviously there's no protection against sexually transmitted infections, so this isn't a good technique for a single woman who might be having intercourse with STI-infected individuals.

What is spermicide, and how does it work?

Spermicides are creams, jellies, or foams that contain a chemical that kills sperm. There's only one chemical that has been approved for this purpose: nonoxynol-9. Spermicides must be inserted into the woman's vagina before intercourse, and even then the pregnancy rate with this technique is approximately fifteen or twenty pregnancies out of one hundred women in the first year of use.

It has been shown that spermicides can irritate the woman's vaginal tissues. This can conceivably make her more susceptible to HIV infection. Because of this, it's now recommended that women not use spermicides for pregnancy prevention if there's any chance that a sexual partner might be HIV infected. The typical-use, first-year failure rate for spermicides is estimated to be 29 percent.[7]

Notes

Chapter One: Where's the Party?

1. H. Weinstock, S. Berman, and W. Cates, "Sexually Transmitted Diseases among American Youth: Incidence and Prevalence Estimates, 2000," *Perspectives on Sexual Repro-ductive Health* 36, no. 1 (2004): 6–10.

Chapter Two: The Big Deal Is You!

1. Linda J. Waite and Maggie Gallagher, *The Case for Marriage: Why Married People are Happier, Healthier, and Better Off Financially* (New York: Doubleday, 2000); R. T. Michael and others, *Sex in America: A Definitive Survey* (Boston: Little, Brown, and Company, 1994), 140–41.

2. M. D. Resnick, P. S. Bearman, and R. W. Blum et al., "Protecting Adolescents from Harm: Findings from the National Longitudinal Study on Adolescent Health," *Journal of the American Medical Association* 278 (1997): 823–32.

Chapter Five: Rules of Engagement

1. Resnick, Bearman, and Blum et al., "Protecting Adolescents from Harm," 823–32.
2. Ibid.

Chapter Six: Questions, Anyone?

1. J. N. Giedd, "Structural Magnetic Resonance Imaging of the Adolescent Brain," *An-nals of the New York Academy of Sciences* 1021 (2004): 105–9; E. Sowell, P. Thompson, and

C. Holmes et al., "In Vivo Evidence for Post-adolescent Brain Maturation in Frontal and Striatal Regions," *Nature Neuroscience* 2 (1999): 859–61.

2. Ed Schor, M.D., *Caring for Your School-age Child* (New York: American Academy of Pediatrics, 1995), 47–48.

3. T. R. Eng and W. T. Butler, eds., *The Hidden Epidemic: Confronting Sexually Transmitted Diseases* (Washington, DC: National Academy Press, 1997), 1–448. Available at www./nap .edu/openbook/0309054958/html.

4. Centers for Disease Control and Prevention, HIV/AIDS Surveillance Report 9, no. 2 (June 1998).

5. Centers for Disease Control and Prevention, "Hepatitis A Vaccination of Men Who Have Sex with Men— Atlanta, Georgia, 1996–1997," *Morbidity and Mortality Weekly Report* 47 (September 4, 1998): 34, 708–711.

6. G. M. McQuillan and others, "Prevalence of Hepatitis B Virus Infection in the United States: The National Health and Nutrition Examination Surveys, 1976-1994," *American Journal of Public Health* 89, no. 1 (1999): 14–18.

7. L. Corey and A. Wald, "Genital Herpes," in *Sexually Transmitted Diseases*, 2nd ed., ed. K. K. Holmes, P. A. Mardh, P. F. Sparling, and P. J. Wiesner (New York: McGraw Hill, 1999), 285–312.

8. M. A. Lynch and R. Ferri, "Health needs of lesbian women and gay men: Providing quality care," *Clinician Review* 7 (1997): 85–117.

9. Linda Eyre and Richard Eyre, *Teaching Your Children Values* (New York: Simon & Schuster/Fireside, 1993).

Chapter Nine: Breaking Free

1. L. Escobar-Chaves and others, "Impact of the Media on Adolescent Sexual Attitudes and Behaviors" (Center for Health Promotion and Prevention Research and University of Texas Health Science Center Houston, 2004), 25–26; J. M. Dempsey and T. Reichert, "Portrayal of Married Sex in the Movies," *Journal of Sexuality and Culture* 4 no. 3 (2000): 21–36; G. M. Wingood et al., "Exposure to X-Rated Movies and Adolescents' Sexual and Contraceptive-Related Attitudes and Behaviors," *Pediatrics* 107, no. 5 (May 2001): 1116–9.

2. Joseph Nicolosi, Ph.D., *A Parent's Guide to Preventing Homosexuality* (Downers Grove, IL: InterVarsity Press, 2002), 162–63.

3. Ibid.

Chapter Ten: Tell Me More

1. Resnick, Bearman, and Blum et al., "Protecting Adolescents from Harm," 823–32.

2. D. A. Cohen and S. N. Taylor et al., "When and Where Do Youths Have Sex? The Potential Role of Adult Supervision," *Pediatrics* 110, no. 6 (2002): E66.

3. Resnick, Bearman, and Blum et al., "Protecting Adolescents from Harm," 823–32.

4. P. R. Reisser, *Focus on the Family's The Complete Book of Baby and Child Care* (Wheaton: Tyndale House Publishers, 1997).

5. Resnick, Bearman, and Blum et al., "Protecting Adolescents from Harm," 823–32.

6. Ibid.

Chapter Eleven: Fools Rush In

1. David Popenoe and Barbara Dafoe Whitehead, *Should We Live Together? What Young Cohabitation before Marriage: A comprehensive review of recent research* (Piscataway, NJ: National Marriage Project, 2002), 8.

2. Resnick, Bearman, and Blum et al., "Protecting Adolescents from Harm," 823–32.

3. Dating tips in this chapter are taken from Joneen Krauth Mackenzie, WAIT training curriculum (Denver: Wait Training, Inc., 2003).

4. Gary Chapman, *The Five Love Languages of Teenagers* (Chicago: Northfield Publishing, 2000).

5. The National Campaign to Prevent Teen Pregnancy, "With One Voice: America's Adults and Teens Sound Off About Teen Pregnancy," (April 2001), http://www.teenpregnancy.org/resources/data/pdf/chrtbook.pdf.

6. Centers for Disease Control and Prevention, "Youth Risk Behavior Surveillance—United States, 2003," *Morbidity and Mortality Weekly Report* 53 (May 21, 2004): (SS-2), 71.

7. National Campaign to Prevent Teen Pregnancy, "With One Voice."

8. National Campaign to Prevent Teen Pregnancy, "Not Just Another Thing to Do: Teens Talk about Sex, Regret, and the Influence of Their Parents," 2000, www.teenpregnancy.org/resources/data/pdf/teenwant.pdf.

9. Ibid.

10. Weinstock, Berman, and Cates, "Sexually Transmitted Diseases among American Youth," 6–10.

11. National Campaign to Prevent Teen Pregnancy, "Not Just Another Thing to Do."

12. D. P. Orr, M. Beiter, and G. Ingersoll, "Premature Sexual Activity as an Indicator of Psychosocial Risk," *Pediatrics* 87, no. 2 (1991): 141–47.

13. Ibid.

14. National Campaign to Prevent Teen Pregnancy, "Not Just Another Thing to Do."

15. Kaiser Family Foundation, "Substance Use and Sexual Health among Teens and Young Adults in the US Fact Sheet," (February 2002), http://www.outproud.org/pdf/CASAFactSheet.pdf.

Chapter Twelve: Free Falling

1. Resnick, Bearman, and Blum et al., "Protecting Adolescents from Harm," 823–32.

2. R. A. Hatcher et al., *Contraceptive Technology*, 18th ed. (New York: Ardent Media, 2004), 395.

3. J. Fitch et al., "Condom Effectiveness: Factors That Influence Risk Reduction," *Sexually Transmitted Diseases* 29, no. 12 (2002): 811–17; J. Fitch et al., *Sex, Condoms and STDs: What We Now Know* (Austin: Medical Institute for Sexual Health, ver. 2.0, 2003): 5–8; National Institutes of Health, "Workshop Summary: Scientific Evidence on Condom Effectiveness for Sexually Transmitted Disease Prevention," (July 20, 2001), http://www.niaid.nih.gov/dmid/stds/condomreport.pdf; S. Ahmed, T. Lutalo and M. Wawer et al., "HIV Incidence and Sexually Transmitted Disease Prevalence Associated with Condom Use: A Population Study in Rakai, Uganda," *AIDS* 15 (2001): 2171–79.

4. Orr, Beiter, and Ingersoll, "Premature Sexual Activity as an Indicator of Psychosocial Risk," 141–47.

5. Teri Reisser, M.F.T., and Paul Reisser, M.D., *A Solitary Sorrow* (Colorado Springs: WaterBrook Press, 1999).

6. Institute of Medicine, *The Hidden Epidemic: Confronting Sexually Transmitted Diseases* (Washington, DC: National Academy Press, 1997), 1–432.

7. Ibid.

8. Giedd, "Structural Magnetic Resonance Imaging of the Adolescent Brain," 105–9; Sowell, Thompson, and Holmes et al., "In Vivo Evidence for Post-adolescent Brain Maturation in Frontal and Striatal Regions," 859–61.

9. Ibid.

10. National Longitudinal Survey of Adolescent Health, Wave II, 1996. For analysis of this data, see The Heritage Foundation, "Sexually Active Teenagers Are More Likely to Be Depressed and to Attempt Suicide," *Center for Data Analysis Report* no. 03–04 (June 3, 2003).

11. Gary Chapman, *The Five Love Languages* (Chicago: Northfield Publishing, 1992).

12. Edward O. Laumann, John H. Gagnon, Robert T. Michael, and Stuart Michaels, National Health and Social Life Survey, 1992 [United States] [Computer file]. ICPSR version. Chicago, IL: University of Chicago and National Opinion Research Center [producer], 1995. Ann Arbor, MI: Inter-university Consortium for Political and Social Research [distributor], 1995.

13. Ibid.

14. American Society of Reproductive Medicine, http:/www.asrm.org/patients/faqs.html.

15. The National Campaign to Prevent Teen Pregnancy, "14 and Younger: The Sexual Behavior of Young Adolescents," (2003), http://www.teenpregnancy.org/resources/reading/pdf/14summary.pdf.

16. Kaiser Family Foundation, "Substance Use and Sexual Health among Teens and Young Adults in the US Fact Sheet," (February 2002), http://www.outproud.org/pdf/CASAFactSheet.pdf.

17. Ibid.

Chapter Thirteen: Moving Out

1. Institute for American Values, http://www.americanvalues.org/html/r-wmm.html.

2. Popenoe and Whitehead, *Should We Live Together?*, 8.

3. Ibid.

4. Ibid.

5. Deborah Graefe and Daniel Lichter, "Life Course Transition of American Children: Parental Cohabitation, Marriage, and Single Motherhood," *Demography* 36 (1999): 205–17.

6. Popenoe and Whitehead, *Should We Live Together?*, 8.

7. Waite and Gallagher, *The Case for Marriage*, 93.

8. Ibid., 110–23.

Chapter Fourteen: Truth or Consequences

1. Weinstock, Berman, and Cates, "Sexually Transmitted Diseases among American Youth," 6–10.

2. X. Castellsague, F. X. Bosch, and N. Munoz et al., "Male Circumcision, Penile Human Papillomavirus Infection, and Cervical Cancer in Female Partners," *New England Journal of Medicine* 346, no. 15 (2002): 1105–12.

3. Centers for Disease Control. "Sexually Transmitted Diseases Treatment Guidelines—2002," *Morbidity and Mortality Weekly Report* 51, RR06 (2002): 1–80.

4. Ahmed, Lutalo, and Wawer et al., "HIV Incidence and Sexually Transmitted Disease Prevalence Associated with Condom Use," 2171–79.

5. Ibid.

6. M. N. Swartz, B. P. Healy, and D. M. Musher, "Late Syphilis," in *Sexually Transmitted Diseases*, ed. Holmes et al., 487–509.

7. Ahmed, Lutalo, and Wawer et al., "HIV Incidence and Sexually Transmitted Disease Prevalence Associated with Condom Use," 2171–79.

8. J. Ambroziak and J. A. Levy, "Epidemiology, Natural History, and Pathogenesis of HIV Infection," in *Sexually Transmitted Diseases*, ed. Holmes et al., 251–67.

9. K. R. Davis and S. C. Weller, "The Effectiveness of Condoms in Reducing Heterosexual Transmission of HIV," *Family Planning Perspectives* 31, no. 6 (1999): 272–79; J. Fitch et al., *Sex, Condoms and STDs*, 5; National Institutes of Health, "Workshop Summary: Scientific Evidence on Condom Effectiveness for Sexually Transmitted Disease Prevention."

10. J. K. Benedetti, J. Zeh, and L. Corey, "Clinical Reactivation of Genital Herpes Simplex Virus Infection Decreases in Frequency over Time," *Annals of Internal Medicine* 131 (1999): 14–20.

11. D. H. Watts, Z. A. Brown, and D. Money et al., "A Double-Blind, Randomized, Placebo-Controlled Trial of Acyclovir in Late Pregnancy for the Reduction of Herpes Simplex Virus Shedding and Cesarean Delivery," *American Journal of Obstetrics and Gynecology* 183 (2003): 836–43.

12. D. T. Fleming, G. M. McQuillan, and R. E. Johnson et al., "Herpes Simplex Virus Type 2 in the United States, 1976–1994," *New England Journal of Medicine* 337, no. 16 (1997): 1105–11.

13. W. Cates, "Estimates of the Incidence and Seroprevalence of Sexually Transmitted Diseases in the United States," *Sexually Transmitted Diseases* 26 (1999) Suppl. 7.

14. B. E. Sirovich and H. G. Welch, "The Frequency of Pap Smear Screening in the United States," *Journal of General Internal Medicine* 19, no. 3 (2004): 243–50.

15. Castellsague, Bosch, and Munoz et al., "Male Circumcision," 1105–12.

16. Centers for Disease Control, *Report to Congress: Prevention of Genital Human Papillomavirus Infection,* 2004; L. E. Manhart and L. A. Koutsky, "Do Condoms Prevent Genital HPV Infections, External Genital Warts, or Cervical Neoplasia? A Meta-Analysis," *Sexually Transmitted Diseases* 29, no. 11 (2002): 725–35.

17. Centers for Disease Control, *Report to Congress: Prevention of Genital Human Papillomavirus Infection.*

18. D. A. Baker, "Hepatitis B Infection in Pregnancy," in *Protocols for Infectious Diseases in Obstetrics and Gynecology*, ed. Mead et al., 208–14 (Malden, MA: Blackwell Science, 2000).

19. F. Sorvillo, L. Smith, and P. Krendt et al., "Trichomonas Vaginalis, HIV, and African-Americans," *Emerging Infectious Diseases* 7, no. 6 (2001): 927–32.

20. Centers for Disease Control, "Sexually Transmitted Diseases Treatment Guidelines—2002," 1–80.

21. M. J. Silverberg, L. Grant, and A. Munoz et al., "The Impact of HIV Infection and Immunodeficiency on Human Papillomavirus Type 6 or 11 Infection and on Genital Warts," *Sexually Transmitted Diseases* 29 (2002): 427.

22. J. Schachter, "Chlamydia Trachomatis Infection of the Adult," in *Sexually Transmitted Diseases*, ed. Holmes et al., 407–22.

23. A. R. Lifson and P. M. O'Malley et al., "HIV Seroconversion in Two Homosexual Men after Receptive Oral Intercourse with Ejaculation: Implications for Counseling Safe Sexual Practices," *American Journal of Public Health* 81 (1991): 1509–11.

24. Ahmed, Lutalo, and Waver et al., "HIV Incidence and Sexually Transmitted Disease Prevalence Associated with Condom Use," 2171–79; J. Fitch and others, *Sex, Condoms and STDs*, 5; National Institutes of Health, "Workshop Summary: Scientific Evidence on Condom Effectiveness for Sexually Transmitted Disease Prevention" ; J. Fitch et al., "Condom Effectiveness: Factors That Influence Risk Reduction," *Sexually Transmitted Diseases* 29, no. 12 (2002): 811–17.

25. R. Platt et al., "Risk of Acquiring Gonorrhea and Prevalence of Abnormal Adnexal Findings among Women Recently Exposed to Gonorrhea," *Journal of the American Medical Association* 250, no. 23 (1983): 3205–9.

26. J. Mann, C. Stine, and J. Vessey, "The Role for Disease-Specific Infectivity and Number of Disease Exposures on Long-Term Effectiveness of the Latex Condom," *Sexually Transmitted Diseases* 29, no. 6 (2002): 344–49; Centers for Disease Control. "Sexually Transmitted Diseases Treatment Guidelines—2002," *Morbidity and Mortality Weekly Report* 51, RR06 (2002): 1–80.

27. Fitch et al, "Condom Effectiveness."

Chapter Fifteen: How Safe Is Safe?

1. R. A. Hatcher et al., *Contraceptive Technology*, 226.

2. J. Fitch and others, *Sex, Condoms and STDs*, 5; Ahmed, Lutalo, and Waver et al., "HIV Incidence and Sexually Transmitted Disease Prevalence Associated with Condom Use," 2171–79.

3. R. A. Hatcher, J. Trussel, F. Stewait, et al., *Contraceptive Technology* (New York: Ardent Media), Table 9-2, 226.

4. Ibid.

5. Ibid.

6. Ibid.

7. Ibid.

Index